A

QTS

meeting the **professional standards framework**

Teaching History

in Primary Schools

Achieving
QTS

meeting the **professional standards framework**

Teaching
History

in Primary Schools

Pat Hoodless

LearningMatters

First published in 2008 by Learning Matters Ltd.

British Library Cataloguing in Publication Data
A CIP record for this book is available from the British Library.

ISBN: 978 1 84445 140 1

Cover design by Topics – The Creative Partnership
Text design by Code 5 Design Associates
Project management by Deer Park Productions, Tavistock
Typeset by PDQ Typesetting Ltd, Newcastle under Lyme
Printed and bound in Great Britain by Cromwell Press Ltd, Trowbridge, Wiltshire

Learning Matters
33 Southernhay East
Exeter EX1 1NX
Tel: 01392 215560
info@learningmatters.co.uk
www.learningmatters.co.uk

Contents

List of illustrations vi

Author statement and acknowledgements vii

1 Introduction: why teach history in primary schools? 1

2 Knowledge and understanding of primary history 11

3 Guidance and support for Key Stage 1 and Key Stage 2 23

4 Planning for progression and opportunities for the development of key skills 33

5 Understanding and using teaching strategies in primary history 46

6 Monitoring and assessment 58

7 Resourcing primary history and collaborative working 71

8 Making the most of links with literacy and mathematics 82

9 E-learning and ICT in primary history 97

10 Creative and innovative approaches: history in the Early Years Foundation Stage 109

11 Creativity and cross-curricular links in Key Stages 1 and 2 120

12 Equality, inclusion and diversity as part of the history curriculum 133

13 Contexts for out-of-school learning in history 145

References 157

Index 163

List of illustrations

Chapter
1	Figure 1	Through the keyhole: a view of the past	4
2	Figure 2	Timeline	14
3	Figure 3	Example of a QCA scheme of work	25
4	Figure 4	Example of a school's long-term plan	34
	Figure 5	Example of a medium-term planning sheet	36
	Figure 6	Example of a short-term plan	39
	Figure 7	Progression in teaching chronology	41
	Figure 8	Victorian bottle	42
5	Figure 9	Teacher-led and child-centred approaches	47
	Figure 10	Cross-curricular links	48
	Figure 11	King Henry VIII	53
6	Figure 12	Example of marked work	64
	Figure 13	Self-evaluation sheet	65
	Figure 14	KWL grid	66
7	Figure 15	Flat-iron	73
	Figure 16	Visual sources	74
8	Figure 17	Fire of London	83
	Figure 18	Put that light out!	87
	Figure 19	A folding book	88
	Figure 20	A Manchester housewife's weekly budget	91
9	Figure 21	Victorian London	99
	Figure 22	Using census data	103
10	Figure 23	A replica Steiff bear	115
11	Figure 24	What I want to know	123
	Figure 25	What was Churchill thinking?	124
	Figure 26	Map of Ancient Egypt	125
	Figure 27	Life in Ancient Egypt	126
	Figure 28	Pottery from Ancient Greece	127
	Figure 29	Model houses	127
	Figure 30	Mind map	131
12	Figure 31	Drawing of Sergeant Lynch	141
	Figure 32	Photograph of Sergeant Lynch	142
	Figure 33	Olaudah Equiano	142
13	Figure 34	Roman site visit	147
	Figure 35	Risk assessment sheet	149

Author statement

Pat Hoodless was formerly Senior Lecturer in History and Education at the Institute of Education, Manchester Metropolitan University. She taught in primary schools in several LEAs across the country for 15 years and then taught curriculum history to trainee primary teachers. Her publications include *History and English in the Primary School* (Routledge Falmer), *Teaching with Text: History* (Scholastic), *Teaching Humanities in Primary Schools* (Learning Matters), and *Ready Resources: History*, and *100 History Lessons* (Scholastic). She also contributes articles on teaching and learning in history to professional and research journals.

Acknowledgements

The author would like to thank Cathy Finney for her chapter on history in the Early Years Foundation Stage, Gail Fulbrook, Jane Bennet, Eleanor Losse and Gemma Rowe for their help in the selection of children's work from their schools, Amy Chapman, a student, for her contributions, and Malcolm Hoodless, who helped with proofreading, photography and citing references.

I would like to thank especially all the children for their examples of work, and the teachers and schools which provided them: Frodsham CE Primary School, Cheshire; Hursthead Junior School, Stockport; and Manor House Primary School, Cheshire.

Finally, the author and the publisher wish to thank the following for their permission to reproduce written material, illustrations and photographs: Qualifications and Curriculum Authority (Figure 3); Private Collection/The Bridgeman Art Library (Figure 11); Pictorial Charts Educational Trust (Figure 16); English Heritage/NMR (Figure 21); © Imperial War Museum (Figures 25 and 32); Birmingham Libraries & Archives (Figure 33).

1
Introduction: why teach history in primary schools?

'It's an adventure!'

Year 3 pupil

About this book

This book aims to provide information, guidance and inspiration for trainee teachers of primary history. It aims above all to assist primary trainees on all courses of Initial Teacher Training in England and other parts of the UK, where similar Professional Standards are in place, to develop their knowledge and understanding of history and their skills in teaching history in the primary classroom. The book draws on examples from the classroom and from whole school curriculum planning to illustrate good practice in primary history as well as indicating ways in which schools are addressing changing principles and ways of working. 'Classroom stories' provide examples of current practice, and examples of children's work indicate the levels of attainment achieved. Key concepts, skills and content for the curriculum in early years settings and primary schools are discussed along with the nature of the subject, both as a distinct discipline and as part of a cross-curricular theme.

The book looks at innovative approaches to history as a leading subject in thematic work, drawing on issues raised in recent documentation, such as *Excellence and Enjoyment – A Strategy for Primary Schools* (DfES, 2003b) and *Every Child Matters: Change for Children* (DfES, 2004c). The Children Act, passed in 2004, made the agenda of *Every Child Matters* a legal requirement. Since then, a series of documents has been published which provides guidance under the Act to support local authorities and their partners in implementing this agenda, such as the Children's Plan (www.dfes.gov.uk/publications/childrensplan).

The book makes links between the revised Professional Standards for Teachers (www.tda. gov.uk), and the statutory requirements for primary history (DfEE/QCA, 1999a). Relevant research background is discussed in each chapter, to assist trainees in tracking their own progress towards achieving Qualified Teacher Status (QTS). The book aims to support those working towards Qualified Teacher Status and also Newly Qualified Teachers (NQTs) in teaching history as well as other teachers and professionals working in education who have identified history and related pedagogy as an area for further development.

The Professional Standards for Teachers

The revised Professional Standards are the framework of requirements for all classroom teachers. Underpinning them are the five key outcomes identified in *Every Child Matters* and the six areas of the common core of skills and knowledge for the children's workforce. A further requirement is that the work of teachers should be informed by the legislation concerning the development and well-being of children (see www.tda.gov.uk, page 1). This book focuses primarily on the Standards for QTS, pointing out opportunities in the teaching of history for meeting the agenda of *Every Child Matters*. There will, where relevant, be reference to the Professional Standards for induction year and main scale teachers seeking further guidance on the teaching of history.

The Professional Standards are set out in three sections: professional attributes, professional knowledge and understanding, and professional skills. This book refers to those standards in each section which have direct relevance to teaching in history. The Professional Standards are shown at the beginning of each chapter, which provides ideas and examples of how to meet them.

Features of each chapter in the book include:

- Chapter objectives;
- Links to the Professional Standards;
- Links to the National Curriculum for history and the Primary National Strategy;
- Classroom stories;
- Practical tasks;
- Reflective tasks;
- Research summaries;
- Summaries of key points;
- Moving on to your next steps in professional development;
- Further reading and websites;
- References.

School history

History is very much alive and in evidence in primary schools today. Roman soldiers, Tudor kings and queens, Victorian workers and inventors, pharaohs and pyramids look down from many classroom walls and corridors. Dates, names and events hang from classroom mobiles, and timelines in many shapes and forms have a place in thoughtful classroom displays. Maybe the most significant reason for teaching history in primary schools is that it motivates children and captures their imaginations, and often their teacher's imagination too. Life in the past is different and sometimes strange, but real all the same, which makes it just that little bit more exciting.

The study of history in school is important for children's conceptual development. They can begin to understand that the past has many different facets and that each era is different from the next, as well as being different from our own. They can begin to understand the vocabulary that accompanies these understandings: age, era, period, time, century, decade, ancient, modern, and all the words used to express our understanding of chronology. The immense concept of time and its measurement can be dealt with directly, giving children a sense of their own identity and place within the eras of social change. They can begin to understand themselves and their own place in society; how they relate to their immediate family and their locality. How change occurs and how changes affect us is a concept at the heart of history, not just what those changes have been, but their significance for people at the time and subsequently. The study of history builds children's understanding of society. They can begin to see how systems of social organisation have grown, why people from different parts of the world may live in their own neighbourhood, why there have been wars, their effects and why conflicts continue to arise. They can see how ideas, customs, habits and fashions have grown. For all these reasons and many more, history is a subject that builds a context for the present in children's minds.

If children 'do' history rather than just 'learn about' it, they will begin to see how our knowledge of ourselves has been gradually assembled over the ages, orally, in writing, and now using computer technology. Children will acquire the skills of the historian, empathy and historical imagination, skill in analysing and interpreting evidence, reasoning and looking critically at information, skill in identifying motives and causes for events, creative skill in building their own image of the past and skill in communicating their understanding to others. It is for reasons like these that there is such a powerful link with subjects such as literacy. Literacy is needed to enable children to access the wonderful treasures from the past through historical sources, non-fiction and literature. The study of history can play a key role in the development of children's higher order language skills, the extension of their vocabulary and their skills in many core areas. Far from subjects such as history becoming 'second class', they should be seen as more important, academic disciplines where the skills of literacy and often numeracy are required as tools for further learning.

History provides a real context for work in other areas and subjects, providing a sound basis for cross-curricular work. Because history is about all human life in the past, it is often referred to as an 'umbrella' subject (Turner-Bisset, 2005a). It can include the history of medical discoveries, engineering and technology, it can also consider social changes, political decisions, geographical exploration of the world, religious beliefs, art, music, sport and the development of learning itself. History therefore is a natural base for the study of other subjects or areas of interest. It can be used as a unifying force, providing a cohesive context and content for cross-curricular learning.

REFLECTIVE TASK

Choose a historical topic that you have learned or read about in the past. Consider different aspects of this topic, such as the cross-curricular links with geography you would need to use or the chronological understanding you would need. Think also about the wider learning, involving moral considerations or issues of equality which might arise in the course of the topic. Think about the opinion that history is an 'umbrella subject' and whether you agree with this view.

What is special about history?

In civilisations across the world, history has been a subject learned by the rulers of society, kings, emperors and the aristocracy. It has always been considered of great importance for those leading their societies to understand their current place in history and the significance of past events in their own and others' societies, to inform their functioning in the present.

History is unique in that it is probably the most abstract subject in the curriculum. Its subject, namely the people who made it, no longer exist. We cannot organise an interview or an experiment, or check our answers, for those who really know are not here. We do have some scraps which they have left behind, but these are a mere fraction of what really existed. To look at a particular time in the past is rather like looking though a keyhole in a door. We can focus on a detail, even in great depth, but we see only a tiny part of the whole fabric of society and life at that time.

Figure 1. Through the keyhole: a view of the past

We can use sources to build up a better picture of what life was like, or of events that took place. However, we have only our own imaginations and skills to rely upon in the creation of our interpretation of the past. We can read written texts, documents and history books, but know that these are only versions of the past, created by someone with a particular view-point or perspective, so that much has to be used with a critical eye and not taken for granted or treated as the true picture of the past. Even primary sources can distort what the past was really like. Overemphasis on particular sources, such as Tudor portraits, for example, can distort children's general view and attitude towards a time in the past, giving them the impression that everyone in Tudor times was very rich and wore furs, silks, jewels and heavily embroidered clothes. What could be further from the truth?

History therefore poses philosophical questions. Can we ever know the truth about what happened in the past? There are often examples of new archaeological finds which constantly disprove the history books. There are regime changes, which bring about the rewriting of history textbooks and 'official' histories. This has happened in societies across the world and throughout time. History is influential in the way it reflects upon current regimes, since it can be seen as part of their very own past, and must tell their story. Some, such as Jenkins (1995, 2003) have gone so far as to suggest that there can be no such thing as history, since all we have is someone else's interpretation. Even contemporary writers in the past, such as Roman historians writing about Boudicca, for example, may have had a particular reason for portraying her in a negative way: they might have believed that women had no place trying to be rulers; they might have personally disliked her; they might have been influenced by the general feeling of antipathy towards her at the time; or they might have been under duress to write what was acceptable to their masters or patrons. Whatever the reason, the question remains, can we really trust what they have written?

History poses moral and ethical questions. It is full of sensitive issues: the horrors of the past, such as beheadings, burnings at the stake, the Holocaust. It cannot avoid past and current issues, such as racism in society, different religious views, conflicting attitudes and different ways of life within society. For young children, there are issues such as family dysfunction, death and bereavement, which are sometimes hard to avoid with a focus on family life prescribed in the National Curriculum. Parental sensitivities might be affected by class visits within the locality, perhaps to a site with unhappy memories, such as war memorials, or to religious sites, which some might object to their children visiting. All such examples carry implications and lessons from history, but how much of this can the teacher suitably raise with children in primary school?

History poses a multitude of questions about the validity of sources. A fundamental question seems to be, 'What is a valid source to use with young children and what is not?' The National Curriculum suggests a wide range of sources under the heading 'historical enquiry'. However, many of these sources are difficult to use and at worst, constitute a potential minefield for the unwary teacher. Stories can be biased, giving a distorted picture of events, or just one perspective. Artefacts can be frustrating, since to derive meaning from them requires skill in historical questioning. Visual sources require expertise in questioning and investigation before much of any significance can be drawn from them. Official documents and statistics are simply too difficult for primary children to access and understand. Historical information books, written specifically for primary school aged children, are often full of inaccuracies, and written by authors with little expertise in the subject them-selves. Popular children's histories, such as 'The Rotten Romans' in the 'Horrible Histories' series (Deary, 1994), may be seen to trivialise significant and tragic events; however well researched, they may not be taken seriously. The internet is a minefield in its own right where, once again, the unwary teacher might make use of unchecked and inaccurate mate-rials. Because history is such an intricate, complex area, dealing with the whole range of human experience, teachers need to take great care in the selection of their teaching resources. This said, history offers possibly more, and richer resources than any other curriculum subject, and if used with care, these can considerably enrich the learning experi-ences of all children.

History develops children's skills in decentring, seeing other points of view, thinking laterally, critically, and comprehensively. One aspect of Piagetian theory which has great value for history is that of decentring. Piaget, in his long study of the behaviour of young children discovered that they tended to behave in a very self-centred way, showing little awareness of other people. Piaget argued that before the age of about seven, children are in a stage of development which does not permit them to take account of the perspectives and needs of others. Yet to study history requires children to do exactly that. The current curriculum requires children to be engaged in learning about others and their experiences, views and attitudes, and so it is the strategies that teachers use to cope with this challenging task that enable children to begin to appreciate the points of view and attitudes of others. In this sense, history can play a major role in children's cognitive, social and emotional development.

REFLECTIVE TASK
REFLECTIVE TASK

Reflect on your own learning of history, your formal education and your incidental learning, such as from a film or book. Consider what made history unique in your education and experience. In what ways has it contributed to your life skills?

The development of children's historical understanding

Clearly there is a link between the development of historical understanding and children's cognitive development. Theories of child development and of cognitive development throughout the primary school years have grown and changed considerably over the past century. Piagetian theory has been challenged and replaced by those, such as Bruner (1974, 1977, 1990), and more recently Steffe and Gale (1995) and Selley (1999), in support of a constructivist theory of education which identifies social and linguistic activity and interaction as a crucial factor in learning. These psychological and educational theories have had considerable influence on the way history is taught in schools, including some profound changes in expectations and requirements. Recent theory has tended to emphasise what children 'can' do and understand, as opposed to looking at their cognitive deficiencies. As a result, time and chronology, along with their associated vocabulary, are now aspects of study in the history curriculum, something unheard of in the mid twentieth century. There is a growing body of research into how children's thinking in history develops, usefully summarised by Hilary Cooper (2000).

A range of strategies is advocated in the teaching of history to match what we know about children's developing capabilities and their different learning styles. Different schools of thought emphasise different ways of learning about the past: some emphasise the use of sources and evidence, seeing history as an enquiry subject (Cooper, 2000, 2007a); others, such as Bage (1999) see history as essentially a narrative, which is best taught and learned through story; Hodkinson (2002) emphasises the importance of teaching chronology; while others point out the importance of the historical imagination (Turner-Bisset, 2005a). There are strong features in each of these arguments, and the selection of appropriate strategies drawn from all of them is perhaps the most logical way of ensuring that all children gain access to the subject. Your choice of resources and strategies might also be influenced by the need to address different learning styles. Visual, auditory and kinaesthetic learners will all gain from an approach which uses a mixture of methods and includes the whole range of historical sources.

How do children learn about history?

When trainee teachers are asked what they know already about historical periods they often begin by professing profound ignorance. However, given time, and the opportunity to think, talk and reflect, they begin to realise that they do actually know a great deal, but they do not know how they know it! Probably this historical knowledge has been derived from incidental learning. For example, much of what children watch on television is rooted in an historical context. Films, drama and educational broadcasts frequently make use of historical settings and it is from these contexts that much informal learning takes place. Literary texts frequently use an historical setting, or if written in the past, are based in one. In addition to this, there is a large amount of popular historical fiction, widely read by children. Children are surrounded by evidence of the past, in old houses, public buildings and monuments, historical sites, palaces, castles and halls, ruins and remains from the past. In many shopping streets there is evidence of social and historical change, with old shop fronts dating back for decades and sometimes centuries, alongside new shops and restaurants, run by recently arrived communities from parts of the world which belonged to the former British Empire.

Older family members may talk about their memories and experiences, acting as a constant source of information about a time unknown to children.

Historical concepts begin to develop at a very early age. Babies begin to learn about the passing of time from their feeding routines, the change from night to day, and as they grow into toddlers, they learn about the cyclic nature of time from the regular pattern of birthdays, holidays and religious festival days. In nursery and infant school, they learn about time through their daily routines, weekly patterns and regular outings to the swimming pool or to the shops with their parents. They know about the constant passing of time from bedtime, lunchtime, dinnertime and playtime in school. Learning about historical chronology is there-fore, in some ways, merely a further development of a process of learning about time that has been taking place in children's experiences since birth.

How much children begin to explore understandings of time, change, causation and inter-pretation, of course, depends on how they are encouraged to think and talk about them. Children's overt skills in articulating their awareness of these aspects of the past varies enormously when they first arrive at nursery or their reception class, probably due to the parental input they have received. If parents have involved their children meaningfully on family excursions to historic sites and museums, asking and answering questions, and talking to children about what they are seeing, then the children's experiences will have been greatly enhanced and their learning reinforced. Such children begin school with a very sophisticated understanding of the past in comparison with their peers. This belief in the importance of social interaction as a vital element in the learning process was first put forward by Bruner (1977). The teacher's task is to recognise what has already been learned and to extend their learning from this point, making it accessible to each child through widening their vocabulary, building their confidence and teaching them the communication skills needed to continue their learning and the ability to express it.

Learning about the past is inextricably linked with language. Meaning for all these random images and impressions of the past is derived through the thinking, talking, reading and writing which accompanies them. Without the vital mediation of language (Vygotsky, 1962) as part of social interaction, our impressions would remain random and undeveloped. Language and the use of English plays a major role in any kind of historical activity. Different models of history teaching all rely heavily on language use, both by teacher and pupils (Husbands, 1996). Skills in history often depend upon skill in the use of language; and speaking, listening, reading and writing frequently play a part in the process of historical enquiry. Indeed it would be difficult to develop in children the process skills of history without the extensive use of this entire range of language skills. Regardless of teaching style, and whether there is a focus on process or content, the links between history and English are natural and inseparable.

Every Child Matters

Every Child Matters places an emphasis on the child and the personalisation of learning. As teachers, therefore, we need to understand the different influences on children, the vast range of sources from which they learn about the past outside the school environment, and the differing levels of support and interaction they might have been offered by their families or other adults – all of which are vitally important in modern approaches to the teaching of history. This is a necessary approach in making links between children's learning in school and the opinions, images and ideas they will have absorbed in an informal way. These links make learning in school 'real' and children are more likely to enjoy and retain their learning because they understand its relevance to everyday life.

Thematic learning can make history 'real' for children, since many learn in a holistic way (Jarvis and Parker, 2005). Children do not naturally break down the world into abstract subjects, but tend to be interested in things such as 'homes and houses', because they are based on 'concrete' concepts which are more meaningful. Children who learn holistically can therefore benefit from history-led thematic work; they can achieve their potential and build up their self-esteem, a vital part of the Every Child Matters agenda (DfES, 2004c). Topics or themes, based on children's own interests are returning to respectability in the primary school curriculum (see, for example, www.qca.org.uk/innovating). Often, these topics link two subjects or make use of the connections between several subjects, and here history has great potential. As a focal point of interest, a historical theme can be used as a suitable basis for much other creative work, in both core and foundation subjects. It can spark ideas for dramatic productions, artistic responses, music and design. History can unify a thematic study by providing the key content and area of interest around which other activities can take place. For example, Grant Bage's powerful argument for story can be particularly useful here where a story can be used to provide a continuous thread throughout the varied activities that can be incorporated into a topic (Bage, 1999).

Excellence and Enjoyment – A Strategy for Primary Schools

As Bage points out, *teaching history is an emotional matter* (Bage, 1999, p19) and it is for this reason that it needs to be a central part of the Primary Strategy and its focus on 'Excellence and Enjoyment' (DfES, 2003b). To many people, history matters very much; it is part of their heritage, their identity and their life. This is also true of many communities, such as those who travelled to look for work in Britain following the Second World War, or those in different parts of Britain, where a local and national identity is of supreme importance. In engaging with the lives of those in the past, hearing their stories and beginning to empathise with their condition, we are engaging emotionally ourselves. It is the significance and emotional weight we give to what we know about history that makes it distinctive and a worthy part of the Excellence and Enjoyment agenda. Although I agree wholeheartedly with the view expressed in *Excellence and Enjoyment* (DfES, 2003b) that *Children learn better when they are excited and engaged – but what excites and engages them best is truly excellent teaching*, I would argue that it is not excellent teaching alone which excites and engages. In the case of history, it is the subject matter itself which is exciting and engaging and which is equally capable of enabling children to use to the full their creative and imaginative abilities.

Outline of chapters

Each chapter is based on one or more of the Professional Standards for Teachers. Chapter 2 focuses on subject knowledge. It considers how encouraging children to 'be historians' provides opportunities for developing their skills and understanding of historical concepts, such as chronology, causation, interpretation and source analysis. Chapter 3 reviews the two major documents which trainees must know and understand in order to qualify for QTS in history, the National Curriculum for history and the non-statutory guidance produced by the QCA, 'A Scheme of work for Key Stages 1 and 2: History' (DfEE/QCA, 1998). It also refers to on-line materials available from the Qualifications and Curriculum Authority (QCA) and Ofsted, the schools inspection service. Chapter 4 introduces the idea of planning for progression in learning history, through sequences of tasks within lessons and units of work. It identifies how concepts such as chronology, and skills such as visual literacy may be developed systematically through a history topic. It looks at short-, medium- and long-term planning and how these are implemented in schools.

Chapter 5 outlines the key pedagogical knowledge that trainees require in order to match teaching strategies to children's developing abilities, to meet their diverse needs, and to ensure an inclusive learning environment. It provides classroom examples of successful strategies and also innovative ways of teaching primary history. It also looks at independent learning in history and the use of personalised learning strategies, perhaps one of the most rewarding aspects of primary school work. Chapter 6 discusses various aspects of assessment: monitoring and assessment; using assessment evidence; use of assessment strategies; feedback and self-assessment; and evaluation of teaching. There is discussion of how assessment information contributes to the evaluation of teaching and the improvement of your own practice. Chapter 7 provides an overview of the range and variety of historical source material that is available in the form of books, the internet, educational publishers, the media, and from library and archive material. The notion of resourcing history includes other adults involved in children's learning. Chapter 8 discusses the wide range of opportunities offered by history for including work on the core subjects of literacy and numeracy. Chapter 9 considers the variety of opportunities for introducing e-learning into the primary history classroom. It outlines resources available on the internet, the use of CD-ROMs, film and television broadcasts. Links with the wider community, other schools, educational organisations and educational establishments in other parts of the world are also discussed.

Chapter 10 considers the requirements outlined for the Early Years Foundation Stage. It focuses on ways of developing young children's sense of time and developing a sense of the past, the major Early Learning Goal for the Foundation Stage, using children's own experiences as a starting point. Chapter 11 explores creativity through cross-curricular work. Opportunities for making links with the arts is a key aspect of this chapter. It also considers the relationship between history and other humanities subjects and links history with wider themes, such as citizenship. Chapter 12 considers the diverse needs of children, from those with differing abilities and learning styles, to those from different ethnic and religious backgrounds. The use of varied teaching strategies is discussed in relation to meeting the widely differing needs of children with special educational needs (SEN). This chapter introduces the notion of making use of histories from other parts of the world and other communities as a starting point for understanding their different cultures. There is also reference in this chapter to children's spiritual, moral, social and cultural development and exemplification of how this can be addressed through history. Chapter 13 looks at learning outside school. Children learn from television, film and drama, literature, art, music and visits to museums and places of historical interest. While much of this learning takes place in the home, or in the company of parents or carers, much can be incorporated into the school's schemes of work.

FURTHER READING FURTHER READING **FURTHER READING** FURTHER READING

Bage, G (1999) *Narrative matters: teaching and learning history through story.* London: Falmer.
Cooper, H (2007) *History 3–11: a guide for teachers.* London: Fulton.
DfEE/QCA (1999) *History: the National Curriculum for England.* London: HMSO.
DfES (2004) *Every child matters: change for children.* London: DfES.

Husbands, C (1996) *What is history teaching?* Buckingham: Open University Press.

Training & Development Agency (2007) *Professional standards for teachers.* London: TDA.

Useful websites

www.canteach.gov.uk/community/itt/requirements/qualifying/standards
    A useful website for general information about teaching and teacher training.

www.dfes.gov.uk/publications/childrensplan
    Website of the Children's Plan.

www.everychildmatters.gov.uk
    Website for the Every Child Matters documentation.

www.bbc.co.uk

www.historyonthenet.co.uk

www.learningcurve.pro.gov.uk_

www.nc.uk.net

www.qca.org.uk/history/innovating

www.schoolhistory.co.uk

www.spartacus.schoolnet.co.uk
    Useful websites for information and ideas on teaching primary history.

www.ofsted.gov.uk
    The website for Ofsted, the official body for inspecting schools.

www.standards.dfes.gov.uk/primary
    Website where information about the Primary Strategy can be found.

www.tda.gov.uk/teachers/professionalstandards.aspx
    Website where information can be found about the Professional Standards for teachers, from initial teacher training to advanced skills levels. (TDA 0313 Professional Standards for teachers is also available as a hard copy.)

2

Knowledge and understanding of primary history

Chapter objectives

By the end of this chapter you should have:

- developed an understanding of the legal requirements placed upon all primary teachers in terms of what they must teach;
- begun to understand the specific requirements for history within the National Curriculum and the links between history and the general teaching requirements of the National Curriculum;
- acquired an overview of the key content, concepts and skills in history at each key stage;
- become aware of some of the major research into how children learn about the past.

Professional Standards for QTS

This chapter will support you as you work towards evidencing attainment against the following Standards:

Q3 (a): Be aware of the . . . statutory framework within which (teachers) work.

Q22: . . . demonstrate secure subject/curriculum knowledge.

The statutory framework: the National Curriculum

The National Curriculum (DfEE/QCA, 1999b) is the statutory document which specifies what must be taught in schools. The various Education Acts, from 1833 to the present day, have helped to shape today's schools and education system. The National Curriculum was the product of a great debate on the state of education in schools in Britain, which had begun during the Callaghan government in the 1970s. There had been criticism of 'progressive' teaching methods in the 1970s and 1980s, which were gaining in popularity, and there was a growing concern over falling standards of achievement. To address these problems the National Curriculum was passed as an Act of Parliament, the Education Reform Act in 1988 and published in 1991. Revisions in 1995 and 1999 have produced the statutory curriculum for history with which teachers work. As a statutory document it has the force of law behind it, and schools must follow its requirements. In history, as in the other curriculum subjects, Programmes of Study, General Teaching Requirements, Attainment Targets and Level Descriptors are set out. The Programmes of Study include 'Knowledge, skills and understanding' and 'Breadth of study', in other words the content, concepts and skills of history which must be taught. Details for the whole of the Key Stages 1 and 2 history curriculum requirements can be found at www.nc.uk.net.

Programmes of Study

The National Curriculum for history (DfEE/QCA, 1999a) is based upon a long tradition of research into historical learning and understanding. It is also the result of considerable disagreement about what should be included in a curriculum for schools. Prior to 1991 there had never been a written curriculum for history and teachers had enjoyed considerable freedom when it came to choosing a historical theme or topic.

Two different views of what was important for children to learn in school had come out of what was known at the time as the 'History debate'. One group felt that the most important thing about history was to know the important events from the nation's past, so that children could have a good understanding of their heritage and how this had developed over time. The other group, however, believed that it was important for children to 'do' history in order to really understand it. This meant that they needed to be able to understand key historical ideas and also to put into practice the skills of the historian. These two aspects of teaching and learning in history have often been referred to as the 'content' versus the 'process' approach: understanding the process of history required children to 'be' historians, using their skills and concepts, while the content approach involved the transmission of an accepted body of knowledge.

When the curriculum was finally agreed and published in 1991 (DES, 1991) it attempted to put together these two opposing beliefs about what school history should look like. It therefore attempted to enable teachers to make links between the key concepts and skills which underpin history as a discipline, with a selection of content areas.

Revision of the history curriculum

The most recent revision of the curriculum in 1999, however, led to some significant changes in the balance between these two ways of looking at history. It considered how encouraging children to 'be historians' provides opportunities for developing their understanding of historical concepts, such as chronology, causation, interpretation and source analysis. There was also an acknowledgement of Britain's changing society and a broadening of outlook, with the addition of references to 'the wider world'. The 'process' concepts and skills, in the form of the 'Knowledge, skills and understanding' at each key stage, were elevated to the forefront, while the required sections of content came second.

Skilful teachers have always known that the two needed to be linked in order to arrive at some meaningful learning in history; however, this is not an easy task to undertake, particularly for those new to the profession. Once understood, however, the history curriculum provides endless opportunities for the development of innovative and creative teaching and learning.

Knowledge, skills and understanding: historical concepts and skills

Taba's research into key concepts in the humanities identified two different types of concept in history: 'organisational' or 'methodological' concepts, which included concepts related to the methods of doing history; and substantive concepts, which covered factual content

(Taba, 1971). Subsequent researchers and writers have used different terms to label these two types, and for more detail on this, see the research section at the end of this chapter.

The 'organisational' or 'methodological' concepts are ideas which organise thinking along specific lines of enquiry and provide some analytical rationale. For example, when studying the six marriages of King Henry VIII, thinking is usually guided by a consideration of the King's reasons for marrying six such different people, and the results can then be grouped under personal or political reasons. In doing this, an historian has used the methodological concept of causation and probably the concept of effect as well if he or she considers the resulting events which arose from these marriages.

The 'substantive' concepts focus on the historical facts. These concepts include ideas and related vocabulary, such as 'war', 'conquest', 'invasion' or 'settlement'. These labels reflect the abstract concept derived from grouping or classifying many different objects into a generalised idea. For example, there could be soldiers, battles, deaths, victories and defeats, all of which, when discussed as a whole, are described as 'war'.

One of the first things a new teacher of history needs to understand, therefore, is how the major concepts which underpin history as a discipline are embedded within the 'Knowledge, skills and understanding' section of the National Curriculum. The following are some of the key concepts in history:

- time and chronology;
- cause and effect;
- change and continuity;
- interpretation;
- historical sources;
- communication.

These concepts need to be identified within each point of the 'Knowledge, skills and understanding' section, so that you are clear which concept you will be teaching when addressing the different National Curriculum objectives.

A new teacher of history also needs to understand how the major historical skills are embedded within the 'Knowledge, skills and understanding' section of the curriculum. Key skills in history, through which children develop their understanding of the major concepts, are an important part of National Curriculum requirements and also feature prominently in the non-statutory guidance for history.

Weaving the concepts and skills effectively into each historical theme is what makes good history teaching. One way to achieve this is to set a key skill or concept as one of your teaching objectives in your lesson plans, ensuring that each part of the National Curriculum requirements is linked together.

Time and chronology

Time is probably the concept which is fundamental to history, more so than any of the others. Since it is an abstract concept, it is known to be one of the hardest ideas for young children to begin to understand. In the past it was widely believed that these concepts were too difficult for children to understand and could not be dealt with until adolescence (Piaget,

1927/1967). Chronology was usually not taught directly for this reason. However, the current National Curriculum requires the teaching of chronology and its related vocabulary, aspects which are the first of the areas to be covered in the 'Knowledge, skills and understanding' section.

Skills in chronology include the ability to:

- sequence and order events and objects according to time; to place them in chronological order;
- use time-related language.

Figure 2. Timeline (Year 5 work)

Consider the way in which you understand the concept of 'time' yourself. Think about what is different between the notion of time and the concept of historical chronology. What does the term 'chronology' mean and where did it originate from? For example, look up the meaning of the Greek word 'chronos'. Draw a diagram or picture to illustrate your understanding of 'time'. Consider how this very abstract idea may be made accessible to young children by showing it in visual or 'concrete' form. Make a timeline of your own life and attach to it pictures and small objects from your personal history.

Cause and effect; change and continuity

Causation and change appear in *knowledge and understanding of events, people and changes in the past* (DfEE/QCA, 1999a: pp104, 105). Knowledge of some content is required in the process of considering what changes took place, why an event happened and what the effects of this event were. It is difficult to talk about change without considering what it was that brought about this change. Teachers therefore need to be constantly raising with children the question 'why?' and also encouraging them to ask 'why?' themselves.

Skills in using the concepts of change and causation include the ability to:

- recognise and explain why events have happened and why people did things, giving reasons for these causes and consequences;
- identify why conflicts arose and how they were resolved;
- identify similarities and differences between different ways of life, different societies and different times in the past.

REFLECTIVE TASK

You have been given the topic 'Home life in Victorian Britain' and are concerned that you will only be looking at the factual detail about how people lived, with a danger of not addressing the skills and concepts required by the National Curriculum. Reflect on what you know about Victorian life and make a note of the opportunities you could create in your planning for raising the question 'why?'

Historical interpretation

The interpretation of the past is another complex idea, which can also involve historical skills. In the curriculum this point refers to the use of different sources which themselves interpret past events in different or distinctive ways. Primary teachers find this concept possibly one of the hardest to teach, largely because of the potential difficulties the idea poses. How can young children appreciate the fact that historians all differ in their interpretations; that they write their histories in very different ways according to their own personal viewpoints or beliefs? For example, a feminist will write a version of history giving a female perspective. All historical writings and sources are influenced to varying degrees by the views and attitudes of their authors and it is vitally important as a life skill that children develop the concept and the skills to enable them to detect the perspectives, bias and prejudices in texts.

Skills in historical interpretation include the ability to:

- interpret and understand sources such as pictures, charts, diagrams, maps, graphs and written texts of many kinds;
- make inferences about the information contained in sources, which is not necessarily obvious or evident. This skill often involves skill in using prior knowledge and making links with other information which is not present at the time. It was called by J.S. Bruner *going beyond the information given*;
- formulate and test hypotheses and generalisations;
- recreate interpretations of the past from sources and the use of historical imagination.

CLASSROOM STORY

One hot summer's day, Sandra's class erupt into the classroom following a playground squabble at lunchtime. She spends some time trying to get to the truth about what has really happened, and eventually realises that each child is providing a different version of events. Since she has a history lesson immediately after lunch, on the reasons for the defeat of the Spanish Armada, she decides to use this incident for teaching about interpretation.

Sandra has two accounts of the failure of the Armada to defeat the English navy and carry out an attack on England. One is written by the commander of the English fleet at Calais, who explains how it was skilful tactics and brave fighting which sent the Spanish fleet running away north. The other is an account by a Spanish commander, who blames his defeat entirely on the terrible weather, especially when passing round the northernmost parts of Britain.

Sandra reads the two accounts with the class and asks them to explain why they think the accounts are different. Did the event really happen in two different ways? Could it be possible that there could be two explanations that are both right, since the events they describe both happened? She compares the different versions of events from this period in the past with what has just happened in school, and asks the children to think about why there are often different versions or interpretations in history.

Historical sources

The notion of a 'source' is a fundamental one in history. The idea encompasses a deeply important concept in history – that of 'evidence'. Sources and the proof they provide are as important to the historian as are 'clues' and 'evidence' to the detective. The concept is also complex, since there is a huge diversity of historical sources, from people talking about their memories, to sets of statistics. Children need to learn how to derive information from historical sources, and this requires specific skills.

Skills in source analysis include the ability to:

- find information from a variety of sources. This skill involves other subsidiary skills, such as close observation, reading, calculation or exploration;
- use questions to derive information from sources;
- sort and classify information into meaningful, useful categories relevant to the enquiry;
- conceptualise new information and link it to previously understood concepts;
- see relationships and connections between pieces of information and the ability to make links with prior knowledge;
- recognise and detect bias. This skill is linked to that of being able to understand the motives of the author of the source and whether these have influenced what has been written or produced;
- evaluate sources used, e.g. to make decisions on the relative usefulness of different sources; to detect whether a source is reliable or biased;
- use empathy, e.g. to understand the values and beliefs of others in the past, even if different from our own.

PRACTICAL TASK PRACTICAL TASK PRACTICAL TASK PRACTICAL TASK PRACTICAL TASK

Build up a collection of sources on one of the history study units to use in the classroom. These might include replica artefacts from a local museum shop, from the school's own collection, and replicas borrowed from a local drama group. For example, for a topic on the Tudors, the following would be useful: a set of prints showing rich Tudor kings and queens, and a set of woodcuts printed from the internet in black and white; a selection of Tudor texts, such as letters, wills, inventories and verse; and finally a small collection of recordings of Tudor dance and church music.

Organising and communicating historical findings

'Communicating their findings in a variety of ways' is perhaps one of the most liberating phrases of the curriculum in the sense that it enables teachers to use as many different forms of communication as they want. Forms of communication include story, drama, role play, presentations, displays, art, music, ICT and many other media.

The organisation of what children have learned encompasses the key historical concepts of analysis and synthesis. Children need to learn how to break down their information in logical ways, and then to be able to reconstruct what they have learned to create an original piece of work, based on accurate source material and logical findings. These ideas underpin all writing and communication of history, and while they are not specific to history, they are an essential feature of the creative work of historians.

Skills in the organisation and communication of history include the ability to:

- organise information in meaningful and logical ways;
- communicate information through an appropriate medium.

Breadth of study: key areas of content

Specific areas of study are set out in the curriculum for each key stage, as follows:

Early Years Foundation Stage

In the Early Years Foundation Stage, the key focus is the development of a sense of time, a very big idea for children only three or four years old. Early years practitioners use familiar methods for introducing these ideas to children, such as personal and family history, objects that are understood by children, such as toys, games and clothes. The people that children know are also used as examples of different ages and relationships.

Although they seem quite simple ideas, these activities are essential for young children to lay the foundations for later learning in history. They begin to build up notions of time, sequence and chronology by realising that people grow older with time. Playing with old toys and dressing up, handling objects and talking about their significance is a precursor to using artefacts as historical sources. Story telling also begins to prepare children for the different historical contexts they will encounter in later history topics.

Key Stage 1

At Key Stage 1 children are taught the 'Knowledge, skills and understanding' through areas of study which focus firstly on their own experience of life, or the lives of their families or other people they know. There is a focus on 'change' in this aspect of the specified content. The focus on people's lives requires children to look at those who lived in the distant past and also at the lives of significant men, women and children from the history of Britain and the wider world. Experiences which are likely to be familiar to young children continue in the study of past events, again either drawn from the history of Britain or the wider world, such as Bonfire Night or the Olympic Games.

Several interesting developments in these requirements took place as a result of the revision of the National Curriculum in 1999. Firstly, there was an increased opportunity for teachers to explore the contribution of people from other nationalities or cultural groups, introduced through the inclusion of the phrase 'and the wider world' in requirements three and four. Also, the notion of a 'significant' person replaced 'famous'. It is important to consider what this word might mean in the context of choosing a character from the past to study (DfEE/QCA, 1999a p104).

The curriculum as specified for Key Stage 1 is refreshingly open-ended. It allows teachers, and children, to identify people and events which are known to them personally. It is only by making history relevant to children that it can possibly have any meaning or significance. Children in the early years have little grasp of the past. They are developing their idea of what 'the past' was, yet they will not see this past anywhere or experience it in any concrete way – their normal mode of learning while young. There is a danger that historical themes and topics might be quite meaningless and far too abstract for them to understand. It is therefore essential that they can relate to history topics in a personal way.

PRACTICAL TASK PRACTICAL TASK **PRACTICAL TASK** PRACTICAL TASK **PRACTICAL TASK**

Look up the dictionary entry for the word 'significant'. Give some thought to this idea and then write down a definition of your own. Finally, compile a list of people from the past, both from British and world history, that you think would be interesting for young children to hear about and who have also made a significant contribution in some way in the past.

Key Stage 2

The breadth of study at Key Stage 2 is quite wide-ranging, and can be difficult to complete in the four years spanned by the key stage. It is more prescriptive than that for Key Stage 1 and lays down specific blocks of history which must be studied, as follows:

- Local history study

- British history
    - The Romans, Anglo-Saxons and Vikings
    - Britain and the wider world in Tudor times
    - Either Victorian Britain or Britain since 1930

- A European history study: Ancient Greece

- A world history study, selected from:
    - Ancient Egypt
    - Ancient Sumer
    - The Assyrian Empire
    - The Indus Valley
    - The Maya
    - Benin
    - The Aztecs

In addition to understanding the need to teach the 'Knowledge, skills and understanding' through these topics, the teacher also needs to acquire some subject knowledge. Without this it will be difficult to see how to link work to the key skills and concepts, and also very difficult to make meaningful links with other curriculum subjects. For example, you would need to know a little about the Roman way of life, their homes and their art to be able to make links with the curriculum for art through Roman mosaics.

Many of these history topics relate to geography, art, music or drama, and, of course to literacy, ICT, and in some cases, numeracy. In many parts of the country, there are links between local history and national topics, such as the Tudors or, very often, the Victorians. There are often opportunities to make use of suitable areas of content from different subjects that overlap, and thus to develop cross-curricular or linked units of work which use processes of learning that are common to two or three curriculum subjects.

Excellence and Enjoyment: A Strategy for Primary Schools

Excellence and Enjoyment: A Strategy for Primary Schools (DfES, 2003b), the Green Paper *Every Child Matters* (DfES, 2003a) and the renewed *Primary Frameworks for Literacy and Mathematics* (DfES, 2006) are a multifaceted response to the principles embodied in the Education Act of 2002. This Act of Parliament outlined the Government's vision for a reformed system of education and was the basis in law of the beginnings of a break from the system imposed a decade earlier.

Excellence and Enjoyment, introduced in May 2003, aimed to introduce a greater focus on the needs and interests of children, shifting away from a subject-based curriculum. It emphasised creativity and innovation and advocated cross-curricular links with the *Primary Framework for Literacy and Mathematics*. Although these documents are not statutory, together with the exemplar schemes of work (DfEE/QCA, 1998) they assist teachers in planning.

Every Child Matters

In 2004, following a wide consultation with people working in children's services, and with parents, children and young people, the Government published *Every Child Matters: the Next Steps* (DfES, 2004b). This was published alongside the formal response to the report into the death of Victoria Climbié, the young girl who was tortured and killed by her great-aunt and the man with whom they lived. The Green Paper built on existing plans to strengthen preventative services by focusing on four key themes. *Every Child Matters* led to an unprecedented debate about services for children, young people and families.

The Every Child Matters agenda led to the passing of the Children Act of 2004, which aimed to put an integrated system at the heart of children's support services. The Children Act set clear principles and targets for all those in the professions working with children. The Government has since produced a number of initiatives, such as the *Children's Plan* (DCSF, 2007) with the purpose of making these principles accessible to all practitioners, such as those in schools, the social services and health workers, to form a 'Children's Workforce'. While the Children Act itself is a statutory document with the force of law, these initiatives provide support and guidance for teachers. They embody a vision set out by the government of the day for the future of all services which work for children, including the educational services.

The centrality of the child as learner, emphasised in *Every Child Matters: Change for Children* (DfES, 2004c), has led to a return to integrated, cross-curricular approaches, similar to those that were popular prior to the introduction of the National Curriculum! It is a widely held belief that young children often learn in a holistic way; in other words they learn through topics which are relevant and of interest to them (Jarvis and Parker, 2005). Thematic approaches which incorporate history as one of two or three subjects are now being advocated and illustrated by various publishers and by the QCA on their website, 'innovating with history' (www.qca.org.uk/history/innovating). There is, of course considerable scope for innovative and creative work, for example when the arts are combined with history, or when history is taught as one of a set of humanities subjects in topics such as 'Remembrance Day' and 'Why has our local shopping street changed?'. Other ways of developing creativity are discussed in more detail in Chapters 10 and 11.

REFLECTIVE TASK

Consider how you might incorporate the agenda of *Every Child Matters* into teaching about the past in the Early Years Foundation Stage. What historical sources would help you address this agenda?

General teaching requirements

There are four general teaching requirements, which need to be addressed where appropriate in history. These are: inclusion: providing effective learning opportunities for all children; the use of language across the curriculum; the use of information and communication technology (ICT) across the curriculum; health and safety.

Key skills, such as problem solving and thinking skills, which may be developed in the course of history schemes of work, are discussed in Chapter 4.

RESEARCH SUMMARY RESEARCH SUMMARY **RESEARCH SUMMARY** RESEARCH SUMMARY

Research into key concepts by Hilda Taba (1971) identified two different types of concept, the first group known as 'organisational' or 'methodological' concepts, and the second group, 'substantive' concepts. This early American research was later developed as part of the Schools Council Project 'Place, Time and Society' by Blyth and Derricot (W.A.L. Blyth, 1976). The project developed the notion of key concepts and introduced the notion of 'process' skills in history. Researchers over the years have used different terms to label these methodological concepts. For example, Nichol and Dean (1977) describe the same concepts as 'syntactic' and Cooper (2007a) refers to them as 'procedural'.

Considerable research has enabled historians to identify key skills in history. Donaldson (1978), among others, carried out research into children's abilities which overturned much of Piagetian theory. This led to research into children's skills in other areas, such as chronology, which questioned Piaget's early views and altered current approaches to teaching. Marwick (2001) has written about the rationale and methodology involved in using sources, Harnett (1998) has looked at the use of pictures as sources, McNaughton (1966) was an early advocate of developing the skills of inferential reasoning when using sources and Hoodless (1994a) has researched into children's reasoning. John West (1981a, 1981d), Hodkinson (2002), Hoodless (1996a, 2002) Barton and Levstik (1996), and Barton (2004), among many others, have all written about different aspects of children's understanding and learning about time and chronology.

REFLECTIVE TASK

Choose one of the key skills or concepts in history and read the relevant research. Reflect on how this knowledge will help you to plan, teach and assess this aspect of history.

A SUMMARY OF **KEY POINTS**

> It is a legal requirement for schools to teach what is specified in the National Curriculum for history.

> The programmes of study cover the factual knowledge, concepts and skills that should be taught. These need to be combined when planning units of work.

> There are two types of key concept in history and the humanities, methodological and substantive.

> There are many historical skills related to these concepts.

> The teaching of history is influenced by the National Frameworks for Literacy and Mathematics and by the agenda of *Every Child Matters*.

> The general teaching requirements of the National Curriculum also relate to the teaching of history.

MOVING *ON* > > > > > > MOVING *ON* > > > > > > MOVING *ON*

Standard I3, Standard I26

You might want to develop further your subject knowledge in specific content areas. There are numerous books and journal articles on each of the topics listed in the National Curriculum which will be of use in this work. Alternatively, you may want to research further into the ways in which children's understanding of the past develops, and again there is a vast literature on this subject. Key journals for both the areas of study are listed in the 'further reading' section below. A third aspect to look into more deeply might be the development of more detailed cross-curricular work in your school, and there is a growing body of literature on this. Each of these interests would contribute to a potential role as history or humanities coordinator.

FURTHER READING FURTHER READING **FURTHER READING** FURTHER READING

Ashby, R and Lee, PJ (1987) Children's concepts of empathy and understanding in history, in Portal, C (ed.) *The history curriculum for teachers.* Lewes: Falmer Press.

Cheminais, R (2006) *Every child matters: a practical guide for teachers.* London: Fulton.

Cooper, H (2004) *Exploring time and place through play.* London: David Fulton.

Professional journals

Primary History
Teaching History
Junior Education
Child Education

Academic journals

Education 3–13
The Journal of Curriculum Studies
The Curriculum Journal
Education
Educational Studies

Useful websites

www.everychildmatters.gov.uk

    The website for the *Every Child Matters* document.

www.nc.uk.net

    The website where you can read and download the full text of the National Curriculum.

www.qca.org.uk/history/innovating

www.ncaction.qca.org

    Two useful QCA websites.

www.standards.dfes.gov.uk

    The website where you can read and download the full text of the Professional Standards for Teachers.

www.teachernet.gov.uk

    A website for teachers which gives a useful summary of government initiatives.

3
Guidance and support for Key Stage 1 and Key Stage 2

Chapter objectives

By the end of this chapter you will have:

- developed your understanding of the non-statutory guidance and support in planning, teaching and assessing the history curriculum;
- considered how to develop the QCA schemes of work in planning history study units;
- considered the value of other guidance and information such as that provided by Ofsted and Teachers TV;
- developed your awareness of the influence of initiatives such as Every Child Matters on the teaching of history;
- notes and examples in the National Curriculum for history.

Professional Standards for QTS

This chapter will support you as you work towards evidencing attainment against the following Standards:

Q14: Have a secure knowledge and understanding of their subjects/curriculum areas and related pedagogy to enable them to teach effectively across the age and ability range for which they are trained.

Q15: Know and understand the relevant statutory and non-statutory curricula and frameworks, including those provided through the national Strategies, for their subjects/curriculum areas, and other relevant initiatives applicable to the age and ability range for which they are trained.

For many years, since the introduction of the National Curriculum (DfEE/QCA, 1999b), teachers have worked under contradictory pressures: one to conform and follow a prescribed curriculum; the other to be innovative and creative, and to develop their own, more customised schemes of work. There is, however, a considerable amount of non-statutory guidance to give teachers a clearer idea and provide exemplary material.

The notes that accompany the National Curriculum for history give guidance on how to interpret the 'Knowledge, skills and understanding' section. For example in relation to 'historical interpretation', the note explains, *People represent and interpret the past in many different ways, including in pictures, plays, films, reconstructions, museum displays, and fictional and non-fiction accounts*. (DfEE/QCA, 1999a, p105). The notes also indicate suitable cross-curricular links that could be made with other subjects. The examples suggest aspects of each of the study units that could be chosen. For example, in the course of studying Ancient Greece, teachers could choose 'arts and architecture' or 'citizens and slaves' as a key focus, where there would be opportunities for comparison with the present day and for work on citizenship and equality.

The QCA schemes of work

The QCA has carried out developmental work which has been of great assistance to primary teachers, provided ideas, examples of planning, resources and references. The first materials which became widely used were examples published as *A scheme of work for Key Stages 1 and 2: History* (DfEE/QCA, 1998). These schemes of work were intended as guidance to assist primary teachers in the development of their own termly or half-termly units of work and were intended to act as a companion to *Maintaining breadth and balance at Key Stages 1 and 2* (QCA, 1998).

The aim of these early publications was to encourage schools not to lose sight of the importance of a balanced curriculum, one in which the whole curriculum would be covered, despite the continuing emphasis placed on improving standards in the core subjects of English, mathematics, science and also ICT. They proved to be a major source of support for teachers struggling to deal with the introduction of the new Literacy and Numeracy Strategies, new requirements to focus on ICT, citizenship, and PE, and further demands for increased detail in yearly and end-of-key-stage assessments.

The first published schemes included 18 units of work, five for Key Stage 1 and 13 for Key Stage 2. In 2000 a further four units of work were added to extend the range of ideas, one for Key Stage 1 and three for Key Stage 2, which built on children's prior learning. The units were allocated to specific year groups, with no suggestion for teaching in that order. The units were intended simply as exemplars, from which teachers and schools might build their own units. They were drawn up in quite a 'skeletal' fashion, with fairly basic ideas for activities and, in some cases, were quite limited and repetitive in the range of ideas presented. While the structure of the units was very clear and useful, much detail was lacking, particularly in relation to the links that could be made with the core and other curriculum areas and the potential links with language development.

The rationale for producing these exemplars is clear: if a school develops its own schemes of work, then these are more likely to meet the particular needs and address the particular interests of the children they are designed for. Local resources, specific interests and learning styles can be planned for if a specific context is in mind when drawing up these plans. The importance of context cannot be overemphasised.

The schemes of work were enormously helpful and teachers across the country gladly took them and used them directly, without taking time to adapt them to suit local needs. In some cases this resulted in a very impoverished experience of history for some children. Teachers in Key Stage 1 would adhere to the units suggested for their age group and rigidly carry out activities that had little appeal to their children and did little to extend their learning about the past. The key message then is that these schemes need to be developed and contextualised. Using your own initial analysis of your teaching context, you will need to revise the outlines provided in the schemes, add different activities, omit others which you feel are inappropriate and reshape the units to suit your own school and locality.

The following example is taken from the QCA scheme of work for history at Key Stage 1 and Key Stage 2 (taken from the QCA website).

History at Key Stages 1 and 2 (Year 3/4)

Unit 7: Why did Henry VIII marry six times?
Section 3: What did Henry VIII do all day?

Objectives

Children should learn:
about the power and importance of a Tudor king;
to identify what monarchs did and did not do.

Activities	Outcomes
Give the children a list of activities combining those that a Tudor king was expected to do, e.g. *hunting, attending church, signing papers, dining in state*, with some that he did not do, e.g. *cutting wood, selling cloth*. Ask the children to sort the activities into two categories; those they think the king did and those he did not do. Ask the children to feed back their decisions and discuss the range of responsibilities of a Tudor monarch.	**Children:** sort information to demonstrate their knowledge of the role and duties of a Tudor king.

Points to note

The role of a Tudor king will be unfamiliar to many pupils. Class discussion should focus on building up the idea of the king's power, his legal and religious role, and the fact that he was surrounded by courtiers.
The discussion could be extended to make comparisons with the role of the monarch today and contribute to citizenship education.

Figure 3. Example of a QCA scheme of work (www.qca.org.uk)

REFLECTIVE TASK

Consider the idea presented in the example above. Devise a longer list of activities that took place in a Tudor castle. Consider what sort of activities the children might find interesting or funny, and which ones would clearly not be considered suitable for a king to do.

Think about the sort of resources you would need to make sure that the children understood about the different roles and jobs of people in a castle. Make a clear contrast between the life of the king (and other rich people) and the life of a servant.

Decide whether this idea would cover just one lesson or more. Could the children really understand these different roles and carry out this activity in one lesson?

Innovating with history

This is a useful resource for teaching history at Key Stages 1 and 2. The guidance on planning on the 'Innovating with history' area of the QCA website, (www.qca.org.uk/

history/innovating) is very clearly set out. Key aspects of planning are explained under the heading 'improving curriculum planning' and case studies from specific localities illustrate the planning process and how this is based on the schemes of work. Under the heading 'contributing to the wider curriculum', there is guidance on making links between history and other curriculum areas such as citizenship, inclusion, ICT, literacy and creativity. The site is regularly updated and new units for the history schemes of work are added from time to time. There are currently several new units which illustrate ways in which schools have combined their work in history with another subject, or how they have adapted an existing unit to incorporate work on areas such as literacy and numeracy, or to suit the particular context of their school. The site also provides links to other sites of value in supporting planning, teaching and assessment.

CLASSROOM STORY

After looking at the QCA website and studying the approach used in 'Innovating with history', Judith decided to design her own unit, linking history with music and dance. In history, the school's long-term plan included, for her year group, a unit on 'Britain and the wider world in Tudor times'. Judith knew, from seeing Hollywood films and TV costume dramas, that music was an important feature of life at all levels of society in Tudor times.

She searched the internet and found that a good selection of tunes was available. She learned that there was less of a distinction between popular music and court music than she had expected. The popular music used by street musicians contained pieces that had their origins in court, just as court composers often used popular tunes for their compositions. Yet a third type of music was that which would have been performed in church, during religious ceremonies.

Judith planned a series of lessons, within which she could make use of her choice of music. She wanted the children to experience the richness and variety of music in Elizabethan times and chose tunes which would have been known to ordinary people as well as ones heard at court. So she decided to focus on the QCA scheme of work 'Rich and poor in Tudor times'. This gave her an ideal opportunity to link the different types of music she had found to each part of her topic. Starting with the well-known characters of the period, she linked her dances and songs with the history of the court and the monarchy. She then looked at the living conditions of the poor and, to accompany this work, she provided opportunities for the children to listen to street dance music and songs. She also wanted to teach her children one of the dances that Queen Elizabeth would have danced. The pavane and galliard were two of the most popular dance forms of the time.

Finally, after a visit to a local early church, she introduced the children to Tudor church music. The children gained an extra dimension in their understanding of the Tudor period through this imaginative approach to the topic.

(For examples of the types of music Judith used, see the list of 'further resources', page 31.)

National Curriculum in Action

The website National Curriculum in Action (www.ncaction.org.uk/) provides further illustrative examples taken from ongoing work in schools. A comment from a teacher on the website points out, *This is one of the most useful resources I've come across to support the National Curriculum*. The materials on the site are supportive in many ways, and particularly in showing examples of children's work and providing good ideas for learning activities and experiences. Each example gives an overview of the lesson objectives and of the planned activities, along with examples of children's work. There are also commentaries which help to clarify how the requirements and guidance can be translated into practice, and which indicate how the work was assessed. Evaluative comment on the effectiveness of the activities is also very valuable.

PRACTICAL TASK PRACTICAL TASK **PRACTICAL TASK** PRACTICAL TASK **PRACTICAL TASK**

Choose one of the examples of children's work from *ncaction* and look at the planning overview and commentary related to it, noting how the activity was set up. Using a different topic and, if possible, one that you will be teaching yourself, plan a lesson, taking account of what you have learned from the *ncaction* example.

Teachernet, Teachers TV and other broadcasts

Teachernet (www.teachernet.gov.uk) and Teachers TV (www.teachers.tv) provide summaries of recent and current developments along with ideas for planning, teaching and curriculum development. Both the BBC (bbc.co.uk/schools) and ITV (www.channel4learning.net/) produce excellent schools broadcasts, with productions that will help to bring history to life in your classroom. It is well worth reviewing what is currently available that will relate to the history topics you are working on. There are also numerous publishers who produce classroom materials and teachers' guides. Other resources for history will be discussed in Chapter 7.

Ofsted: reports and recommendations

Ofsted produces annual reports which give a good overview of the state of the different curriculum areas in schools. There are several recent reports and articles on primary history, its strengths and weaknesses and recommendations for future development. These are very helpful in their succinct analysis of what now needs to be the focus in primary schools and where improvements can be made. There is an important overview of progress between 2003 and 2007, *History in the balance* (Ofsted, 2007). Its main recommendations are the need to:

- revise the curriculum for history to improve children's understanding of chronology and their awareness of the 'big questions' of history;
- ensure a balance in the curriculum between a compulsory core of knowledge and skills with a more flexible element which can be relevant to local needs;
- pay attention to coherence and progression;
- ensure the history curriculum reflects the principles of *Every Child Matters*, providing children with the historical knowledge and skills to understand the world in which they live.

(Ofsted, 2007, p5)

In particular, primary schools should:

- evaluate their current provision for history and consider how it can best meet the needs of all pupils and help them to understand the world in which they live;
- establish a clear rationale for learning history topics which enables pupils to develop some understanding of chronology, create a narrative and understand the wider implications, or 'big picture' of what they have studied;
- clarify their understanding of the principles and aims of the National Curriculum for history and ensure progression in pupils' knowledge and skills;
- ensure that there is 'workable assessment' to support the above;
- ensure the linking of key stages to provide better coherence and progression;
- improve links with other subjects where appropriate, particularly literacy, numeracy, ICT and citizenship.

(Ofsted, 2007, p6–7)

Recent Ofsted reports and publications are available in full on the news section of the Ofsted website: http://ofstednews.ofsted.gov.uk.

Recent initiatives

Since the year 2000, there have been several significant new educational initiatives produced by the Government. These have begun to influence the primary history curriculum and how it is delivered.

All Our Futures

Following complaints of excessive workload from schools, there was a move to slim down the curriculum. What this meant, in practice, was that schools were relieved of the pressure to cover the whole curriculum in the same degree of detail. This led to a reduction in the time spent on the foundation subjects and in particular on subjects such as history. The humanities and the arts began to suffer more than other parts of the curriculum that were considered more important.

In response to these developments, publications such as *All Our Futures: Creativity, Culture and Education* (NACCCE/DfEE, 1999) focused heavily on the importance of stimulating creativity in areas of the curriculum such as the arts. Research has pointed to the significance of learning different subjects in stimulating different skills, attitudes and qualities in a child (Gardner, 1993). For instance, the arts are considered important in stimulating children's creative skills and in satisfying a need for creative opportunities in their school work. Musical activities were believed to stimulate the brain and even enhance children's skills in subjects such as mathematics. Gardner highlighted the variety of 'intelligences', suggesting that children needed the opportunity to explore the world in all its different forms in order to develop their skills.

Excellence and Enjoyment: A Strategy for Primary Schools

Published in 2003, *Excellence and Enjoyment* (DfES, 2003b) built on the notion of linking subjects and building opportunities for creativity into the primary curriculum. It set forth the goals of empowering primary schools to *take control of their curriculum* in order to revise their work in a creative way relevant to their children's needs; to *use the freedoms they already have to suit their pupils and the contexts in which they work*. The overall strategy which encompasses the literacy and numeracy frameworks aims to support the whole curriculum in the same way as support has hitherto been provided for the core subjects.

A key feature of the guidance was its aim of helping schools to *design broad and rich curricula which make the most of links between different areas and provide opportunities for children to have a wide range of learning experiences*. In particular there was a focus on schools being *creative and innovative in how they teach*. Observations in schools had found increasingly that, although children were engaged in written work, there were too few opportunities for them to talk and build up their skills in oracy, and that there was a lack of enthusiasm and commitment on the part of both teachers and children to subjects such as history.

Every Child Matters

The agenda of *Every Child Matters: Change for Children* (DfES, 2004c) has influenced planning and teaching in primary history. Part of a long-term programme of change, this document clarifies how the emphasis in guidance for schools has shifted from covering specified curriculum content, to meeting the needs of the child. The overall well-being of children and their achievement in school as a means of future success are key concerns of this guidance. Underpinned by the principle of personalisation in terms of the range of wider services offered in the support of children, Every Child Matters requires that the needs and interests of individual children are addressed and that every child should succeed, regardless of their background. Teachers need to be aware of the significance of these initiatives and weave the objectives and key features into their history teaching.

History is an inclusive subject, with strategies to meet all types of learning style and special needs, including the gifted and able. It is a wide-ranging subject and children with English as an Additional Language (EAL) and those from different ethnic and cultural backgrounds can also feel included in the curriculum, if content is carefully selected and thoughtfully employed (see Chapter 12).

The history curriculum is most effective when it is adapted to meet local needs and is relevant to the school and its children. There are, of course, examples of schools where this approach has been maintained consistently in the past. Those with a strong tradition of work in the foundation subjects tended to continue to work on themes and topics which had been established for some time. One class teacher I observed maintained her belief in the importance of making links across the curriculum, and continued to teach her topic on 'Roman Britain' in a highly cross-curricular manner, which at the same time made considerable use of local Roman resources, sites and remains. The topic was both meaningful and exciting for her classes.

PRACTICAL TASK PRACTICAL TASK **PRACTICAL TASK** PRACTICAL TASK **PRACTICAL TASK**

For many years, Judith had based her Year 5 history study on a residential visit to a local Roman town. The class would visit the museum and local heritage centre, enjoy a river trip, walk around the Roman walls, visit a site where they met a Roman soldier and, in the evening go on a town trail and listen to ghost stories from the past. Once back in school, the children worked on their history topic. Judith linked most of the other subjects in the curriculum to the theme for the rest of the term.

Make a note of the cross-curricular links Judith might have made with literacy, mathematics, geography and ICT.

The Primary Framework for Literacy and Mathematics

The *Primary Framework for Literacy and Mathematics* (DfES, 2006) aims to ensure that the principles of *Every Child Matters* and *Excellence and Enjoyment* are put into practice in schools. *Excellence and Enjoyment* promoted the view that *what excites and engages them best is truly excellent teaching*. The learning of literacy and mathematics as part of the whole learning experience, and not in isolation from the rest of the curriculum, is a principle that underlies the renewed frameworks. Examples of the close links that can be made between these core areas and history are indicated in Chapter 8.

RESEARCH SUMMARY RESEARCH SUMMARY **RESEARCH SUMMARY** RESEARCH SUMMARY

Holistic learning

The principles advocated in recent initiatives can be seen in research going back to the early 1960s, which emphasised the development of the 'whole child' (Peters, 1967) through a well balanced education. This has not just been a philosophical argument, however; research in the United States found that the brain's two hemispheres appeared to have different functions; the left concerned with more logical, analytic thought, and the right with more 'holistic' capabilities, such as being able to recognise whole images and spatial movement. It was concluded that the two halves work as a whole dynamic system, with both hemispheres contributing in different types of activity. Different areas of the brain were found to work together on different activities. Transferable skills were found to cross between apparently quite unrelated subjects, such as music and mathematics (Fox and Gardiner, 1997). Creative, insightful thinking often occurs as a result of the interaction between different areas of learning or activities, such as between drama and writing. The forming of intelligence, it was believed, was a result of the use of the whole brain, not just one part of it. It was argued, therefore, that there needed to be a revision of curriculum requirements for this kind of learning to take place, through greater flexibility to ensure that children's needs could be addressed and also through opportunities to combine areas of learning to enhance such opportunities and to promote creativity. (For further detail on creativity, see Chapters 10 and 11.)

A cross-curricular approach to history

The Enlightenment of the seventeenth and eighteenth centuries in Europe emphasised the importance of deductive reasoning and rational decision-making, a key aspect of historical enquiry. History also makes use of creative thinking in order to create interpretations and hypotheses about the past. While many dispute that creativity can be taught at all, and argue that it is an innate ability, the authors of *All Our Futures*, the NACCCE Report (1999) maintain that it can indeed be taught, and explain why and how. They also argue that creativity is not unique to the arts, but is also a key feature of humanities subjects such as history.

W.A.L. Blyth carried out research into the cross-curricular links between and within the humanities subjects. Much of this work was published as a Schools Council Project, *Place, time and society* (1976), and was discussed in his book, *Making the grade for primary humanities* (1990). The NACCCE Report argued that balance in the curriculum was essential and that time and resources were needed equally for subjects such as history as for literacy and numeracy. Provision for arts and humanities, the report argued, was being rapidly eroded, and also for creativity in other areas such as science. It was argued that all areas of learning are equally important since they differ in the modes of knowledge that they generate and in their forms of study. The report called for explicit provision in these areas in order to form a fully developed, well-educated person.

A SUMMARY OF **KEY POINTS**

> The National Curriculum contains non-statutory guidance in the notes and examples provided for the history curriculum.

> QCA schemes of work are a valuable support and source of ideas for planning. However, they need to be treated as examples only, and should be developed as appropriate according to your teaching context.

> The recently introduced 'Innovating with history' website has some useful exemplars of ways of combining and adapting units for a more cross-curricular approach.

> The ncaction website is also a most useful source of examples of children's work and of how this has been assessed according to National Curriculum levels of attainment.

> Teachers TV and other broadcasts can provide additional support and guidance for teaching history.

> Cross-curricular approaches and creativity have been advocated in the NACCCE Report, as well as in *Excellence and Enjoyment*, *Every Child Matters* and the *Primary Framework*.

MOVING *ON* > > > > > > MOVING *ON* > > > > > > MOVING *ON*

Standard I15, Standard I16

Look further at the potential of history for cross-curricular work, and of the ways in which it might be combined with the teaching of the core subjects such as literacy to enhance skills in all of this area. Identify the literacy skills which might overlap with work in history. Read the research background to the ideas behind cross-curricular teaching and learning and particularly take note of points raised by Ofsted in their recent reports at http://ofstednews.ofsted.gov.uk. Consider the role of the curriculum coordinator in fostering this work in school.

FURTHER READING FURTHER READING **FURTHER READING** FURTHER READING

Beard, R (2003) Breadth, balance and the literacy hour, *Primary History*, 34: 9–11.

DfES (2004) *Every child matters: change for children in schools*. London: DfES. This is specifically about the role of professionals working in education and will be the last relevant part of this initiative for you to read.

Freeman, J and Weake, J (2004) Engage, innovate, motivate with QCA's new website for history, *Primary History*, 38: 16–17.

Harrison, S (2004) Ofsted Report on primary history. *Primary History*, 37: 15–16. Although this is an old article, the points it makes about good practice in teaching history are still very relevant.

Further resources

Arbeau, T (1967) *Orchesography*. New York: Dover Publications. An excellent practical guide to Elizabethan dancing, giving the steps and melody lines to several popular dance forms.

CDs

Music and dance:

Musicians of Swanne Alley, *Elizabethan Ballads and Theatre Music.* Virgin Veritas, 0724348207920.

David Munrow, *Renaissance Danseryes*. Virgin Veritas, 0094635000320. Two collections of popular tunes and courtly pieces.

Church music:

Early English Choral Music. Naxos, 8.505079.

A collection of five CDs of various composers, available separately.

(NB: Be aware of copyright restrictions.)

Useful websites

www.bbc.co.uk/schools/

www.channel4learning.net/

> The BBC schools website and the Channel 4 website contain useful broadcasts and other information.

www.qca.org.uk/history/innovating

> This website also includes information on developments in other curriculum areas, such as art, where links have been made with history units.

www.everychildmatters.gov.uk

> The website for the *Every Child Matters* document.

www.ncaction.org.uk/

> A QCA website with good examples of children's work and assessments of these.

http://ofstednews.ofsted.gov.uk

> You can find Ofsted reports on this website.

www.standards.dfes.gov.uk/primary/frameworks

> The website where you can read and download the *Primary Frameworks for Literacy and Mathematics*.

www.teachers.tv

> Contains broadcasts and useful information.

www.teachernet.gov.uk

> A website for teachers which gives a useful summary of government initiatives.

4

Planning for progression and opportunities for the development of key skills

Chapter objectives

By the end of this chapter you will have:

- acquired an understanding of short-, medium- and long-term planning in history;
- considered ways of planning for progression in children's learning in history;
- explored how key concepts and skills can be developed within a well-planned sequence of history lessons.

Professional Standards for QTS

This chapter will support you as you work towards evidencing attainment against the following Standards:

Q22: Plan for progression across the age and ability range, designing effective learning sequences within lessons and across series of lessons...

Levels of planning

Three levels of planning take place in schools: long-, medium- and short-term planning. Long-term planning covers the work of the whole school in a subject and gives a brief overview of what is covered in each year and each key stage. Medium-term plans are referred to as 'units of work', 'schemes of work' or 'history studies'. These give more detail and show how a topic or theme in history is developed, normally over a term or half term. Short-term plans are the lesson plans made for individual classes or groups for each lesson or activity and include most detail. While you will initially be involved in short-term planning, it is useful to understand the whole planning process.

Long-term planning

Long-term plans are usually drawn up by the subject coordinator for the whole school, their main purpose being to ensure that there is some coherence, variety, breadth and balance in the experience of the children over their primary education. Long-term plans help teachers avoid any unnecessary repetition of topics and are useful in providing evidence that National Curriculum requirements are being met.

An issue raised by the report, 'History in the balance' (Ofsted, 2007), however, is that coherence and progression are often lacking in the long-term plans for primary history. The example given in the Classroom story below illustrates quite a sudden break between work that is largely focused on the child's own experiences in Key Stage 1 and that in Key Stage 2, which focuses on more distant historical topics.

The report also comments on the way that pupils dart from different periods and back again with little apparent rationale for doing so. There may be good reasons for this apparently random organisation of topics and themes, such as the availability of resources or local museum provision, but plans such as this give little evidence of such reasoning. The report raises questions about the way in which the curriculum is structured and about the rationale for that structure, which should be apparent in planning.

CLASSROOM STORY

A school's history coordinator was given the task of updating the medium-term plan created by her predecessor. She was concerned about how effectively it addressed the issue of chronology. She looked at the timing of different themes and wondered whether these would provide children with a clear idea of the passing of time.

History	Term one	Term two	Term three
Year 1	Our toys		Our school
Year 2		Our local area	Seaside holidays in the past
Year 3	The Romans in Britain	What was it like for children in the Second World War?	
Year 4		A Viking case study	Rich and poor in Tudor times
Year 5	How did life change in our locality in Victorian times?		Ancient Greeks
Year 6		The Aztec civilisation	What can we learn about recent history from a study of the life of a significant person?

Figure 4. Example of a school's long-term plan

PRACTICAL TASK PRACTICAL TASK **PRACTICAL TASK** PRACTICAL TASK **PRACTICAL TASK**

Consider how chronology might be more effectively addressed and revise the plan.

Medium-term planning

A medium-term plan shows the objectives or learning outcomes – what the teacher wants the children to learn by the end of the unit of work or scheme of work. More detailed than long-term plans, they are usually written by the class teacher or by a team of teachers working with a number of classes in a year group on the same theme, sometimes with the support of the subject coordinator. They are working documents for the teacher or team of teachers to use and amend, for example, as new resources become available. All levels of planning require preparation, the collection of ideas and resources, and subject specific knowledge suitable for teaching the subject and assessing children's learning. This information needs to be shown in the medium-term planning.

Beginning to plan a unit of work

There is no one correct way of planning a unit of work in history. However, there are some principles that are worth keeping in mind:

- Consider the topic you are going to teach, such as 'Britain since 1930' and identify a key concept in history that you can use to organise teaching and learning;
- Taking into account the children's learning needs and interests, formulate an overarching question to guide their work, such as 'How has life changed for children in Britain since the Second World War?';
- Select sources and other resources that will be useful in addressing this question;
- Devise a sequence of related questions as a focus for each lesson within the unit;
- Plan teaching and learning activities for each lesson, ensuring there is continuity and progression in the learning of content, concepts such as 'change', and skills;
- Plan a motivating first lesson to set the context of the topic, such as a broadcast, story or class visit;
- Make a note of cross-curricular links with the *Framework for Literacy and Mathematics* and with other curriculum subjects;
- Plan opportunities for assessment;
- Devise an appropriate way to conclude the topic, where children can share and celebrate their learning.

It is important at this stage to link the skills, concepts and factual content together around a central question, which is likely to interest the children. Useful examples of schemes of work based on key questions are provided by the DfEE/QCA (1998). Further examples of medium-term plans for each subject can be accessed at www.standards.dfes.gov.uk, and other websites with sample planning are listed in the 'Useful websites' section below. Useful general guidance and advice on planning can also be found on the Nuffield primary history website (http://primaryhistory.org/leadinghistory).

The example on pages 36–7 of some initial medium-term planning for a unit covering half a term's work is largely based on the QCA Schemes of Work for History, Unit 6A, but incorporates two new lessons on the grounds that the new objectives will make better cross-curricular links and will also relate to local resources more effectively.

Short-term planning

Short-term planning refers to the planning of individual lessons by the class teacher. For example, a lesson on Roman settlements would be part of a larger medium-term plan based on the National Curriculum study, 'Romans, Anglo-Saxons and Vikings in Britain'. Apart from showing the teaching and learning activities that will take place, a key aspect of the lesson plan is to show your learning objectives. These will be based on National Curriculum requirements and may also include objectives related to literacy or perhaps another curriculum subject if there are cross-curricular links throughout the topic.

Objectives, often expressed as key questions, are the knowledge, skills or understanding which you will want the children to have learned by the end of the lesson. These are the

YEAR: 4	TERM: Autumn	SUBJECT: History: What was it like to live in Roman Britain?					
Wk/date	Key learning objectives/ questions: what I want the children to learn this week	Activities: how am I going to achieve this?	Who has over/ under achieved?	Assessment of progress	How will assessment inform future planning?	Evaluation: how well did the lesson meet the objectives?	What would I do differently next time?
1	**Why do people move away from where they were born?** • relate their own experience to the concept of settlement • recognise that people moved to different areas long ago and had the same reasons as people have now	Discuss experiences of moving home, in Britain or from abroad, using maps. Discuss reasons and make bar chart to show common reasons. Discuss why immigrants, emigrants and refugees move.	Two children over achieved; three under.	Most children met the objectives, but many struggled with reading maps and new words.	Focus on map reading; introduce key vocabulary. Monitor the five children noted more carefully. Plan extension tasks for the more able.	Met objectives.	Plan key vocabulary and skills work more carefully.
2	**Who invaded and settled in Britain a long time ago?** • use the terms 'invade' and 'settle' • place the Celtic and Roman periods on a timeline • understand that the Romans invaded and then settled in Britain	Develop understanding of 'invade' and 'settle'. Give children cards to group with these terms, eg *stay, arrive, conquer, land, visit, remain.* Ask children to explain reasons for choices. Establish that people have been invading and settling in Britain for a long time. Place labels and pictures on timeline, sorting pictures into Roman and Celtic groups, and identifying invaders.					
3	**Who were the Celts and who were the Romans?** • select and record information about Celtic and Roman ways of life using a variety of sources • compare these ways of life	Provide information and pictures of the Celts and Romans. Ask children to complete a grid, with the headings: 'How they did things', 'Celts', 'Romans'. In the first column, children list aspects such as dress, belief, language, towns, farms, technology, art. Compare the two ways of life using words, pictures or sentences in the other columns.					

Figure 5. Medium-term plan

4	**Why did the Romans settle where they did?** • use maps and ICT to investigate types and patterns of settlement in Roman times • discuss and record reasons for these patterns	Use the webpage http://www.roman-britain.org/places/_roman_britain_layermap.htm. Children discuss aspects of Roman settlement, eg military, domestic, manufacturing, towns. Provide groups with a map of Roman Britain which shows the physical geography. Groups discuss possible reasons for settlements to have been located where they were, e.g. towns near the coast. Ask them to note and list their ideas to share in the plenary.		
5	**How did the Romans change Britain?** • use evidence that tells us about life in Roman Britain • ask and answer questions about what survived from the Roman settlement of Britain	Visit to a Roman site. Before the visit, tell the children that the Romans introduced some of their customs and ways of life, e.g. *towns, baths, new forms of religion and farming methods.* Tell them that the Celts responded by building villas and adapting Roman styles of pottery and dress. Ask children to suggest what they would like to find out about on their visit. Develop a list of questions for them to use at the site. At the site look for evidence of Roman lifestyles. Help the children to answer the prepared questions.		
6	**What do we know about the Roman way of life?** • organise and communicate their historical findings using skills in literacy and ICT	Ask the children to create a classroom display, or produce a child's guide to the site they visited on paper or in the form of a webpage to the site they visited.		

Figure 5. Medium-term plan

learning outcomes that you will be able to assess against your objectives, to identify which children have not met them, and which have exceeded them (see Chapter 6).

Your own knowledge of history is important otherwise you will not be clear in setting objectives and assessment tasks. In planning an activity, decide which of the 'Knowledge, skills and understanding' links most closely and logically to what you want the children to learn.

To reduce the amount of time spent on paperwork, many teachers now use their detailed medium-term plans directly for teaching lessons. However, trainee teachers will need to demonstrate that they can write appropriate, detailed lesson plans in history and also how their work in history links with work in other areas. For example, see the links made in the example of a Year 3 plan on page 39 (shown in italics).

In evaluating a lesson, you will need to say how effective your teaching strategies, classroom management and use of resources were, as well as commenting on how far the children met your objectives and how you might change your approach next time.

PRACTICAL TASK PRACTICAL TASK **PRACTICAL TASK** PRACTICAL TASK **PRACTICAL TASK**

Choose one event or idea from a history study unit that might form the basis of a lesson. Show how you would make a link between the 'Knowledge, skills and understanding' and the lesson content. Indicate how you might link literacy or another curriculum subject. Use the planning sheet on page 39 as an example and, if possible, test out your plan in school.

Planning for progression

Ofsted (2007) points to a lack of progression in primary history teaching, particularly in teaching and learning about chronology. Little rigorous research has been carried out into children's developing skills and understanding in history; however, there are some indications from research of the ways in which children's learning develops.

Progression in subject knowledge: content

As early years practitioners know, young children in the Early Years Foundation Stage can only remember and handle a limited number of pieces of information at a time. They might only be able to deal with two pieces of information at once, in order to make comparisons between them. In Key Stage 1, they are likely to be able to retain sufficient detail to cope with four or more pieces of information. This ability underpins the National Curriculum requirement to *recognise why people did things, why events happened and what happened as a result*, and to *identify differences between ways of life at different times* (DfEE/QCA, 1999a, p104).

For example, a Year 1 child, who has not yet begun to develop skills in information processing and finds factual information hard to remember, might comment, after hearing the story of the Gunpowder Plot, 'Guy Fawkes was bad.' There is one simple piece of information in this sort of statement, with little reasoning involved.

Year 3 History Lesson Plan: Roman Britain. Lesson 2

Previous Knowledge and Understanding *(refer to specific learning which has taken place in this area and any misconceptions the children may have had)*
Knowledge of the Roman invasions and of the meaning of the words 'invade' and 'settle'.

Specific Learning Intentions *(what you intend the children to learn, with links to National Curriculum and Primary Framework if appropriate)*
• to use maps and ICT to investigate types and patterns of settlement in Roman times. History NC: 4a, 4b, 8a; Geog NC: 1a, 1b, 1c, 6d; ICT NC: 5b.
• to discuss and record reasons for these patterns. Primary Framework for Literacy: Y3, strands 1, 9.

Planned Learning Experience *(how the children will learn what you intend them to learn, how are you personalising the children's learning, how will you use any other adults in your classroom?)* *(ensure you identify clearly how you will use speaking and listening strategies and ICT where appropriate)*	Process of assessment *(how you will assess your selected children? e.g. observation, written outcomes, notes on discussion etc.)*	Success criteria *(criteria by which children can measure their achievements and set future targets for themselves)*	Evaluations *(the appropriateness of your planned learning experience and your selected teaching strategies)*
- Look at aspects of Roman settlement, such as military, domestic, towns etc. *using ICT and whiteboard* with the whole class. (Differentiated questioning.) - *Links with geography:* Provide a map of Roman Britain which shows the physical geography. Ask groups to discuss possible reasons for settlements being located where they were, e.g. towns near the coast or on rivers or estuaries; forts at strategic points. Additional support for the less able group. - *Links with Primary Framework:* Children make notes to list their ideas to share with the class in the plenary through Speaking and Listening.	Observation during initial and plenary Speaking and Listening to note children's responses, and marking children's written notes	• Children interpret and discuss their maps effectively • They locate different types of Roman settlements on the map • They create logical, clear notes	

Next Steps (Assessment for Learning)
For the children identified *(make use of feedback from the children, listening to their voices)*

For you as a teacher *(how will you improve your questioning, modelling, etc.?)*

Figure 6. Short-term plan

However, a Year 2 child, in talking about the same story with his teacher says: 'I think that Guy Fawkes was very bad when he tried to blow up Parliament because he would have hurt all the people inside.'

A comment like this shows that this child is able to link together in his mind a number of different pieces of information: his opinion about Guy Fawkes, what Guy Fawkes tried to do, and the likely effects. This child is therefore making links between three pieces of information, one based on his own point of view and another making a causal link. These links are apparent from the language he uses: 'I think'; 'because'.

By the end of Key Stage 2, a child of average ability would be expected to write a paragraph about an event in the past, incorporating as many as seven or eight separate pieces of information, and making links of different kinds between them. The National Curriculum requires that they *identify and describe reasons for, and results of, historical events*, and also *describe and make links between the main events, situations and changes within and across the different periods and societies studied* (DfEE/QCA, 1999a).

PRACTICAL TASK PRACTICAL TASK **PRACTICAL TASK** PRACTICAL TASK **PRACTICAL TASK**

Study this example of a child's talk comparing two stories about Queen Boudicca. Analyse the information processing involved, such as the number of pieces of factual information it contains, the number of opinions, and any other features of interest.

I think this is more respectful to her because in the 'Rotten Romans' book, it calls her 'Big Boud' and stuff, and it says her husband was 'a great wimp', and so on. In this one it says, as though the king did the right thing. So I think that is kind of a lot more harsher – in this one it says like 'he did the right thing'.

Year 6 pupil

Children are expected to use their knowledge of the past to develop a sense of period – the characteristic features of the periods and societies they study. They will need to have retained this knowledge sufficiently to make comparisons with the present day or with another historical period. The website National Curriculum in Action (www.ncaction.org.uk) gives good examples of levels of work and expectations.

Progression in understanding historical concepts

Key concepts such as time and chronology, continuity and change, cause and effect and interpretation all involve historical subject knowledge and skills. Children need to develop an understanding of their meaning in order to be able to use them effectively. Using the concepts of chronology and change, which are often linked, the following example shows how a school curriculum might consistently build up children's concepts through carefully planned work which, at each stage, raises the level of expectation and attainment.

End of Early Years Foundation Stage	Developing a sense of time	Introduction of time-related vocabulary; stories; relating objects to people in the past, or to people of different ages; beginning to place two or three objects in time order – older/ newer

End of Key Stage 1	Place events and objects in chronological order; use common words and phrases; identify differences between ways of life at different times	Using a sequence line to include a larger number of objects, pictures or words; children required to use time-related vocabulary; stories; 'then' and 'now' photographs; family trees
End of Key Stage 2	Place people, events and changes into correct periods of time; use dates and vocabulary relating to the passing of time; identify and describe reasons for changes in the periods studied	Using and constructing a detailed timeline including several dates and showing key events of the period; children required to use time-related vocabulary, including in written work; writing stories, producing charts and extended writing showing changes within and between periods studied

Figure 7. Progression in teaching chronology

Complementing these activities within year groups, there would need to be a general school or class timeline, where children could be encouraged to place in the correct periods their work or research. This would help them see the chronology of the historical periods covered in school and also bring coherence to their understanding of chronology and change.

Progression in the ability to use historical skills

For progression in the development of historical skills to be clearly planned and taught you need a sound understanding of what these skills are and how they relate to thinking skills in general. Fundamental to the study of history, as Marwick (2001) has cogently argued, is the use of sources. Since it is essentially a problem-solving task, source analysis makes use of many problem-solving, or thinking, skills which include:

- close observation;
- making verbal associations with what has been observed; labelling;
- sequencing;
- posing questions and devising answers;
- linking new information with existing knowledge;
- identifying relationships;
- classifying and analysing information;
- making inferences;
- organising and synthesising findings to create an account or hypothesis.

Time and practice are needed for children to develop these intellectual skills and they work at different levels of attainment in using them. For example, in using an artefact, such as the old Victorian codd bottle below, children are able to produce responses at many different levels. An Early Years Foundation Stage child, aged four, might comment that 'It's green and heavy.' Here she is using observational skills and labelling her observations, producing a simple, literal response. A Year 6 child, aged 10, who has been studying the late Victorian period might know that this kind of bottle was used at that time. She might be able to place it in its historical framework and make well-informed inferences about its use:

Figure 8. Victorian bottle

It's an old bottle – I can tell because it's worn and looks different from modern bottles. It's made of thick, strong glass. We learned in our history topic that people could get back money when they took the empty bottles back to the shop. It would have been hand-made, so was quite an expensive thing to make. It probably held fizzy drinks of some kind because it has a marble inside it that I think would have been a stopper, held up by the fizz in the drink.

This 10-year-old has observed carefully, questioned what she has seen, analysed her observations and then organised her ideas to produce a good explanation of the object. Her complex language reflects the thinking that has taken place. She has also made a number of inferences about it, that is, observations for which there is no direct evidence, but which can be assumed or worked out from what evidence there is. Information processing, reasoning and creative thinking have all been used in this one illustration of a simple historical enquiry.

Between these two levels of skill in source analysis, there are many stages of development, which need to be carefully planned and assessed as the child moves from year to year. The use of sources features in every historical topic, and they can be used to encourage children to develop their powers of observation and inference.

Developing thinking skills in history

A vast amount of research has been carried out into what thinking is and how it takes place, since it is the basis of new learning. The research in psychology has resulted in a major distinction between 'behaviourist' learning theory and 'cognitive' learning theory. Behaviourist theory, characterised by Pavlov's dog and Skinner's rats, judges learning as a specific outcome or behaviour that can be measured or tested. Cognitive theorists, however, believe that new learning is stimulated by thought and a hierarchy of thinking skills, which interact with language, and also depend on maturation; learning is seen as a developmental process. These theories have influenced educational theory and practice, including teaching and assessment in history.

The thinking skills listed in the 'general requirements' of the national Curriculum all link clearly to the history curriculum. These general skills are:

- information-processing;
- reasoning;

- enquiry;
- creative thinking;
- evaluation.

These skills contribute to problem solving, a key skill which is required to be taught across the curriculum. History is very much a problem-solving subject.

REFLECTIVE TASK

REFLECTIVE TASK

Consider:

What is thinking?

What does 'thinking' entail?

What goes on during thinking?

Thinking skills specific to history

These general thinking skills relate to specific skills in history. Chronological skills require the use of skills in information processing in order to sequence events logically. Information processing is used when handling all forms of historical data, from statistics about population growth to diary extracts. Reasoning is one of the most commonly used skills in history, particularly in solving problems. Reasoning skills enable children to make inferences and deductions, to use precise language in their explanations, and to make judgements and decisions informed by evidence. Enquiry skills are the basic tools of the historian, while creative and evaluative thinking is required in the use of sources, forming conclusions from judgements made about them and compiling personal interpretations of events. The outcome of developing all these skills is the ability to solve problems and to 'do' history.

Key skills

There are six key skills that are involved in teaching and learning in all parts of the curriculum. Communication and application of number are considered in Chapter 8 and information technology in Chapter 9. This section looks at how the other three skills of 'working with others', 'improving own learning performance' and 'problem solving', listed in 'Promoting skills across the National Curriculum' apply to history (DfEE/QCA, 1999a, p20–21).

'Working with others' is a common feature of classroom work in history. Children will readily share their thoughts and bounce ideas off each other when faced with a challenging task such as source analysis. Consequently, the most effective way of using source materials such as artefacts with young children is to enable them to play with them, talk about them and form conclusions about them when working either with a partner or in a group. Shared and collaborative reading and writing activities offer children support with difficult tasks in history, which they might otherwise fail to address satisfactorily.

Children enjoy improving their own learning performance in history in several ways. They can gain a great sense of achievement by remembering events and dates. They can also carry out self-evaluation in their written work and edit and redraft their writing using word processing packages on the computer. They especially enjoy improving their work if it is to be collected in their own project book or 'best' book.

If well taught, history is always a problem-solving subject. Unravelling the causes and reasons for people's behaviour in the past is a mystery which children very much enjoy. Piecing together their own ideas about the past is an exciting and rewarding part of the process of history and is a real problem-solving activity.

RESEARCH SUMMARY RESEARCH SUMMARY **RESEARCH SUMMARY** RESEARCH SUMMARY

Taba (1971) researched the use of objectives in planning and teaching, otherwise known as 'advance organisers'. These have now come to be known as 'learning outcomes' or 'learning intentions'. It is generally thought that teaching strategies which use them are more effective. Ofsted (2007) has identified the fact that where a teacher's subject knowledge is good, teaching, learning and children's attainment is improved.

Piaget (Inhelder and Piaget, 1958) devised the idea of learning 'stages' through which a child passed as they matured, understanding abstract concepts only in the 'formal' stage during adolescence. Bruner (1977) established the idea of the 'spiral curriculum', whereby children could return regularly to the same concept but, at each encounter, develop their understanding to a deeper level.

Bruner (1974, 1977), Blyth (1976), Coltham and Fines (1971), Levstik and Pappas (1987), Cooper (1991), Hodkinson (1995), Hoodless (1988), among many others, have investigated children's thinking in history. Thinking skills are now a part of the general requirements in the National Curriculum.

A SUMMARY OF **KEY POINTS**

> **Long-term planning is an outline plan for teaching and learning in history for the whole school.**

> **Medium-term planning is for work on a topic, which might cover a term or a half term, within one class. Medium-term plans are often called 'units of work'.**

> **Short-term planning is a lesson or activity plan for one class or group.**

> **Progression is important in learning historical subject knowledge, historical concepts and historical skills.**

> **Thinking skills are widely used in good history teaching and learning, where children use sources and engage in problem solving.**

> **The National Curriculum key skills can be incorporated into history teaching.**

MOVING *ON* > > > **>** **>** **>** MOVING *ON* > > > **>** **>** **>** MOVING *ON*

Standard 126
Ofsted has identified that effective teaching and learning in history are frequently related to teachers' subject knowledge. Choose a history study unit for which your subject knowledge is limited and work at improving it through reading and research. Use your new knowledge to plan in more detail for progression in that unit of work.

FURTHER READING FURTHER READING **FURTHER READING** FURTHER READING

Fisher, P (2002) *Thinking through history.* Cambridge: Chris Kington.
Hodkinson, A (1995) Historical time and the National Curriculum. *Teaching History,* 79: 18–20.
Wood, S (1995) Developing an understanding of time-sequencing issues, *Teaching History,* 79; 11–14.

Useful websites

www.standards.dfes.gov.uk.
   This site contains examples of medium-term planning.

www.ofsted.gov.uk/publications

A useful source of all of Ofsted's recent publications.

www.globalgateway.org.uk

A website that provides guidance and information on sharing information and ideas with partner schools and on making international links with schools around the world and links to other websites.

www.ncaction.org.uk

Good examples of children's work at different stages.

http://primaryhistory.org/leadinghistory
www.qca.org.uk/history/innovating

Websites that are useful in supporting your planning.

www.roman-britain.org/maps/militarylayermap.htm

Excellent interactive map of Roman Britain, which can be changed to show towns, forts, mines, etc.

5
Understanding and using teaching strategies in primary history

Chapter objectives

By the end of this chapter you will have:

- considered the key pedagogical knowledge that you need to match teaching strategies to children's diverse needs;
- understood the need for strategies which provide opportunities for children to develop their skills in oracy;
- considered examples of various strategies and innovative ways of teaching primary history;
- considered creative ways of combining subjects to deliver history objectives.

Professional Standards for QTS

This chapter will support you as you work towards evidencing attainment against the following Standards:

Q10: Have a knowledge and understanding of a range of teaching, learning and behaviour management strategies and know how to use and adapt them...and provide opportunities for all learners to achieve their potential.

Q14: Have a secure knowledge and understanding of their subjects/curriculum areas and related pedagogy to enable them to teach effectively across the age and ability range for which they are trained.

Q25(a): Use a range of teaching strategies...

Q30: Establish a purposeful learning environment conducive to learning...

Teaching and learning approaches

History is a very broad subject, which embraces many other subjects and which can be taught using a wide range of strategies. The choice of teaching and learning approach, however, is dependent on the needs of the children and also the content of the unit of work; teaching strategies and styles need to be appropriate to the sort of learning you want to take place.

Teacher-led lessons and child-centred learning

There is always a tension between the amount of teacher input in a lesson and the amount of opportunity for children to work independently. One way of visualising the range of strategies which might be used is to think of the different styles of working as a scale, moving from teacher-led approaches to child-centred learning:

Teacher-led				Child-centred
Teacher exposition, through story-telling, scene setting, explanation etc.	Teacher-led question question and answer	Teacher's knowledge of children's interests and experience used to set tasks	Teacher consults children on their interests and negotiates tasks	Children choose their own topics for study
Teacher-designed task for children to complete	Teacher-designed task for children to complete	Children carry out teacher's tasks, but with some autonomy	Children engage in agreed research or tasks	Children engage in individual research
Teacher summary of what has been achieved during the lesson	Teacher leads feedback session, to which children contribute	Children feed back within a structure set up by the teacher	Children create presentations with teacher support to feed back to the class what they have learned	Children create their own presentations to feed back to the class what they have learned

Figure 9. Teacher-led and child-centred approaches

In recent years the style of the literacy and numeracy hours has influenced the rest of the curriculum, and it has become common for a traditional three-part lesson to be planned and led by the teacher, as in the first section of this matrix. However, teaching styles vary considerably, and some teachers have the skills to sustain an approach like the one in the last section, where the child takes the lead throughout. Obviously, the child would have to be a competent, confident learner, and have some experience of independent working. The more able children in the final years of their primary schooling are capable of, and thoroughly enjoy, working in this way.

Some teachers aim to enable children to attain greater independence in their work during the course of a topic. Teacher-led activities would predominate at the outset, with a gradual increase in the amount of child-centred, personalised learning as the children gain confidence. By the end, the most able children could be working independently on aspects of their own choice. This approach to learning is one that probably comes closest to meeting the aims for more personalised learning of the Every Child Matters initiative (DfES, 2004c).

Subject-led and cross-curricular work

Similarly, there is a whole spectrum of ways of planning and teaching units of work and lessons, ranging from the pure history lesson to one which has historical content, but incorporates other subjects. For example, a Year 3/4 topic on the Romans, which had been planned with the resources available locally, made use of a range of subjects in the curriculum:

Activity	Cross-curricular link
Chronological work on placing the Romans in time, using Roman numerals	Link with numeracy and number lines
Discussion about invasion and settlement	Link with geography through map work
Making comparisons between aspects of life in Celtic and Roman Britain, using a variety of resources	Link with literacy through scanning texts and marking extracts; engaging in shared work Link with literacy through vocabulary and talk
Comparing sources about Boudicca that contradict each other	Link with literacy through making a comparison of two accounts of Boudicca which give different viewpoints; identifying

	language features which demonstrate these differences
Using a range of written sources Ask and answer questions about what survived from the Roman period	Link with literacy through converting brief notes made during the visit into connected prose Link with ICT through searching for information on a selected website
Presenting their findings from research in a variety of ways	Link with ICT through use of presentation software Link with art through drawings and paintings in different media

Figure 10. Cross-curricular links

Other units of work, which illustrate ways of combining work in history with other subjects can be found at www.qca.org.uk/history/innovating. There is guidance and the facility to create your own schemes or units of work from the original examples created by the QCA.

The use of a cross-curricular approach to planning, of course, makes a considerable difference to the range of teaching and learning strategies that can be employed, as well as to the hugely extended range of resources and materials that then become available through accessing other subjects. For example, art and music are excellent sources for historical study, and the wealth of resources that come with the inclusion of these subjects can enrich the child's learning immensely.

PRACTICAL TASK PRACTICAL TASK **PRACTICAL TASK** PRACTICAL TASK **PRACTICAL TASK**

Access a unit of work from one of the internet sites recommended and identify the cross-curricular links that have been made within it.

Establishing a purposeful and appropriate learning environment

The environment in which children learn can also significantly affect the quality of the learning that takes place. Levels of interest, pace of learning and conceptual understanding are all influenced by both home and classroom contexts. These contextual factors are many and varied, and a significant proportion cannot be controlled by the teacher, such as the degree of support provided for the child out of school, their emotional and physical well-being when they arrive in school, or their stage of intellectual development. A secure working atmosphere, achieved through sound relationships and good classroom management, are fundamental. The physical organisation of equipment and resources can drastically affect the flow and pace of lessons and these factors need careful thought.

The organisation of the children into pairs or groups who can work together effectively, or for a specific purpose, is also important. For example, you may wish to organise groups according to their ability if there is a substantial amount of reading and writing. On the other hand, mixed ability groups might enable the children with weaker language skills to be supported by the more able. Work might link with out of school activities and you might decide that friendship groups would be the most useful organisation.

Good displays and illustrations can prompt interest and questions. A timeline, to which children refer and add information in the course of a topic, can help to bring coherence to their understanding of a period. Interactive displays can be a valuable part of a lesson; children might construct the display themselves, adding to it and using it as reference material during lessons. The classroom atmosphere can be enhanced by attractive, colourful and artistic displays. These soften the environment and bring into the classroom features of the outside world, linking real life and classroom learning. For example, some of the most exciting display work I have seen has been that in small primary schools in rural areas, where natural objects from the forest or farmland have formed part of the fabric of the classroom. By enhancing and enriching the learning environment in these ways, those children with emotional or learning difficulties will be supported through additional tactile and visual input.

ICT can be an additional feature of this kind of environmental enrichment. Through the use of rich visual images and sound using an interactive whiteboard, the classroom can incorporate aspects of daily life that are familiar to the children, forming a link between home and school. Images drawn from relevant areas can be used as a backdrop to topic work as well as for specific input into lessons. Books, posters and objects, including historical artefacts and replicas, are frequently used within displays to motivate the children and provide them with additional resources for learning. By writing to parents and carers in advance of starting a new topic, many useful items can be gathered for display.

One of the most valuable functions of a good display, however, is to celebrate children's learning. Their own work needs to be a growing part of displays as the topic progresses and eventually the purpose of the classroom display is to exhibit all the work they have completed. Colour, texture and the use of 3D displays can boost children's self-esteem enormously, both because they see the importance attached to their work and also that the teacher values their efforts by including them in the very fabric of the learning environment.

Using a range of teaching and learning strategies

Teacher exposition

The most common way of beginning a lesson is in the form of the teacher giving an introduction to the whole class in the form of 'teacher-talk', where the teacher presents a topic, idea or an area of content, either verbally or using presentation software such as PowerPoint. The teacher can, at this point, review prior learning, explain the lesson objectives and give an outline of what the children will be doing. These 'advance warnings', described as 'organisers' (Taba, 1971) help to focus the children on their tasks and also enable them to attune themselves to the content of the new lesson. This kind of 'tuning in' has been found to be beneficial to learning and has become part of regular practice in primary schools.

In history, when starting on a new topic or theme, a useful strategy is to begin by asking the class what they already know. Children can sometimes be quite surprising in their specialised knowledge, and this can provide a starting point for further work and also useful information for the teacher in terms of the level of knowledge and understanding to expect when planning further tasks. It is often helpful also to model a task that you want the children to carry out, especially if it is new to them. For example, you might want them to devise some questions about an object or picture, and so a useful starting point would be to carry out this activity using another object before asking the children to carry out the task themselves.

REFLECTIVE TASK

REFLECTIVE TASK

You are a trainee teacher and you have been given a world history study to plan. You are concerned about the best way to introduce this topic to the class, since it is based on a very distant place. There are few first-hand sources easily available to use and there is no museum in your area which covers this topic.

Consider what might be the most effective ways to introduce your chosen world history topic in the light of these constraints.

Research and investigative work

Questioning

Questioning is a key part of enquiry-based, investigative learning, a style of learning which lies at the heart of work in history. Teacher questioning takes many forms: closed questions, requiring a specific answer; open-ended questions where a number of responses are accep-table; key questions, which set up an enquiry; and subsidiary questions, which seek a more detailed response. At first, the teacher needs to model and prompt the type of questions for children to use. These need to be useful questions in the way they derive information from sources, such as 'who might have used this, what might have been its function?' These questions ask for a range of possible answers, so that discussion and further thought can take place. Children's responses could be recorded on the whiteboard and saved for later use. Eventually children will realise that there are alternative answers and they will begin to think about likelihood and eliminate the least likely solutions. A reasoned, thoughtful answer should finally be the result. A range of English Heritage pamphlets has been produced to provide ideas for developing questioning skills, such as *Learning from objects* (Durbin et al, 1990).

Participating in the questioning process is an important skill, but the most important one is that of being able to *initiate* the questioning process. Children need to be encouraged to use questioning themselves as a purposeful way to solve problems. Children need to be auton-omous in their enquiries, able to instigate and conclude a piece of enquiry work, first with support and then independently. In some small-scale research that I have carried out myself, I have concluded that it is those children who have an enquiring approach and ask their own questions who are the ones most likely to arrive at a sensible solution to a problem (Hoodless, 1988). The development of information processing skills requires a gradual intro-duction to using sources, first scaffolded and then gradually encouraging the children to work with more independence. Language, mathematical skills and data processing skills are, of course, all crucially important in enabling the child to access resources and interpret information (see Chapters 8 and 9).

Teacher-designed enquiry and children's learning styles

Enquiry tasks designed by the teacher need to include differentiation for ability; tasks may include similar content, but will be framed in different ways, usually according to the reading ability of the groups or individuals they are for. Tasks may also be differentiated to suit different learning styles. For example, visual sources might be provided for children who have visual learning as a preferred style. From the research of those such as Gardner (1993, 2006) we know that people have a preferred, or dominant style of learning. Some respond better to a *visual* cue, some to *auditory* stimuli and others to *kinaesthetic* cues. These styles are sometimes abbreviated as 'VAK'. While it is crucially important that children should not be permanently classed as 'visual' learners and then not challenged in other ways, it is useful for teachers to ensure that they provide the entire range of opportunities for a class of children, so that at some point, each child will be presented with materials appropriate to their learning style.

PRACTICAL TASK PRACTICAL TASK **PRACTICAL TASK** PRACTICAL TASK **PRACTICAL TASK**

Look up the work of Howard Gardner and look into the meaning and uses of VAK. Design an activity for three groups which makes use of VAK.

Paired work – talk partners

Teacher-designed tasks can be for pairs of children working together. Tasks could include picking out the key points from a short piece of text, discussion, or 'talk partners', or creative activities such as producing a piece of creative writing together. Paired work can be supportive of the less able learners and also generate more ideas and a higher standard of work than when children work alone.

Group work – enquiries and problem solving

Galton has carried out detailed studies of the effects and educational benefits of group work (Galton and Williamson, 1992). Group tasks can include open-ended enquiries using books or internet sources, or specific enquiries using sources which children will discuss and analyse with a particular question to guide them. The group will continue their task by agreeing on a solution and presenting their agreed conclusions to the class. Groups might also be given the task of creating a dramatic representation of an event, a piece of display work, music or part of a newspaper. Collaborative work of this kind has social and emotional advantages, and also enables the child to develop their thinking about the past and learn from their peers.

Whole class work

Whole class work could include tasks set by the teacher, such as a piece of comprehension work, or a written task, which is similar for all the children in the class. Tasks such as these are often useful for assessment purposes. Shared and guided writing are strategies that can be used effectively in history lessons where the content of a written task is challenging and teacher support is needed. Investigative work can also be carried out as a whole class, through teacher-led questioning and answers provided by the children.

Individual work

There are many ways of developing individual work in history, such as research and enquiry into an individually chosen topic, book making, diary writing, or creating ICT presentations. When they first start to undertake individual work, children of all ages require guidance, structure and support, otherwise they might resort to copying work from published sources. They need to know how to find information and then how to use it to inform their own enquiry. Young children embarking on individual research will need to have suitable websites selected for them and have help in identifying appropriate sections in books.

They will also need guidance in devising questions to guide their work. The KWL grid is a useful strategy for supporting them, since the first task in creating it is to complete the questions they want to answer. The grid also enables them to monitor their findings and to evaluate what they have found out at the end, helping them to engage in self-assessment. Support will be needed in making brief notes and then in turning the information into the required form.

In communicating their findings, they will need support and direction. For example, if creating their own book or website, they will need guidance and direct teaching of the skills and knowledge needed to produce such a response; this teaching could be provided for the whole class and then used by individuals. There are opportunities here for cross-curricular work with a genuine purpose in this kind of personalised learning.

Using sources

The National Curriculum for history, first published in 1991, ensured that primary children were enabled to learn in a variety of ways. The requirement to make use of a range of sources enabled teachers to focus on first-hand experience, thus making use of children's different strengths, interests and types of intelligence.

Sources for the study of history can be either 'primary' or 'secondary' and both can be used with the whole class, with groups, pairs or individual children. Primary sources are those which were written or made at the time or in the period being studied, while secondary sources are those created later and which make use of primary sources for evidence and information. Primary sources might include, for example, original artefacts, portraits, paintings or written texts made at the time. Original toys and domestic objects, or replicas of these, are often used in teaching primary history. Secondary sources range from books written by historians giving their interpretation of a period or event, to dramas and film, based on other accounts.

Working with artefacts

Artefacts can be used in a wide variety of ways. One artefact can be the subject of a whole class lesson, where the teacher leads questioning and models the types of useful questions to ask. Groups or pairs of children can work well together if an open-ended question is set to encourage them to investigate a number of artefacts, such as 'What do these objects tell us about the people who used them?' Once skilled in this kind of source analysis, individuals can ask and answer their own questions on the significance of an artefact.

Artefacts provide kinaesthetic learning experiences for all young children, who enjoy learning from concrete, visual experiences, an appropriate style of learning for primary age children according to Piaget (1926, 1928). They are particularly appropriate, however, for children with special needs and those who have a preference for this style of learning. Artefacts enable children to make physical contact with the past and children can use their imagination to understand what it would have been like to use them. This kind of imaginative activity could be described as play, an essential activity and part of the learning process for all primary children.

Artefacts also make use of many aspects of the sensory curriculum, in that they enable children to feel the texture and weight of an object, to test its degree of warmth or coldness, and even to smell things that it might have been associated with in the past, such as an old iron, which still had the dust and smell of ashes from when hot coals were put inside it to heat it up. All children benefit from such experiences, if they are enriched by discussion and explanation by the teacher or by peers.

The use of artefacts helps children develop their intellectual skills, such as those involved in making detailed observations, seeing relationships, making inferences and arriving at a potential solution to a set problem. They derive great enjoyment from using artefacts as props in scenes and dramas (Hoodless, 1994b).

Using visual sources

When people think of an historical period, such as Tudor times, they often recall visual images: King Henry VIII, black and white house, sailing ships and 'men in tights'. Pictures are important for children with a preferred visual style of learning, but they are also impor-

Figure 11. King Henry VIII

tant for all young children. Historical images, in the form of paintings, portraits, photographs, film and so on, help the child begin to build up a concept of period and a sense of time.

Images often convey messages in the form of symbolism. For example, the many elaborate portraits of wealthy aristocrats painted through the ages convey the message of their worth and importance in society. Tudor pictures often contain significant symbolic messages. For example, the image of Queen Elizabeth Ist in the Armada Portrait emphasises her importance as the leader of a world power, symbolised by the Queen's hand on the world (www.bbc.co.uk/history/british/tudors/armada_gallery). Much can be inferred by children from these portraits, such as the fact that many people could not read, and so pictures had to convey other messages, in this case, propaganda. A similar message is conveyed in the woodcut shown on page 53 of King Henry VIII.

Pictures are important cues when children begin to read and therefore 'picture reading' is a key part of early literacy. Children learn many reading skills from 'picture reading', such as observing detail, scanning and focusing on important points, eventually relating them to the written text in early picture books. Harnett (1993) has carried out research into children's developing skill and historical understanding in the course of using visual sources.

Using written sources

There is great excitement and pleasure involved in the immediacy of using primary written sources at first hand, from collections such as the diary of Queen Victoria (Hibbert, 2000). The issue of bias needs to be raised, of course, since writers would have been heavily influenced by current events and their own opinions. Secondary accounts are also useful in providing opportunities to learn about interpretation and bias. It is virtually impossible to create an historical account without including in it your own views and beliefs, or the attitudes and values of the age in which you live. Often, people write with clear bias or prejudice that depends on their situation, which 'side' they are on in a conflict or debate, or their personal views.

These sources provide close links with the Literacy Framework (DfES, 2006) where awareness of different points of view is also an objective. There is therefore a need to encourage the *critical reading* of texts by children, something that is also an important life skill (Hoodless, 2006). Through exposure to a wide range of texts children can begin to understand how people are influenced by their own time and how this affects their writing. Children can build upon this experience by writing their own interpretations of events they have studied.

Oral history

One of the most exciting activities for young children is to have a 'visitor' come into the classroom to share their memories and experiences. They can come to talk about their work experience in the past and explain how things have changed, or they can describe the toys they used to play with, before there were computer games and PlayStations, or they can talk about what it was like to be a school child after the Second World War. Local groups and history societies will also be able to help with locating the right person for your oral history lesson.

This kind of oral history work can also be carried out at home, where children can interview their parents, grandparents or carers and record the memories they have of the past. There is information about aural sources on the internet, from the Oral History Society (www.ohs.org.uk/), the British Library (www.shop.bl.uk/) and on CD-ROM, such as Ready Resources (Hoodless, 2003a).

Using the built environment

Victorian houses are a primary source and are interesting for children to study. You can use a local history walk in order to examine the details of the buildings, note which look 'old' or 'new', and note the features of the old buildings. Back in school the children can then use maps and the relevant section of the census data for the area to find when the old houses were built. They can also find detailed information about the people who lived in them at that time, thus learning about another important source and making use of their skills in literacy.

Historical sites and museums

In addition to their collections, many museums are developing interactive displays and guided visits combined with activities using sources, so that they are becoming a major resource for first-hand experiential learning. In museums such as Styal Mill (www.quarry-bankmill.org.uk) or the Gladstone Pottery Museum (www.stoke.gov.uk/museums/gladstone) children are guided through practical activities, often by people experienced in working in those industries. Reconstructions through drama and audio-visual displays help to bring the past alive for young children. They can see people in similar costumes to those worn in the past, and can hear the noise made by the machinery and experience the oily smells while watching how it works. Similar re-enactments are often to be found in palaces, castles and stately homes, where children can experience such things as a 'Victorian Christmas' (Fisher, 2005). Reconstructions of the past are an important source of historical learning, and this approach is discussed in Chapter 11.

Science, music, art and design technology also provide excellent sources for the study of history and further detail on these cross-curricular links can also be found in Chapter 11.

Sensitive issues

Sensitive issues often arise in history, particularly when using sources. These can be on a small or grand scale, ranging from personal experiences to major events such as the Holocaust. They can include controversial and divisive issues, touching on race and class, for example, which need sensitive treatment. Whatever their nature, they need to be taken seriously by trainees and newly qualified teachers who need to be aware of the sensitivities of children and also of the possible impact of dealing with sensitive issues in the wider school community and on parents and carers. A planned government report on the teaching of these issues is described in *Primary History* (Wilkinson, 2006b).

RESEARCH SUMMARY RESEARCH SUMMARY **RESEARCH SUMMARY** RESEARCH SUMMARY

The background

The Plowden Report (1967: paragraph 620) maintained that history was far too abstract a subject for young children to understand and it was argued that children's sense of time was not sufficiently developed at primary school age for them to be able to grasp historical content or sequence past events. By the 1970s and 1980s, however, research into how young children actually acquire historical concepts and understanding began to develop.

Bruner emphasised the central roles of language and social learning in children's cognitive development (Bruner, 1977, 1990). Other research followed, suggesting that children were more capable than had been assumed, depending on the type of approach used to teach them; if the content of their lessons was familiar to them, they would be able to understand. Examples of new research that had more positive findings includes, among many others, the work of West (1981a, b, c) Coltham and Fines (1971), Levstik and Pappas (1987) and Cooper (1991). The findings drawn from this more optimistic recent research are evident in the eventual requirements of the National Curriculum for history.

Classroom organisation

Different teaching styles have been discussed by Galton (1980, 1992, 1998) and were the subject of intense debate within the discussion paper which came to be known as the 'Three Wise Men Report' (Alexander, Rose and Woodhead, 1992). Galton and others studied methods of teaching and classroom organisation in the Oracle Project of the 1980s. They examined closely the ways in which teachers were using group work and found that many teachers were struggling to implement effective teaching using these strategies. They recommended that fewer group activities should be planned to take place at one time. More recent studies have now been published (Galton, 1998), using exactly the same research tools and commenting on changes, or lack of them, since their first enquiries 20 years earlier.

Using sources

Coltham and Fines (1971) have studied widely the use of different teaching strategies, ways of organising learning and the use of sources in teaching history. Turner-Bisset (2005a) has looked at a range of strategies for approaching the teaching of primary history in a creative way. She discusses in detail the creativity that can be achieved in the history curriculum through the use of sources and cross-curricular links such as through story-telling, drama, music and dance.

A SUMMARY OF **KEY POINTS**

> There is a wide range of teaching approaches from teacher-led lessons through to child-centred learning.

> Schools use both subject-focused and cross-curricular thematic work. In the foundation subjects, thematic work is becoming more widespread, where topics include two or more subjects.

> Establishing a purposeful and appropriate learning environment can contribute to motivation and good-quality learning in history.

> The range of teaching strategies includes teacher exposition, question and answer, investigative work organised for the whole class, pairs, groups or individual children, the use of sources and children creating their own reconstructions of the past. These can be dramatic, visual, spoken, ICT based or written.

> Historical sources are a good stimulus for children's own creative work.

MOVING *ON* > > > > > > MOVING *ON* > > > > > > MOVING *ON*

Standard I29a

In teaching history lessons, make a note of the kinds of language children are using during their activities, such as questions which they have devised themselves, tentative language, or terms to do with concepts of time. Consider how you might provide greater opportunity in your unit planning for this kind of language use to take place. For example, problem-solving activities encourage children to use questioning and speculative language when they are talking about possible solutions, thus providing them with opportunities to develop this specific kind of language.

FURTHER READING FURTHER READING **FURTHER READING** FURTHER READING

Barnsdale-Paddock, L and Harnett, P (2002) Promoting play in the classroom: children as curators in a Classroom museum, *Primary History*, 301: 19–21.

Claire, H (2004) Oral history: a powerful tool or a double edged sword?, *Primary History*, 38: 20–23.

Cooper, H (2004) *Exploring time and place through play*. London: David Fulton.

Disney, A and Hammond, D (2002) Questions you always wanted to ask about using historical maps. *Primary History*, 32: 22–23.

English Heritage (1998) *Story telling at historic sites.* Northampton: English Heritage.

Hoodless, P (2004) Questions you always wanted to ask about history and written sources. *Primary History*, 37: 25–26.

Lomas, T (2002) How do we ensure really good local history in primary schools? *Primary History*, 30: 4–6.

Mills, M (2003) Questions you always wanted to ask about accessing archive sources, *Primary History*, 34: 24–25.

Useful websites

www.bbc.co.uk
  Useful for visual sources.

www.ohs.org.uk/
www.shop.bl.uk/
  Useful for sound recordings.

www.qca.org.uk/history/innovating
  A useful reference website for looking up the new schemes of work and for making your own modifications to create your own schemes.

www.pcet.co.uk
  This educational supplier produces a wide range of charts, maps, timelines and photo packs for use in the classroom.

www.quarrybankmill.org.uk
www.stoke.gov.uk/museums/gladstone
  Examples of museum websites.

www.freeict.com/index.php/Science,_Geography_and_History
www.bbc.co.uk/history/interactive/
www.ict.oxon-lea.gov.uk/weblinks/pri_history.html
www.coxhoe.durham.sch.uk/Curriculum/History.htm
www.kented.org.uk/ngfl/subjects/history/index.htm
home.freeuk.com/elloughton13/index.htm
www.britishmuseum.org/explore/introduction.aspx
  These websites have examples of games and simulations for history.

6
Monitoring and assessment

Chapter objectives

By the end of this chapter you will have:

- **developed your understanding of strategies for monitoring and assessing children's learning in history;**
- **considered examples of methods of record-keeping and assessment;**
- **begun to appreciate how assessment information can be used to inform practice;**
- **begun to understand the difference between formative and summative assessment;**
- **considered ways to use assessment for learning by incorporating opportunities for assessment, feedback and pupil self-assessment at the planning stage;**
- **begun to consider the process of reflection on your own teaching.**

Professional Standards for QTS

This chapter will support you as you work towards evidencing attainment against the following Standards:

Q11: Know the assessment requirements and arrangements for the subjects/curriculum areas they are trained to teach...

Q12: Know a range of approaches to assessment, including the importance of formative assessment.

Q13: Know how to use local and national statistical information to evaluate the effectiveness of their teaching, to monitor the progress of those they teach and to raise levels of attainment.

Why assess work in history?

Since the introduction of the National Curriculum (1999b) and the National League Tables for Primary Schools (www.direct.gov.uk/en/Parents/Schoolslearninganddevelopment/), there has been a growing emphasis on assessment and children's attainment at the end of each key stage, but only in the core subjects. Despite this, there are important reasons why assessment needs to be carried out in subjects like history. Teacher assessment is necessary so that children's progress can be reported to parents with some degree of accuracy. It is needed to inform planning and also to inform future teachers of your class. The demands upon teachers in carrying out their own assessments in a subject like history can be considerable, particularly if the teacher has only an initial grasp of the subject. For these reasons, it is important that you begin to acquire a clear understanding of what needs to be assessed, how it might be assessed and the purposes of that assessment.

Monitoring and assessment

While 'monitoring' and 'assessment' are related and are often linked together, these terms do, in fact, involve different processes.

- **Monitoring** involves the teacher on a day-to-day basis carefully observing children and their progress, along with reviewing their work to build up a picture of their learning – it is part of the assessment process.

- **Assessment** is a central part of planning, teaching and learning, and involves using a range of strategies to collect evidence about children's progress. These include strategies drawn from behaviourist learning theory, such as direct observation of children's responses to tasks, and cognitive theory, such as exploring children's understanding by using questioning (see Chapter 4). Judgements are then made about the level of attainment achieved in relation to the National Curriculum Attainment Target for history. This target contains a number of statements about the achievement of children reaching levels 1 to 5 (which mainly apply to primary level) and the 'best fit' is made by comparing what is known and recorded with each of these statements.

There are different types and functions of assessment.

- **Formative assessment or assessment for learning**: this involves the day-to-day monitoring and assessment of children's progress. Formative assessment notes specific strengths and weaknesses with a view to identifying development strategies and targets aimed at addressing children's individual needs. It is clearly important in the process of identifying children with special educational needs and also in helping children to carry out self-assessment and set personal targets. It includes regular marking of children's written work and giving regular feedback to help them improve their work. Formative assessment can also inform your planning and teaching when included in your evaluations.
- **Summative assessment**: this assessment summarises children's attainment and takes place at the end of the year or key stage when a significant stage of learning has been completed. Examples of this in history would be the assessment of children against the statements made in the National Curriculum level descriptions at the end of Key Stages 1 and 2. The purpose of this assessment is to gather information to report to parents or the child's next teacher.

Monitoring

An important task for the teacher during lessons involves monitoring children's performance in relation to the activities and learning objectives. The importance and complexity of monitoring is clearly emphasised by Kyriacou (1998), who notes how monitoring learning while teaching is a particularly demanding activity. During a lesson it is natural for the physical process of teaching to dominate the teacher's mind but monitoring skills must be applied simultaneously as part of the teaching process. Effective monitoring skills take time to develop but it is important for trainees to be aware of the teacher's role in this area.

Monitoring can take place in a whole class teaching situation where a priority is to ensure that children understand new knowledge and skills. Careful observation of children's body language and analysis of their answers or questions can give an indication of how the lesson content and activities are being received by the class. Evidence of misunderstanding or difficulty on the part of the whole class, or of groups or individuals, may necessitate a change in teaching method. If the children are working individually or in groups, monitoring can take place by looking at examples of work and questioning children to ascertain their level of understanding. Here there is an opportunity for the teacher to give individual or group support and to deal with any misconceptions. Constructive feedback and discussion which supports the children in their learning is an important part of the overall monitoring process.

Assessment

Assessment against the criteria set in the National Curriculum aims to set a general standard, against which the attainment of children can be judged. They can then be recorded as meeting the expected level of attainment; failing to do so; or exceeding it. This type of assessment is referred to as 'criterion referencing' and it aims to set clear standards and goals for all, regardless of locality, background or differing interests and abilities. It is the basis of the assessment requirements of the National Curriculum, and as such aspires to ensure equality of opportunity across the country. You may also wish to assess children's progress in cross-curricular skills such as creativity, which is discussed in Chapter 11.

What are we assessing in history?

Content

Factual content, such as names, dates and key events was, in the past, favoured as the basis for assessing children's understanding of history. This is not surprising, since it is probably the simplest type of knowledge to check through the use of easy question and answer tests. What any historian would say, however, is that this simplistic view and this type of activity does not, in fact, constitute a proper assessment of children's knowledge or understanding of the subject. What are the other things that we need to assess then?

Historical skills

If children have been appropriately taught, they will have begun to develop some of the skills of the historian. Skills such as using dates and chronological terms can be set as historical objectives and can then be assessed. Similarly, change and the causes and effects of change are objectives which need to be assessed. Skills in understanding interpretations of the past, source analysis and communication in history are all key aspects of the skill of the historian, which are to be found in the National Curriculum and which can be set as lesson and unit objectives, for later assessment.

Concepts

Key concepts, such as time and chronology, causation, change and historical interpretation need to be assessed. However, these are difficult to judge, since concepts are not clear-cut; they are acquired, developed, and children's understanding of their complexities grows over time. Assessment of these complex ideas is therefore much more complicated than simply ascertaining whether a child can remember a date or a reason for a specific incident. It is more a process of determining which stage of understanding they have attained, and this can be judged, to some extent, through the use of the Attainment Target for history (DfEE/QCA, 1999b). You need to look at a child's achievements, in terms of their written work, their spoken comment and their engagement with practical tasks, in order to make a statement about their level of understanding. Your idea of their level can then be compared with the statements made within the Attainment Target to arrive at an assessment of their stage of development in this particular area.

PRACTICAL TASK PRACTICAL TASK PRACTICAL TASK PRACTICAL TASK PRACTICAL TASK

Refer to the National Curriculum in Action website (www.ncaction.org.uk) and scan through some of the examples of children's work provided in the section on 'items of work'. Choose two or three which clearly focus on one of the history objectives, such as historical enquiry using sources, or interpretation. Refer to the National Curriculum Attainment Target, which is to be found at the back of the National Curriculum Handbook, or on the website. Use the level descriptions and compare the statements in these with your own judgement of the level of work in each example. Then go to the sections of the website which show how the examples have been assessed ('commentary' and 'about this entry') to check how accurate your assessment was.

Using level descriptions, or 'levelling'

Summative assessment is carried out at the end of each unit using the level descriptions from the Attainment Target for history. These are also the basis for making judgements about pupil performance at the end of Key Stages 1 and 2. Level descriptions describe the subject knowledge, skills and understanding which children working at that level should be demonstrating. At Key Stage 1 the majority of children are expected to work between levels 1 and 3, achieving a level 2 at the end of the key stage. At Key Stage 2 the majority of children work between levels 2 and 5, usually attaining level 4 at the end of the key stage. Some may exceed these levels or fail to achieve the average level of attainment. When deciding on a particular level description, careful consideration needs to be given to the adjacent levels so that the 'best fit' is achieved using several pieces of a child's work.

A good working knowledge of level descriptions is important since a key part of the assessment process is ensuring that a child is performing at an appropriate level for their age. Ofsted subject reports have voiced concerns in relation to history; in the 2000–2001 report it was noted that in some cases teachers have only a vague idea of what may reasonably be expected of pupils (Ofsted, 2002).

A good critique of the Attainment Target and level statements is to be found in Nichol (2004). Nichol points out the flaws in the current statements and refers to the CHATA Project (Concepts of History and Teaching Approaches), carried out by Lee, Dickinson and Ashby (Ashby, Lee and Dickinson, 2002; Lee, 1992). This project identified a model of progression for learning and understanding in history and Nichol suggests this would have produced a more coherent, progressive set of statements which could have been used at a national level.

Use of assessment strategies

Setting assessment tasks

Good practice in history teaching is characterised by the use of a wide variety of teaching and learning styles and related resources, which are appropriate to the lesson objectives. Assessment tasks, which make use of both behaviourist and cognitive approaches, need to be devised so that children of all abilities are able to demonstrate what they know and what they can understand. For example, in finding out what children in Year 2 understand about chronological sequencing, a useful assessment task would be to give them a set of sequencing cards to place in time order on a simple timeline. The amount of information provided, such as visual links between events, text or dates, can be varied according to the children's abilities. Observation and discussion as to their reasoning for placing the cards in a particular order will provide valuable assessment information.

Key Stage 1 assessment activities suggested in Bage (2000) include observation of how effectively children use a class timeline or display to explain what is different from today. The teacher can ask children to write a book caption, museum notice or label about an artefact, explaining what this evidence tells us about how it was used. Bage explains how history assessment activities should allow children to engage in a range of responses, such as interpreting pictures, researching, drawing, and questioning as well as writing.

Observation

By watching children at work and listening carefully to their talk, you can quickly build up a picture of their level of understanding. For example, do they work confidently at their tasks; do they use appropriate vocabulary; do they need continual support? Observation can cover knowledge, skills and understanding, oral communication skills and working as a member of a team. Skill is needed in managing the class effectively in order to have time to record your observations. Brief written notes from observations and marking can be recorded using an appropriate recording sheet. A possible format can be found in Hoodless (2003b, p83).

CLASSROOM STORY

A Year 2 class were studying the lives of significant people and for this lesson the children were looking at the achievements of Mary Seacole. Small groups were using pictures, maps, timelines and written accounts. While keeping an overview of the whole class, the teacher spent about 20 minutes observing a group of lower ability children who were looking at an artist's impression of Mary Seacole tending wounded soldiers at the front line. Observations were targeted at individual children, since the teacher was keen to observe the historical knowledge, understanding and skills demonstrated by the child. Conversations amongst the children were carefully listened to and the teacher engaged in discussion with individual children to assess their understanding. The teacher made written notes about the children using a structured observation sheet.

One child was reluctant to participate and did not offer any opinions about what Mary Seacole was doing in the picture. Noticing this, the teacher moved to sit next to the child and engaged her in conversation about the picture, targeting simple questions at her to see what her response would be. After a short while, it became apparent that this child had not really understood the focus of the activity, nor did she have a clear understanding of when the events shown in the picture took place.

When evaluating the outcomes, the teacher realised that she had not adequately prepared the class with enough contextual background prior to setting the group task, and she concluded that this had disadvantaged the lower ability groups. For her next lesson, she took this into account, noting the names of children she now knew had struggled with today's activity, and planning specific guidance and questioning for these children at the start of the lesson to ensure that they had fully understood the context and the purpose of their tasks.

Using discussion and questioning

Whole class discussion and questioning can be a useful form of formative assessment, particularly at the start of a new topic, when it can tell you quite a lot about the children's level of knowledge. It is important to make use of open-ended questions, where scope is left for children to devise their own answers. This allows for a wide variety of responses and also tests the children more fully, ensuring that what they say is entirely their own. The quality of language used and its historical accuracy is generally an indicator of how well children understand a topic or theme. Their approach to discussing their conclusions also tells you a great deal about their ability to reason and think about the sources of evidence those conclusions are based upon. This may not be true of all children, however, such as those with learning difficulties. Adapting tasks for children with SEN is discussed in Chapter 12.

Marking

The marking of children's work provides information to children and parents as well as the teacher. All types of work need to be marked, including drawings, models, timelines or sequences, notes or labelled diagrams, since if the planned activity has taken account of the need for assessment there will be an opportunity to use each piece of work children produce. There are some important points you need to be aware of as a trainee:

- Locate the school marking policy; schools will usually have a clear marking policy giving guidance to teachers.
- When setting a task which will be marked, make it clear to the children what will be the focus for marking. This will of course be the learning objectives of the lesson and children need to know what is expected of them.
- Comments on work should relate to specific learning objectives. These may link with another subject, such as English, if cross-curricular work has been the focus of the lesson.
- Marking needs to recognise the achievement of learning objectives and the effort put into the work but also identify any weaknesses or misconceptions.
- Provide children with clear advice on how they can move forward.
- Remember that marking should be a two-way process, a dialogue between child and teacher. Opportunities should be created for discussion with individual children about marked work. Children need time to reflect and to engage in self-assessment.
- Marking provides an excellent opportunity for gathering evidence about children's progress. Problems or misconceptions may be identified and inform future planning and teaching.
- Marking and other forms of formative assessment needs to be positive and constructive so that the child is encouraged and motivated to try to progress further.

REFLECTIVE TASK

Look at the example on page 64 of marked work on the reasons for Germany going to war in 1939. Reflect on the kind of information and feedback that the child has received.

Feedback and self-assessment

Feedback

Feedback and self-assessment, both key aspects of assessment for learning, are closely related to each other. The spoken or written feedback provided to a child after you have marked their work needs to refer to the history objectives. There must be comment on how well the child has met these and also suggestions as to how future work might be improved. Secondly, feedback needs to encourage the child to reflect on what they have learned. Ideally, it is a good idea to discuss your written feedback with the child to provide an opportunity for the child to begin to engage in self-assessment as a natural part of the process. This, of course, is not always possible, and so the stimulus for reflection needs to be in your written comment, or encouraged through the use of another strategy, such as the setting of personal targets for each child.

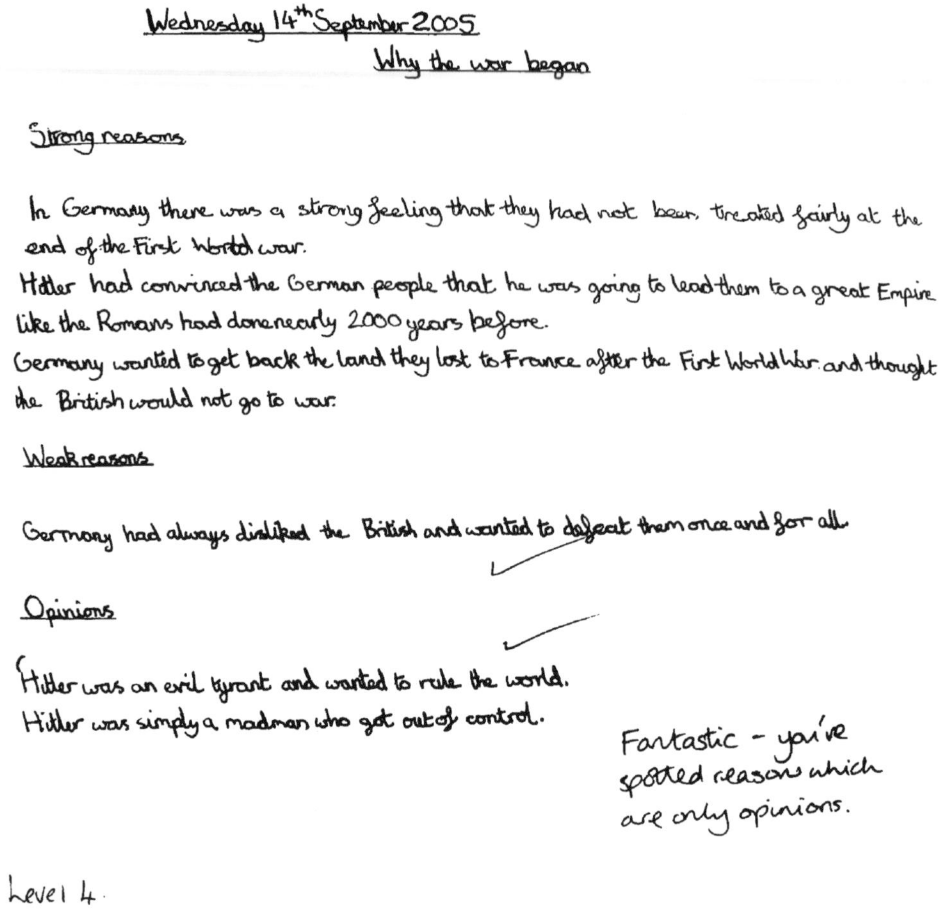

Wednesday 14th September 2005

Why the war began

Strong reasons

In Germany there was a strong feeling that they had not been treated fairly at the end of the First World war.

Hitler had convinced the German people that he was going to lead them to a great Empire like the Romans had done nearly 2000 years before.

Germany wanted to get back the land they lost to France after the First World War and thought the British would not go to war.

Weak reasons

Germany had always disliked the British and wanted to defeat them once and for all

Opinions

Hitler was an evil tyrant and wanted to rule the world.
Hitler was simply a madman who got out of control.

Fantastic – you've spotted reasons which are only opinions.

Level 4.

Figure 12. Example of marked work (Year 5 work)

Self-assessment

The process of self-assessment involves children reflecting upon their own learning, good practice which should be encouraged to allow ownership of their own learning. Self-assessment for children, however, needs to be kept simple and manageable. At Key Stage 1 a popular approach is for children to indicate if they have coped well with a piece of work by drawing a smiley face or putting their thumbs up or down.

At Key Stage 2 children could be encouraged to comment at the end of a unit on what they think they have learned in terms of new knowledge and skills. This could be done through the use of a KWL grid (see Figure 14, page 66). Through this approach children are encouraged to identify their strengths and areas for development which can be translated into targets. For self-assessment to be effective the teacher has a key role to play ensuring that the children are continuously made aware of the learning objectives. Weekly targets allow the child to review their progress regularly and set their own targets. An evaluation sheet at the end of the task is also a useful strategy, particularly for the more able child.

Evaluation

I made: <u>an Anderson shelter</u>

1. What did you want your shelter to be like in the beginning?

2. How well does it do the job you want it to?

Brilliant ☐
Good ☐
OK ☑
Poor ☐

3. What are your shelters good points?

My shelters good points are the farm that is near by, and the door knob.

4. What could you improve?

I could proberly improve the shelter by maybe having some people in the shelt

5. What problems did you have when making and how did you solve them?

How to stand up the shelter then. I solved it by using some stronger card!

6. You are now the expert. What advice would you give to someone else making it?

Always keep your disghn deisghn simple.

7. If your teacher said you could make it again, what would you do differently?

I would have a detachable roof.

Figure 13. Self-evaluation sheet (Year 5 work)

Plenaries

End of lesson plenaries provide an excellent opportunity for assessment. By focusing on the learning of a few children during each lesson plenary, through directing questions and recording responses, it is possible gradually to build up a good picture of the learning attainment of a whole class. Questioning aimed at target groups or individuals needs to be planned carefully, of course, to ensure that assessment is both manageable and effective.

Using assessment evidence

Recording and reporting

Recording and reporting are both important outcomes of the assessment process.

- **Recording** is the development of written documentation showing the progress children have made. Assessments made against the criteria set in the Attainment Target for history are recorded on each child's profile, as well as being added to the overall class and school records.
- **Reporting** involves giving feedback to parents and other professionals whether through written reports or orally at parents' evenings or staff meetings.

Record-keeping

There are several purposes of maintaining an effective record-keeping system, which is the responsibility of the history coordinator:

- to record pupil progress and achievement in relation to the learning objectives;
- to record children's misconceptions;
- to use assessment evidence for modifying future planning;
- to provide information about individual children for preparing reports to parents.

What kinds of records might be useful? Consider the following:

- a portfolio of children's work demonstrating progression of the class in the subject area;
- individual achievement in relation to learning objectives; 'tick sheets' are a simple method and are not overly time-consuming to complete while marking work;
- space for recording observations, for example, to denote a particularly good standard of work or to highlight specific learning difficulties. Various record sheet formats are in use in schools and the Class Record Sheet and Individual Pupil Record Sheet found in Lomas et al (1996) are interesting examples.

Decide which of these you might use and whether you might use a combination of methods. Add any other ideas you may have.

Reports

Reports for history will probably be relatively short compared with those for the core curriculum but they need to be soundly based on assessment evidence and comments need to be carefully considered. There are a number of points to bear in mind when writing reports.

- Reports should be supportive and positive about the child's efforts.
- Reports need to be written in a style which is clear and understandable for parents.
- Children's progress in relation to subject knowledge, skills and understanding is the key focus of a report on history, and areas for improvement should be highlighted and targets identified.

PRACTICAL TASK PRACTICAL TASK PRACTICAL TASK PRACTICAL TASK PRACTICAL TASK

Some examples of comments on history from school reports are given below. Identify how well they relate to the Attainment Target for history. Consider what you might put if you wished to improve them.

Year 5 History

James responded enthusiastically to our topic on Ancient Greece. He enjoyed acquiring the relevant knowledge and listening to Greek myths and legends.

Year 3 History

The main topic this year has been the Tudors. A visit to the Tudor stately home was very worthwhile. Sarah worked very hard throughout. She was very interested in artefacts and used reference materials effectively in her work. She appreciates that the past is relevant to the present.

Using assessment information

Assessment for learning

Assessment for learning (AfL) aims to make use of classroom assessment to raise children's achievement. There is some useful guidance on this on the website of the QCA (www.qca.org.uk/qca_4334.aspx). Ten principles apply to AfL, including the need to make sure that learners are aware of the aims behind what is being taught. They should also be made aware of how they are being assessed in order to enable them to work towards improving their performance. Feedback should support their learning and contribute to their progress and their desire to achieve.

Assessment opportunities should be planned in order to enable the teacher to build up a detailed profile, or portfolio, of each child's attainment. Using the monitoring strategies mentioned above you will gradually begin to build up records and your knowledge of each child's understanding of history. Armed with detailed knowledge and understanding of their children's abilities, teachers are in a better position to plan for the next stages of learning, using their assessments to plan with greater accuracy for the child's future learning.

Using local and national data

League table results show the performance of each school, organised by local authority. They are the results of the tests in English, mathematics and science taken by children in the final year of primary school. They also show 'value added' scores, which indicate how much a school has improved. You can combine this general information with comment on a school's work in history, found in the Ofsted school reports (www.ofsted.gov.uk/reports/). Local information on children's services is also available from this site. By comparing the performance and comment on quality of teaching with your own, you may find opportunities for improving aspects of your own history teaching.

Evaluation of teaching

Evaluation of teaching is a part of the planning and assessment cycle. Lesson and unit evaluations are carried out by each teacher, involving reflection on the effectiveness of their teaching strategies, and the quality of learning that has taken place. This sort of evaluation is used to develop and improve practice in individual classrooms and also within a whole school, where the curriculum coordinator is responsible. Assessments of individual children and whole class assessments are a significant source of evidence which should help to inform future planning. A review of the content and delivery of Key Stage 2 history units would be an example of evaluative assessment at whole school level.

When carried out by head teachers and Ofsted inspectors, the main function of evaluation of teaching and learning is also to improve practice. The wider purpose of evaluation by inspectors, however, is the building up of local and national records and reports. The current Standards encourage trainees, NQTs and experienced teachers to use local and national statistical information to assist them in evaluating the effectiveness of their teaching, to monitor the progress of those they teach and to raise levels of attainment.

RESEARCH SUMMARY RESEARCH SUMMARY **RESEARCH SUMMARY** RESEARCH SUMMARY

While there has been some academic research into progression in children's historical abilities (see, for example, Ashby, Lee, and Dickinson (2002), Barton, McCully and Marks (2004)), most specific comment on assessment can be found in the inspection reports produced by Ofsted. Recent reports are listed, along with their websites, in 'Further reading' below. There is comment on schools' emphasis on literacy and numeracy and the consequent limited curriculum time available for history. Ofsted (2005) also refer to the underdeveloped state of the assessment of history, pointing out that many teachers are not well enough informed to set appropriate work. Inspectors found that:

Assessment remains an area of weakness. Not only is assessment insufficiently used to support pupils' progress, but neither is there clarity about the standards attained that can be used for other purposes. So, for example, there are problems when pupils transfer to secondary schools.

http://live.ofsted.gov.uk/publications/annualreport0405/

'History in the balance' (Ofsted, 2007) draws on four years of research in both primary and secondary schools. Once again, there are concerns expressed about the assessment of the subject in primary schools. The report states that there is little teacher assessment in primary schools, and that children's progress is faltering, since teachers are unsure about the standards expected in history. Several areas for development in primary schools are identified, including assessment and more opportunities for children to take responsibility for their own learning.

A SUMMARY OF **KEY POINTS**

> Monitoring and assessment need to be carried out systematically and regularly. Monitoring involves the day-to-day checking and observation of progress, and assessment includes judgements made at the end of a unit, year or key stage.

> There are a number of different assessment strategies, including observation, setting assessment tasks, self-assessment by children, discussion and questioning with peers or teacher, and marking. These contribute to judgements about the progress of individuals.

> Recording and reporting result from the assessment process. Record-keeping is important in keeping track of the progress of children and whole classes, and also supports evaluations of teaching. Reporting to parents about their child's progress is a requirement for all curriculum subjects.

> Assessment for learning informs future planning and contributes to teacher evaluations.

> Evaluation of teaching, carried out by each teacher, involves reflection on the effectiveness of their strategies, and is used to develop and improve practice. It is used for the same purpose by head teachers, inspectors and advisors, and also for the purpose of building up local and national records and reports.

MOVING *ON* > > > > > > MOVING *ON* > > > > > > MOVING *ON*

Standard I11, Standard I12, Standard I14

Read the most recent reports from Ofsted and the QCA and note the key issues and findings that they include. Reflect on these issues and consider the role of the history coordinator in working on them in their own primary school. Discuss with peers the approaches that could be used by the coordinator and the constraints on developing them, such as teachers' concern about lack of time for history. Draw up an action plan for the school whose main focus is the development of rigorous assessment in history.

FURTHER READING FURTHER READING **FURTHER READING** FURTHER READING

Cooper, H (2007) Thinking through history: assessment and learning for the gifted young historian, *Primary History*, 47: 36–38.

Freeman, J (2001) Monitoring, evaluating and planning the history National Curriculum: the role of the QCA, *Primary History*, 29: 9–11.

Jacques, K and Hyland, R (eds) (2007) *Professional Studies: Primary and Early Years.* Exeter: Learning Matters.

Jones, E (2004) Optional assessment materials for history at Key Stage 2, Primary History, 36: 8–9.

Useful websites

www.direct.gov.uk/en/Parents/Schoolslearninganddevelopment/
  You can find information about the National League Tables on this website.

http://live.ofsted.gov.uk/publications/annualreport0405/4.1.5.html
  The annual report of Her Majesty's Chief Inspector of Schools 2004/05.

www.ncaction.org.uk
  Useful examples of children's work also showing how they have been assessed and levelled against the history statements of attainment.

www.ofsted.gov.uk/publications
  Ofsted publications including conference reports.

www.qca.org.uk/
  QCA information and guidance on assessment for learning.

7
Resourcing primary history and collaborative working

Chapter objectives

By the end of this chapter you will have:

- **developed your awareness of the range of resources available for teaching primary history;**
- **considered the value of children working with primary sources in history;**
- **developed your awareness of the role of other adults in children's learning;**
- **developed your awareness of the importance of collaborative working with colleagues.**

Professional Standards for QTS

This chapter will support you as you work towards evidencing attainment against the following Standards:

Q25a: . . . use a range of . . . resources . . . which meet learners' needs and take practical account of diversity and promoting equality and inclusion.

Q5: Recognise and respect the contribution that colleagues, parents and carers can make to the development and well-being of children and young people and to raising their levels of attainment.

Q6: Have a commitment to collaboration and co-operative working.

Q20: Know and understand the roles of colleagues with specific responsibilities, including those with responsibility for learners with special educational needs and disabilities and other individual learning needs.

Published resources and historical sources

Secondary sources

Secondary sources are those which are written or produced some time after the events, so history books and reference materials, for example, are secondary sources. There is a vast range and variety of secondary source material available in the form of books, the internet, educational publishers, the media, and from libraries and archives. It is, of course, most important to take note of the quality and appropriateness of the resources you select and use. They need to address the requirements of the National Curriculum for history, be up to date, free from political or social bias and prejudice and should promote and exemplify equality and inclusive practice. This last point can include gender, race, religion, language, culture and social class. All of these different aspects of society in the past need to be equally and fairly represented in the resources and sources that you use.

Published materials

Historical 'information' books are a useful form of secondary source for history; children can begin to make use of their research and information processing skills in searching through them to find the appropriate chapter, page and paragraph, and also in making use of the index, for the topic of their enquiry. Children will need much guidance and support when beginning to use reference books on their own, gradually learning how to locate the information they need by themselves, and progressing to using an index and library resources. Literary texts and poetry often use history as their context and contain historical information or allusions. Secondary sources such as textbooks, stories, newspaper accounts and documents containing different versions of events giving different interpretations all need to be introduced to children. Through exposure to a wide range of texts they can begin to understand how people are influenced by their own time and how this affects their writing in many different ways. Children can build upon this experience by writing their own interpretations of events in the different genres they have studied.

Many educational publishers include some history titles in their book materials, and these often contain extracts from primary sources of information. There is a wide range of publishers that produce books and resources with different emphases, some of which are:

- Oxford University Press, whose 'Oxford Connections' series contains a children's book on the Romans, Children in World War II, Victorian Children and the Greeks, and an accompanying 'teacher's notes' book for each title. The series aims to make links between literacy and history and helps develop children's skills in writing and thinking.
- Cambridge University Press have produced an ICT resource in conjunction with Hitachi, for Victorian Britain and the Vikings. This series has two components: CD-ROMs and on-line links, which include stories, videos and a range of other visual and auditory materials.
- Scholastic produce several series for primary history: 'Horrible Histories', a humorous version of the past; and other series, such as: '100 History Lessons', 'Ready Resources History'.
- Pearson/Longman produce a series called 'Book Project', which, although essentially a literacy scheme, includes some books that have links with the Tudors and the Victorians, while others are thematic, such as 'transport', 'toys', 'homes', etc.
- Hodder Wayland Publishing Ltd have various series, such as 'All about' and 'Past in Pictures', which cover most of the study units. 'History Starts Here' covers the Ancient Romans, the Egyptians, Greeks, Aztecs, Victorians and Tudors. There is also the 'Heritage' and 'Illustrated World' History through Poetry series, published by Hodder Children's Books.
- Fulton Publishers (now Routledge) are producing a 'Literacy through History' series, but with few titles as yet.
- Heinemann, now part of Pearson, produce the 'Picture the Past' series; History Topic Books, which focus on Roman Britain; 'Life in the Past', which looks at aspects of life in Victorian times, such as schools, homes, the seaside and toys; 'Explore History' which includes pupils' books and CD-ROM, and covers the Key Stage 2 units; 'Primary World Book Web', which is a package of on-line resources for different ages and abilities.
- Dorling Kindersley's 'Eyewitness Guides' are useful for detailed visual information and are much enjoyed by primary children of all ages.
- Folens produce several series of books for primary history, such as: 'Accessing Primary History'; 'Primary History'; 'History in Action'; 'Photopack series'; 'History Highlights'; 'Accessing Whiteboard Plus' and 'Primary Specials'.
- A & C Black also produce several series, including: 'Ace Place'; 'Developing History'; 'Flashbacks'; 'Real Lives'; 'Tough Jobs' and 'What Happened Here?'
- TAG Learning produce a series called 'Digital Time Traveller', which includes books on the Romans, the

Victorians, and castles.
- Anova Books (formerly Batsford) produce a wide range of books and series on historical themes, such as 'Costume History' and 'Women in History'.

The BBC (www.bbcshop.com/) and other organisations such as English Heritage (www.english-heritage.org.uk/) also have large publications lists, which can be accessed on their websites.

PRACTICAL TASK PRACTICAL TASK **PRACTICAL TASK** PRACTICAL TASK **PRACTICAL TASK**

Choose a non-fiction book on history on a Key Stage 2 topic. Think about how a Year 4 child, carrying out some independent research, might use this book. Consider what guidance and structure they might need for this work, and what you might do to ensure that they used the book effectively. If possible, try out these ideas in the classroom.

The internet
The internet is an unimaginably rich resource for history. If used with caution, it can be a very valuable resource indeed. However, there are a great many pitfalls in this 'minefield' of information. For further discussion and examples from the internet see Chapter 9, where reference is made to a wide range of ICT-based resources for each unit.

Primary sources

Artefacts
Artefacts can be original objects from the period being studied, or they can be replicas, made in modern times; in other words, they can be either primary or secondary sources. There are, of course, many types of artefacts. They can include small objects, such as a piece of jewellery from the Indus Valley civilisation, or an industrial building, built in nineteenth-century England. As Sallie Purkis points out, even large buildings are artefacts (Purkis, 1993b).

Families and others in the community are most generous in helping provide resources. If you send out a letter to parents, families and carers, asking if they would lend their mementoes, from the Second World War, for example, you will probably receive a great deal of support. However, it is important to check that they are all safe (I once had a very dangerous 'trench digger' sent in) and to return, with thanks, any that you feel could be a health and safety problem. It is also vitally important to list each item and its owner, and to ensure that they are all kept in a secure place. Equally, people are pleased to help you acquire objects, as far back as late Victorian times, such as old flat-irons, or you can purchase items from museum shops, 'antiques fairs' or second-hand shops very cheaply. For example, the flat-iron shown in Figure 15 was very inexpensive to buy, yet it has been a source of interest and learning for many primary children.

Figure 15. Flat-iron

It is difficult, of course, to find objects going back to earlier periods in time or to remoter history. However, there are organisations and local authorities which produce packs of replicas, such as those found at www.northlincs.gov.uk/ or www.cambridgeshire.gov.uk/leisure/archaeology/.

While they are usually a little more expensive, even one of these can enhance your teaching about the Romans or Ancient Egypt. Replicas of objects from Ancient civilisations can also be found in museum shops, such as the shop for the British Museum (www.britishmuseum. co.uk/). A visit to a suitable museum, which provides 'hands on' workshops, can be an additional way of enabling your class to experience objects from the past at first hand.

Visual sources

Visual sources include pictures, paintings, photographs, portraits, sketches, film and video material, television broadcasts, and so on. There is certainly a very wide variety to choose from. Visual sources are readily available in books, on the internet and from educational suppliers, such as the Pictorial Charts Educational Trust (www.pcet.co.uk).

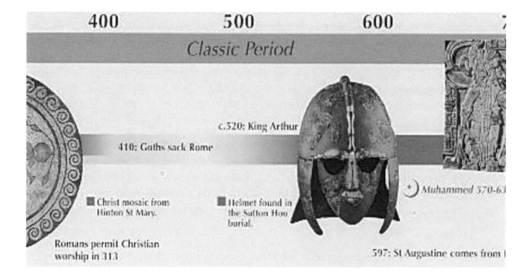

Timeline

Toys

Figure 16. Visual sources (www.pcet.co.uk)

A helpul visual source is the photograph. Pictures taken of children growing up are always useful in the Early Years Foundation Stage and Key Stage 1 for studying children's own lives and those of their families. A sense of the past can then be developed through looking with the children at paintings and photographs showing families at other times in the past. The national Media Museum, based in Bradford, has a large free collection of materials and a selection which can be viewed on-line (www.nationalmediamuseum.org.uk/).

Film and broadcasts are widely used in schools. 'Moving Memories', sets of original film footage dating from the beginning of the twentieth century, are available from The North West Film Archive (www.nwfa.mmu.ac.uk/). The major TV channels all produce useful programmes for history lessons. However, care is needed in using them, since they need follow-up work which has been planned to encourage discussion and interaction, otherwise the learning experience risks becoming very passive. Broadcasts are listed on websites such as www.onthebox.com.

Written sources
In addition to books and internet sources, written sources include diaries, letters, news-papers, documents, wills, play scripts and poetry. There is a major link with literacy in the range of written forms and styles that history provides, and the value of literature cannot be overemphasised. Reading works or extracts from authors and writers such as Dickens or Anne Frank provides a vivid experience of people's lives and opinions, all of which helps children build up a picture of different eras in the past. They are also an excellent stimulus for children's own imaginative creative writing. While many historical texts and literary works are difficult for young children to read and engage with, they do provide some challenge for the gifted and talented children in a class.

Censuses, street directories, numerical and statistical data, graphs and charts are all forms of written source which can be useful as part of a history topic. For further information on sources related to literacy and mathematics, see Chapter 8.

Oral history
Oral history, discussed in Chapter 5 above, is an important primary source for history, providing some of the most immediate and exciting information. The Oral History Society (www.ohs.org.uk) provide on-line advice on interviewing and interview techniques.

Music, art and architecture
Music, songs and dance are further first-hand sources of evidence. Rosie Turner-Bisset's book is an excellent source of information on suitable songs, music and dance for primary children to use, and provides guidance on how to use these sources with children (Turner-Bisset, 2005a). The use of music is discussed in more detail in Chapter 11.

Art and architecture in all its many forms are excellent primary sources, providing an insight into what a past society was like. Portraits are widely used in schools, particularly those of the monarchs through the ages. A huge selection is available on the website of the National Portrait Gallery (www.npg.org.uk/), and others are available on other museum websites. Family portraits at different times in the past, along with pictures of homes, forms of trans-port, or costume, are all to be found in the works of art made at the time. Other artwork, such as statues from Roman times, woodcuts made in the Tudor period, illustrations for the books of Dickens, or sketches depicting child labour in nineteenth-century inspectors' reports, show people and their lives in the past. Lowry's industrial scenes or film clips from the twentieth century are excellent sources of information about the environments in which people lived and worked.

Works of art encourage children to observe closely and to think critically about what they see, asking and answering questions to further their understanding of the contextual background. They also greatly facilitate the study of historical interpretation and help children understand that the past has been represented in many different ways. For example, certain well-known characters, such as Guy Fawkes, are represented in different ways depending on whether he is seen by the artist as a villain or a hero.

People

The contribution of colleagues, parents and carers in supporting learning
The potential value of contributions by teaching colleagues, support staff, parents and carers in supporting learning cannot be overstated. From the head teacher of the school to the school secretary and caretaker, all staff may be in a position to contribute their knowledge, skills and memories of past times to children learning history, and it can be helpful to make use of this potentially huge fund of expertise.

History coordinator
The subject coordinator for history is the key point of contact when you arrive as a new teacher in a school. They will be able to inform you about the school's policies towards history, marking and assessment, and give you an overview of the topics covered and the order in which the units are taught at Key Stages 1 and 2. It is useful to have an overview of this sort, since the work you do in your own class can then be linked to the work of children in the previous and following years. The coordinator will also be able to help you to locate resources and plan your history unit(s) for the year, providing you with the school's long-term planning and also medium-term plans prepared by previous teachers in your year group. You can also seek advice and support once you have drawn up your lesson plans. Many schools now simply work from the detail provided in their unit plans and your coordinator will be able to advise you on their current practice.

CLASSROOM STORY
Rosemary had just started working in a new Key Stage 2 class, and being very keen on history, she set to work on her history planning as soon as she knew what topic she would be teaching that term. She drew up a very clear, concise medium-term plan, showing how her class would progress over the half term covered by the plan, particularly in their understanding of chronology. She then created a set of eight detailed lesson plans, using the work in her unit plan as the basis of each one. Where she could, Rosemary linked literacy and numeracy to her work in history and also made cross-curricular links with geography and ICT.

Once these plans were completed, she took them to the head teacher for approval before starting her teaching of the unit. However, to her dismay, the head passed them back to her after a few minutes, saying that she should really have talked about all this with the humanities coordinator. Quickly finding the coordinator, Rosemary discovered that in her new school, lesson plans were not required, since the school had adopted the policy of simply linking literacy with work in other subjects using the Literacy Framework Planning Tool. Teachers then worked directly from their unit

---

plans, which were all that was required. Rosemary realised that she needed to think and act more as a team member in order to avoid spending too much time planning in isolation only to find her planning was not really appropriate.

Special needs coordinator

The 'Senco', or special educational needs coordinator, is also an important colleague in terms of planning and teaching. Their work largely focuses on developing the literacy and numeracy skills of those children with special educational needs (SEN); however, it is possible to link some of this work to your plans for history. For example, if you are planning work on a history unit, such as 'myself' or 'my family', it can be a useful practice to draw up a list of the key words that you will be introducing in the course of the topic. These can then be shared with the Senco, and used in the planning of any support staff working on literacy with children from your class.

Teaching assistant

The teaching assistant (TA) is another very valuable source of information in the classroom. Teaching assistants often have considerable experience and knowledge of the locality, and can therefore make a very valuable contribution to planning, preparation and the provision of resources and ideas. They can also enhance children's experience of an historical topic with the different perspective they may bring to it.

PRACTICAL TASK PRACTICAL TASK **PRACTICAL TASK** PRACTICAL TASK **PRACTICAL TASK**

You are carrying out some work on the Victorians, which makes use in the next lesson of a number of visual sources. You have collected a range of sketches, portraits and photographs showing aspects of the lives of children in the period, and want the children to investigate the pictures, asking and answering questions of their own. In previous lessons of this sort, you have noticed that the teaching assistant has focused on helping the less able children to write labels and short sentences, but has struggled to engage the more able children in discussion. You are aware that this is necessary for the children to devise and answer questions and extend their skills in source analysis. Consider what guidance you could give to the teaching assistant to enable her to achieve these goals.

Working alongside the teaching assistant is becoming an important aspect of the role of the class teacher. It is important to support and guide the teaching assistant in order to ensure that their skills are deployed as effectively as possible within your classroom, particularly during PPA (planning, preparation and assessment) time, when tasks need to be specified. Such tasks might be most effective if they are designed to build upon and extend learning that has taken place in earlier lessons on history, such as continuing research work for a history topic book, continuing to develop skills in source analysis by working with different sources, working on literacy tasks which relate to earlier history work or work which is to follow, and so on. It is also important to include the TA in planning work and in ensuring that any assessment feedback they might gather is clearly recorded so that it can be incorporated into your own assessment records. You can find out more about the role of teaching assistants and higher level teaching assistants (HLTAs) from the website www.tda.gov.uk/support/hlta.aspx.

Nursery nurses

Nursery nurses are responsible for looking after the social and educational development of young children. Their work involves planning and supervising activities and keeping parents up to date with their child's progress. Collaborative working with your nursery nurse is essential to achieving secure and effective development of the language related to historical understanding, the talk that needs to accompany historical enquiry, and the numerical skills that will eventually enable children to understand historical chronology and timelines.

Support staff

Other support staff include play workers, learning mentors and specialist support staff who work with children with English as an Additional Language (EAL) or learning difficulties such as autism. Play workers plan, organise and supervise activities inside and outside school. So, if you are working in an early years setting, you need to involve these workers in any activities you might devise to extend children's understanding of history, such as enabling children to talk about historical objects in a display, or telling stories from the past. Learning mentors support any children who may be underachieving. Their role is to help children overcome barriers to learning caused by social, emotional and behavioural problems. Once again, although they are likely to be mostly engaged with work in the core areas of literacy and numeracy, opportunities to make links with history need to be pointed out and planned. Caretakers and cleaners can also often have a role to play in history lessons, particularly if they have worked at the school for some years and can talk about how the school or the local area has changed over time.

English as an Additional Language(EAL) support staff

EAL support colleagues are trained to ensure that effective learning takes place across the curriculum. They will have studied, and will understand, the factors involved in planning and delivery to enable bilingual learners to make progress in all curriculum areas while developing their knowledge of English. You can assist them in this task by sharing your planning in history with them, along with, for example, the key ideas and related vocabulary that you will be using in your history topic. This enables access and engagement with history for all learners, in particular those from minority ethnic groups, where English is an additional language.

Parents and carers

Parents, carers and relatives are an important element in the learning process. By making links with learning inside and outside the classroom, you can deepen and extend children's understanding and motivation considerably. Some children struggle to make links between what they learn in school and 'real life', and this is where those with an interest in supporting learning outside the classroom become vitally important. Parents and others can contribute in many ways, but sometimes it is necessary to make a deliberate attempt to involve them. Newsletters and other forms of communication are a useful way of informing them about your current and forthcoming topics in history. They can then make a positive contribution, for example, in the form of sending in resources, arranging to speak to the class, providing materials or coming into school to help make costumes for a play, or work with ICT with the children.

More important than this form of support, however, is the kind of work directly with the child that enhances their learning. For example, parental interest in children's topic work can extend to helping them find resources on the internet or in the local libraries, taking them on family visits to relevant museums or places of interest, or working with them to put together timelines, books, stories or accounts sent from school as homework. They can also be an invaluable resource on school outings, helping to enrich the children's learning by engaging them in talk and asking and answering questions. One of the most interesting ways of involving parents and others is to send home the children with interview schedules, so that they can record the adults' memories with their help, for use in the children's personal or class projects. Sharing the results of all this work is probably one of the most enjoyable primary school experiences, with parents, carers, grandparents etc. all being invited to a class assembly, a play or a presentation to celebrate the successful outcome of the children's work.

Sharing effective practice

Working as member of a team is an increasingly important aspect of primary school practice. Planning, preparation and the location and use of resources is often carried out as part of a year group team of two or three teachers, and work on whole school planning and assessment is frequently discussed by the whole staff team. It is therefore important to regard yourself as part of the team when you are working on your history units, sharing ideas, planning and resources with colleagues, as well as learning from their ideas and practices. If possible, it can be very beneficial to visit other classes and observe the way colleagues work on their history themes, thus building up good practice within a school.

REFLECTIVE TASK

Use some of the suggested websites to explore the possibilities for educational visits based on history. For example, consider the potential of a visit to Hampton Court Palace in terms of children's learning (www.hrp.org.uk/). Devise a theoretical plan for a visit which you might include within a topic on the Tudors. Consider in particular how you would deploy support staff and other adults.

RESEARCH SUMMARY RESEARCH SUMMARY **RESEARCH SUMMARY** RESEARCH SUMMARY

All the DCSF's official research documents are on-line at www.dfes.gov.uk/research/ . This website can be a useful source of information when you are carrying out personal research for your initial teacher training course and also for other courses leading to teaching qualifications.

The National Teacher Research Panel is a group of practising teachers who work to promote teaching as a research-informed profession, and to ensure that researchers take the perspectives of teachers into account. Their website has more information about their work and some resources for teachers: www.standards.dfes.gov.uk/ntrp/. The research area of TeacherNet has useful information about education topics: http://www.teachernet.gov.uk /research/ and various resources such as articles, reports, texts, statistics websites and on-line databases are available at http://www.teachernet.gov.uk /research/ resources/. These topics include areas such as the role of teaching assistants.

The National Foundation for Education Research (NFER) produces well-researched publications and reports, some in hard copy and others on-line at www.nfer.ac.uk/. These include research into issues such as meeting children's needs, current trends in education, community cohesion and social inclusion.

A SUMMARY OF **KEY POINTS**

> There is a vast range of resources for primary history, including published materials, but these need to be selected with care to ensure that they are free of strong bias and that they meets the requirements of your school's policies.

> Historical sources, both primary and secondary, are some of the most interesting and motivating but, again, these need to be used with caution to ensure that children are provided with a balanced picture of the past.

> Places, such as the local area and historic sites, provide motivating and often interactive displays and re-enactments.

> People, such as teaching assistants and other school staff, parents and carers can be a vitally important resource in terms of providing more personalised support and extending children's learning.

MOVING *ON* > > > > > > MOVING *ON* > > > > > > MOVING *ON*

Standard 15, Standard 16, Standard 120, Standard 121, Standard 129

You might wish to think about developing links in the school's long-term planning between history and wider cross-curricular themes such as equality or inclusion. One of the aspects of history planning that you will need to review is the resource collection that is available in the school. In reviewing this, consider how the resources you have to date will enable teachers to make the cross-curricular links you envisage. How will you support the 'human resources' in the school in adapting their work to incorporate new resources and initiatives?

FURTHER READING FURTHER READING FURTHER READING FURTHER READING

Halewood, J (2000) A treasure trove of local history – How to use your local record office, *Primary History*, 24: 10–12.

Hammond, P (2004) A load of old rubbish. Using Victorian throwaways in the classroom. *Primary History,* 36: 12–16.

Harrison, S and Woff, R (2004) Using museums and artefacts, *Primary History,* 37: 18–21.

Mills, M (2004) Using digital photographic images in the classroom, *Primary History,* 36: 30–35.

Whitworth, K (2006) Discovery visits: What's new at English Heritage for schools?, *Primary History,* 43: 14–17.

The Autumn 2003 issue of *Primary History,* 'Learning through Museums and Galleries', is entirely devoted to the use of museums.

Useful websites

www.britishmuseum.co.uk/
www.northlincs.gov.uk/
www.cambridgeshire.gov.uk/leisure/archaeology/.
   Sources of replica artefacts.

www.english-heritage.org.uk/
www.bbcshop.com/
   Useful for published materials.

www.hrp.org.uk/
   Website for the Historic Royal Palaces in London, which has some good interactive graphics.

www.nationalmediamuseum.org.uk/
   Website of the National Media Museum, which has some free on-line materials.

www.npg.org.uk
   National Portrait Gallery website.

www.nwfa.mmu.ac.uk/
 The North West Film Archive has remarkable original film footage.

www.ohs.org.uk
 Website of the Oral History Society.

www.onthebox.com.
 Lists TV broadcasts.

www.pcet.co.uk
 Useful posters and charts.

http://www.schoolsweb.gov.uk/locate/professionaldevelopment/research/
 Useful for research background.

www.tda.gov.uk/support/hlta.aspx.
www.teachernet.gov.uk/
www.nfer.ac.uk/
 Further information is available on these websites about the role of other adult support in the classroom and current educational issues.

8
Making the most of links with literacy and mathematics

Chapter objectives

By the end of this chapter you will have:

- considered the range of opportunities offered by history for including work on literacy and mathematics;
- considered the links between the history curriculum and language and the potential for developing skills in both subjects;
- considered the links between the history curriculum and mathematics and the potential for developing skills in both subjects.

Professional Standards for QTS

This chapter will support you as you work towards evidencing attainment against the following Standards:

Q15: Know and understand the relevant statutory and non-statutory curricula and frameworks, including those provided through the National Strategies;

Q17: Know how to use skills in literacy and numeracy... to support their teaching;

Q 23: Design opportunities for learners to develop their literacy and numeracy skills.

History and literacy

The use of language across the curriculum

Language and thought are so closely related as to be inseparable (Vygotsky, 1962; Bruner, 1990). Theorists see the development of skills in language as part of learning to think, not simply a by-product of it. Indeed, Bruner argues that it is social interaction and the language associated with it that promotes the development of thinking skills. He sees learning as an active process in which learners use their knowledge and understanding to construct new ideas.

The specific language skills of reading, writing, speaking and listening are embedded within the National Curriculum for history, which requires children to develop their skills in communication throughout the primary school. At Key Stage 1, children should be able to select from their knowledge of history and communicate what they have learned in a variety of ways through talking, writing or using ICT. At Key Stage 2, they are expected to have extended their skills considerably. They should recall, select and organise historical information; use dates and historical vocabulary; communicate their knowledge and understanding of history in a variety of ways, such as through drawing, speaking, writing or by using ICT. Progression in teacher expectation is important in setting increasingly challenging objectives to raise the level of children's attainment. Close links with the revised *Framework for Literacy* will assist teachers greatly in planning for this progression (DfES, 2006).

The links between history and language are many and varied since history is a subject which makes much use of language in all its forms. Most history is studied through the use of texts and oral accounts. Children's skills in communication are therefore developed continually in history in the course of reading, listening, writing and speaking, all skills without which it would be very hard to study history (Nichol, 2000). All of the teaching strategies used in teaching primary history relate either directly or indirectly to skills in the use of both verbal and written communication.

Many schools are now making use of history-related activities and sources in the literacy hour. For example, deciding whether statements are fact, fiction or opinion, are aspects of both subjects. By learning to read and understand texts within the literacy lessons, children are then able to make better use of written sources in their history. In schools where such links between the two subjects have been established by coordinators, Ofsted has made very positive comment (Ofsted, 2007).

The National Framework for Literacy and the history curriculum

In places, there are similar requirements within the *Framework for Literacy* and the history curriculum. For example, within the 'narrative strand' in Year 1 of the Framework, there is reference to traditional stories and recount texts, both of which might easily relate to learning about the past. Information texts are mentioned every year up to Year 4. Later years also include content such as myths and legends (Year 3), stories with historical settings (Year 4), older literature and classic/narrative poems (Year 5) and in Year 6, biography and autobio-graphy. All of these clearly have links with history, or offer the potential for historical content and context to be used for work in literacy.

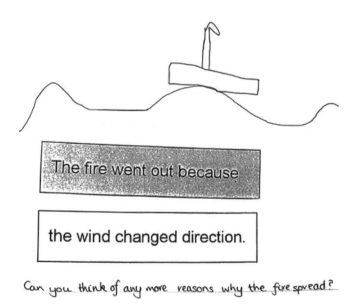

Figure 17. Fire of London (Year 1 work)

Links with historical skills are evident in the objectives set for each year group in the *Framework for Literacy*. For example, the Early Years Foundation Stage objectives refer to the skill of using talk 'to organise, sequence and clarify thinking', focusing on the skill of sequencing, which begins to develop in the early years. These early understandings might contribute specifically to children's developing skills in understanding historical sequencing and chronology in later years (Hoodless, 2002). The example of work in Figure 17 illustrates how learning at Key Stage 1 can build up an understanding of causation.

Developing literacy skills through history

The conjunction of skills between the two subjects is extensive, with skills such as the following clearly providing opportunities for work in history throughout Key Stages 1 and 2.

- Reasoning: children need to be introduced to, and to use for themselves, the language of reasoning. Such language includes the use of 'because', 'so', 'when...then', 'if...then'. In looking for connections and reasons in history and in using sources, children will need to use this type of language in an increasingly specific way to communicate their understanding, thus making use of their literacy skills.
- Exploring interpretations: the language of reasoning also underpins the comparison of different interpretations of events. For example, a child might argue that Guy Fawkes was a bad person 'because' he was prepared to kill people to try to get what he wanted.
- Using the past tense correctly: many children over-generalise when converting words from the present into the past tense. Verbs such as run, or went, become runned or wented. This is generally not due to any lack of intelligence on the part of the child, simply lack of exposure to the correct forms, and history can provide the context for this kind of necessary exposure and practice.
- Sequencing: this important concept has its own set of key vocabulary, which children will need to learn and use. This includes terms such as 'before', 'after', 'next', 'last', 'first', 'second', 'third', and so on.
- Using evidence and sources: this is a key part of the history curriculum, and where written sources are involved in studying the past, there are numerous opportunities to make links.
- Inferring writers' perspectives: this is also a major part of work in the history curriculum. An understanding of the perspective, prejudices or bias of an author is vitally important to historical enquiry, since it can greatly influence the 'evidence' from that source.
- Comparing different types of texts: again, history relies upon the use of a number of different sources to provide a broad and balanced view of a past period or event. In literacy, children might focus on the technical features of different texts; in a history lesson their comprehension and significance, such as the different viewpoints or interpretations they reveal, would be a major part of how they might be used.
- Understanding underlying themes, causes and points of view: a further major part of the history curriculum links with this objective. Analysing why things happened in the past is a very similar skill to that outlined in the *Framework for Literacy*.
- Comparing how writers from different times and places present experience and use language: this skill in literacy can significantly enrich children's understanding of the past. Differences in styles of writing and communicating attitudes are an important part of understanding past societies.
- Communicating the results of historical enquiry: this aspect of the history curriculum enables children to develop skills in composing non-fiction and extended writing, note-making, lists, charts and diagrams, poetry, instructions and the wide variety of genres for which texts from history serve as a model.

There are many examples of these links in books and journal articles on primary history. Cooper, in her chapter on 'History, the curriculum and communication skills', gives a number of examples from practice and a detailed analysis of the links between literacy objectives and historical thinking (Cooper, 2007a, p94–96). There are other practical examples in the form of plans and case studies, such as Issue 41 of *Primary History* (Historical Association, 2005), which focuses entirely on the links between history and literacy.

PRACTICAL TASK PRACTICAL TASK **PRACTICAL TASK** PRACTICAL TASK **PRACTICAL TASK**

Using children's books from a library, or sources from the internet, find two different types of text which relate to the same historical theme or event. Using these texts as learning resources, plan activities which link history and literacy to test out in the classroom.

Wider links with English

Talk

Talk, involving questioning and discussion, is vitally important in historical enquiry. Talk, both with their peers and teachers, enables children to internalise the skills and related language uses that are fundamental to the study of the past. These include the use of appropriate vocabulary, tenses, descriptive words and phrases, the language of time and problem solving. For example, it is often through discussion and the use of questions they have themselves formulated that children are able to solve problems effectively (Hoodless, 1994a). Children can learn a great deal of new language by means of the process of 'instrumental enrichment' (Fuerstein, 1980); they operate as an apprentice, absorbing the kind of talk they hear the teacher using and beginning to use it themselves.

Children's talk, particularly in answering focused questions, can reveal a great deal about the level of their historical knowledge and understanding. Talk is a useful tool for assessment of progress in the course of a unit of work. For example, if key words have been identified and noted on your unit of work, a useful assessment task would be to monitor the children's growing use of this vocabulary in their own talk. A particularly valuable activity is to monitor children's ability to ask their own questions, and the appropriateness of their questioning.

Storytelling and oral history

Probably the most ancient and widely used activity in communicating history, especially with children, is the use of story and story-telling. It is an art that has been used in many different cultures across the world, for example, the Vikings and their sagas, and is still a popular method for introducing a topic to a class or for developing further their involvement and knowledge of content and contextual detail. Children can relate their own experiences to what they hear and begin to identify and empathise with the experiences of the characters in the story. Story-telling is a fairly skilled activity, however, and you will need to carry out some research into the context and content before you embark on a session. You will need to practise some of the skills involved in engaging your young audience. Children are always more engaged and excited by the face-to-face interaction of listening to a story directly told, rather than listening to something read from a book. Your stories can be enhanced by facial expressions, gestures, the use of different 'voices' and, of course, visual images. John Fines has written and researched extensively into this aspect of teaching history (Fines and Nichol, 1997) and has used story dramatically in a way calculated to give rise to a range of other activities.

Introducing a 'visitor' in the classroom, or an 'expert', perhaps from the local museum, can create an exciting and memorable learning experience. Hearing personal memories recounted can make history more 'real' for those children who find it difficult to empathise with people's experiences in the past, and listening carefully is a skill which they can develop as part of their work in literacy. Listening is a skill specifically mentioned as a strand in the core learning outlined throughout the primary phase. For example, in Year 2, they are required to 'listen to a talk by an adult, remember some specific points and identify what they have learned', whereas by Year 4 they should 'listen to a speaker, make notes on the talk and use notes to develop a role-play' (DfES, 2006). All of these literacy requirements apply to good practice in history teaching. Claire (2004b) provides some useful advice and information on the use of oral history along with references to other more detailed work.

Drama

What children often enjoy most is the creation of their own dramas, scenes or role-plays. Dramatic activities provide opportunities for children to engage with issues from the past that might be difficult to work with in other ways. Through the process of rehearsing their scenes, or thinking through their part in a role-play activity, children internalise and clarify their thinking about issues chosen for study, such as the moral issues surrounding the conflicts between Boudicca and the Romans. The resulting ideas, discussions and debates are an excellent opportunity to integrate work in citizenship with that in history (Hoodless, 2003b, Chapter 10).

Re-enactments in museums or at historic sites, TV and film dramas also contribute in motivating children to absorb new knowledge, ideas and understanding of issues that have faced societies through the ages. Cooper (2007a) describes an occasion when she performed herself as 'teacher-in-role', a most powerful tool in the classroom. Hot-seating in this way can provide an exciting means of conveying necessary background and factual detail. Freeze-frames and other techniques are described in the case studies provided in *Primary History* (Historical Association, 2008).

Reading: the links with literature and non-fiction texts

There has recently been a revival of interest in the value of fiction and story as a source for understanding about the past (Hoodless, 1998b; English Heritage, 1998; Bage, 1999; Vass, 2005b). Often used as an on-going book, read to the class by the teacher to accompany a topic, historical fiction plays a significant role in establishing the context and providing children with some detailed information about their history topic. Stories written about the past can also convey an understanding of more abstract features of the past. Some recent small-scale research of my own has shown that children in Key Stage 2, when working with a medium that is familiar and understandable to them, can demonstrate quite advanced understanding of aspects of the past, such as the very different values and attitudes that were held (Hoodless, 2006). For example, in reading stories set in the early part of the twentieth century, children noticed the great deference paid to a character such as Boudicca, because of her status as a queen, while at the same time indicating that members of the present royal family might not be treated by the media in such a way. Story and literature can fire children's imagination and enthusiasm for the past and can be a more memorable source if used as part of an historical theme.

Non-fiction written sources are perhaps one of the most important and widely used of all historical sources. They include all written documents dating from the past – a very large category indeed. Joan Blyth was an early advocate of making use of these links (Blyth and Hughes, 1997). In *Using Written Sources in Primary History* she considers non-fiction to include non-fiction *information books, reference books, such as encyclopedias, history dictionaries and atlases, and ICT-based sources*. She has also advocated the use of original texts written in the past as a means of introducing children to different genres and authentic historical sources (Blyth, 1998). Turner-Bisset (2005a), in her chapter on using written sources, gives a detailed overview of the written sources that can be used, from personal documents, such as diaries, certificates, bank cards and so on, to inscriptions on gravestones or gaol records.

Writing in different genres

Many schools are beginning to take advantage of the great range of useful exemplary source material which history can provide. Husbands (1996) and others have highlighted the exceptional potential of history to provide a variety of different genres which children can use in their writing and different audiences for whom they may write. Children can produce inventories, reports, narrative accounts, letters, newspaper pages, questionnaires, books, stories, interviews and descriptions. They can be guided and their efforts scaffolded in a number of ways, for example by using 'writing frames' and storyboards (Wray and Medwell, 1998).

Creative writing and poetry offer the possibilities of real creative links with history. History, as Jon Nichol points out, is a creative art (Nichol, 2005). It provides a vast range of models for writing and the careful use of written sources can have a profound influence on the quality of children's work. Poetry is a major form of writing in which emotions and thoughts can be expressed, and there are many examples of this in history. For example, the poetry of Walter de la Mare is full of historical allusions, which can be explored and used in children's own poetry.

The important links between English and history in terms of creativity and imagination enable the child to engage in writing set within an historical framework. In the example below, historical sources had been used in studying the use of propaganda during the Second World War, and this activity required children to design a poster using instructional text.

Figure 18. Put that light out! (Year 5 work)

Vocabulary

The extension of vocabulary is a feature throughout the *Framework for Literacy*, and here history can contribute widely. If they are encouraged to use sources, such as books, the internet, charts, documents, oral sources, and so on, children are exposed to a wide and varied range of vocabulary. The task of the teacher is to identify important vocabulary which will be useful to add to the children's repertoire. To ensure that these new terms are learned you will need to plan to introduce this vocabulary to the class, and include it in your written plans. Ensure that you plan to use it yourself and also that the children have opportunities to use it in their own 'active' vocabularies at some stage. Check by listening to their talk to see whether they have incorporated the new words in their own discussion or answers.

REFLECTIVE TASK

Choose an historical theme from the National Curriculum which is likely to be popular at Key Stage 2, such as 'Britain and the wider world in Tudor times'. Consider what key vocabulary might be needed by children in your chosen year group when studying a topic from this period. Select 10 or 12 key words which you feel would be most relevant. Plan for these to be incorporated into a unit of work on your chosen topic. You will find the vocabulary suggested in the QCA schemes of work a useful example of the type of words to think of (DfEE/QCA, 1998). However, this is unlikely to be adequate for a specific topic, such as a study of the Spanish Armada, or Shakespeare's England.

Understanding, using and making books

Last but not least, history provides one of the best opportunities for developing in children a great love of books. One of the best ways to instil this love is to encourage children to make their own (Johnson, 1998). Once a child's very best pieces of work on a historical topic have been collected together in a hand-made book and embellished with their best artwork, they will not forget the pleasure of creating, reading and sharing their work. Children can learn about the important features of books when they make their own, including the purpose of the contents pages and the index. Books can be very simply made from a sheet of folded paper, like the example below. However, Johnson illustrates many varied and inventive ways of creating books, from the most simple to the very complex, such as pop-up books and books with carefully made binding.

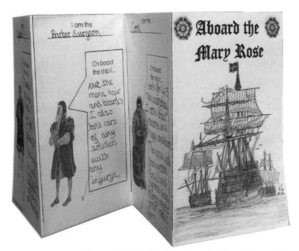

Figure 19. A folding book (Year 5 work)

History and mathematics

The links between history and the *National Framework for mathematics*

While many schools are now making links between history and literacy, the links between history and mathematics have been less well-developed. In many cases, they are there, but are perhaps not acknowledged. Schools sometimes see potential links between mathematics and subjects such as geography, which are perceived as more 'technical' or 'scientific', when in fact, there is an equally good case for making the connection with history. Cooper provides a list of the links between mathematics and history from the Foundation Stage to Year 6 (Cooper, 2007, p101).

Using and applying mathematics

In the Foundation Stage children are expected to learn how to sort objects and justify their decisions, skills which apply very much to early learning in history. For example, children need to understand how to group objects which relate to people of different ages, such as a baby's bottle, or an old slipper belonging to a grandad. They can then be asked to say why they have grouped these objects together.

At Key Stage 1, children gradually begin to extend their skill in using numbers and also begin to understand how information can be represented in lists, tables or simple diagrams, such as timelines, timetables, or lists of reasons for an event. They begin to understand the relationship of pattern to number. Colin Miller (1998) points out how the work of Pythagoras has influenced and informed modern mathematics, and points to a link between his interest in number patterns and this part of the mathematics curriculum.

Number systems from the past are a constant source of interest for children in the early years of Key Stage 2. The number systems used by the Romans or the Aztecs, for example, and by our own fairly recent ancestors (pounds, shillings and pence) are useful in consolidating children's understanding of place value. For example, old pennies were counted in 12s – 12 pence made one shilling – while there were 20 shillings in one pound. Children can learn that 10 is not the only basis for a counting system, and that earlier peoples have used many different types of number bases. Money, and calculations involving money, can be included in work on shops and shopping both in the past and the present.

CLASSROOM STORY

Jean thought that her Year 3 class would enjoy linking their work in mathematics to their work in history, and knew they would enjoy working with Roman numerals, which they had just learned about during a museum visit. She set them the following sums to do, having made sure to start with that they remembered what the numbers up to 10 looked like. She questioned them carefully about how the Romans had worked out how to make up numbers like 4 and 9. She pointed out that in early Roman times, the number 4 would have been written as 'IIII', but the Romans later worked out that it could be written 'IV'. Jean also pointed out that the children needed to write their answers in Roman numerals if they were to get them right. They would also need to work out how to write and read some numbers greater than 10.

Roman numerals: I = 1, II = 2, III = 3, IV = 4, V = 5, VI = 6, VII = 7, VIII = 8, IX = 9, X = 10

III +	VI +	IX −	XX −	I ×	IV ×
IV	V	II	IV	VI	II
———	———	———	———	———	———
———	———	———	———	———	———

Number plays a vital part in using timelines in Key Stage 2, where calculations may be needed to work out the lengths of reigns, the lengths of wars or spans of time. Various types of evidence from the past are often recorded in the form of charts and diagrams, such as the census records. Children need to learn how to interpret these charts and also how to create their own. These are skills very closely related to those required for using charts in mathematics.

Number puzzles and magic shapes, such as magic squares, were known to the Ancient Chinese and cultures in Asia and the Middle East. These are discussed in detail in a fascinating article by Colin Miller (1999b), where you will find examples to try out with your class. Their historical significance, such as the belief that they had magical properties, is also quite fascinating.

There are many ways of linking an area of content such as Roman Britain, for example, to mathematical skills, as you will see in the example below.

CLASSROOM STORY

Jane was in her first year of teaching, and found that she was to be responsible for teaching about Roman Britain to a Year 3 class. From her training she knew that she must try to link together the skills, concepts and knowledge that children would be learning in order to meet the requirements of the National Curriculum for history.

Jane looked at the National Curriculum document and thought about her class. She had seen their assessments from the previous year and had met them on two occasions. She knew that they were quite immature and probably did not have a very secure understanding of the concept of chronology. She also realised that there would be an opportunity to link her teaching of history with some work on numeracy. Jane therefore planned to create both an historical timeline and a number line. She hoped to be able to compare the two in order to help the children understand how historical timelines work, their links with number, and how they can be 'read'. She planned to develop the children's vocabulary in history, by teaching them time-related terms and by using these as key vocabulary in her lesson plans.

Counting and understanding number

Number skills developed in the Early Years Foundation Stage and in Key Stage 1 contribute to children's work with time charts, timetables, calendars and timelines. They also use their developing skills in counting and calculation when working on local history, where they might be recording the numbers of steps, windows or other details in buildings, part of their understanding of how building styles change over time.

By Year 3 children are expected to be able to read, write and order whole numbers to at least 1,000 and position them on a number line (DfES, 2006). These skills all relate directly to the ability to understand and use dates and conventional timelines, since there would appear to be an obvious link between a grasp of number up to 1,000 and an understanding of chronology. In Years 4, 5 and 6, children are expected to learn about positive and negative numbers and where they would appear on a number line, again a topic linked closely with an understanding of the BC/AD divide in historical chronology. Children's understanding of number can only be enriched by putting these somewhat abstract notions into a practical context such as that of the passing of time and its measurement.

There are numerous historical records about the lives of ordinary people, particularly in Victorian times, and the use of these sources can often be enhanced by a sound knowledge and understanding of mathematics. For example, in studying how the poor spent their household incomes, a child might be introduced to sources such as 'A Manchester Housewife's Weekly Budget' (Royston Pike, 1966). This list, shown in Figure 20 below, demonstrates shows how much the housewife could spend on different types of food for her family, and, more interestingly, what she had to spend most of her income on – food. The child could find what percentages or fractions of her total earnings would have been spent on each type of commodity and compare these with a present-day weekly shopping list.

Consumption by the Week, of different Articles, by her Husband, herself, and five Children

	£	s	d
Butter, 1½ lb. at 10d		1	3
Tea, 1½ oz.			4½
Bread she makes herself; buys 24 lb. of flour, barm, salt, and baking, cost		4	6
Half a peck of oatmeal			6½
Bacon 1½ lb.			9
Potatoes, two score a week, at 8d a score		1	4
Milk, a quart a day, at 3d a quart		1	9
Fresh meat on Sunday, about a pound			7
Sugar, 1½ lb. a week at 6d			9
Pepper, mustard, salt, and extras, say			3
Soap and candles		1	0
Coals		1	6
Rent of house, per week		3	6
		18	1

	£	s	d
Alleged total of weekly income	1	5	0
Deduct foregoing expenses		18	1

	£	s	d
Leaves for clothing, sickness of seven persons, schooling, etc., a surplus of		6	11

Source: From the examination taken by MR COWELL in the Lancashire District; Factory Commission Report; P.P. 1833, vol. XX, D I, pp. 39–40

Figure 20. A Manchester housewife's weekly budget (Royston Pike, 1966, p53)

PRACTICAL TASK PRACTICAL TASK **PRACTICAL TASK** PRACTICAL TASK **PRACTICAL TASK**

Work out from the above list the percentages of total income that were spent on different items such as food or coal.

Knowing and using number facts

Understanding how to count on and back, particularly in 10s, helps children to work with timelines and to understand how these can be divided into decades. In fact the use of a timeline based on decades could help children in Key Stage 1 with their learning in mathematics. Knowledge of addition and subtraction facts and place value will similarly assist children in their use of timelines and in their ability to calculate spans of time.

Miller (1999a) has identified cultures such as the Ancient Egyptians, who used the process of doubling as a method of multiplication. He points out a clear link, in his article 'Mathematics from history', between history and this section of the mathematics framework. His ideas are interesting, not only from the perspective of teaching history, but also as an exciting new strategy for linking number work with history.

Calculating

At Key Stage 2 children could use their knowledge of number facts in work on local history. For example, in learning about the complex style of windows in Elizabethan and Georgian buildings, they might want to know how many panes were used to make up the large windows that became fashionable in those times. To be able to recognise the advantages of using multiplication facts in their calculations in preference to extended addition would not only save them a great deal of time during a field work study, for example, but also reinforce their learning in mathematics. Number facts would also help considerably when looking at statistics about populations in the past, such as those about disease, birth and death rates, or immigration and emigration.

Understanding shape and space

An understanding of shape, and of how it is used in architecture, is helpful in local history. When working on the identification of buildings from different periods, recognition of particular shapes is particularly helpful. Shapes can be identified such as triangles and pyramids, often seen in Georgian buildings, along with symmetrical designs, such as are seen in the wide Georgian crescents of town houses. These mathematical concepts transfer in a most valuable way to environmental work where design is a focus for learning and where changing designs and styles are a feature of a lesson or unit of work.

Map reading becomes an important aspect of teaching and learning in history in Key Stage 2, when the world history units begin to be covered. The location on a map of places described, and the description of events such as the crossing of the 'Ocean Sea' by Christopher Columbus in 1492, all require the use of detailed maps and, where possible, globes of the world. The understanding of grid references can be deepened and related to real-life situations by making use of it in map reading and drawing in relation to these history units. Local history topics also rely heavily on the use and understanding of maps and the four compass points, and here the use of grid references to pinpoint the position of buildings and places of interest is even more important.

Measuring

The measurement of time is an aspect of mathematics which has probably the closest links with history. The Framework for Mathematics requires that in the Early Years Foundation Stage, children learn to *use everyday language related to time; order and sequence events and measure short periods of time*. *Knowledge and understanding of the world* in the Curriculum guidance for the Foundation Stage includes the development of a sense of time as one of its early learning goals.

At Key Stage 1, the National Curriculum for history requires that children *place events and objects in chronological order* and *use common words and phrases relating to the passing of time*. In Years 3 and 4 of the Framework for Mathematics, there is work relating to estimating time intervals and clock time and, in Year 4, constructing tables and charts, and learning to read and understand different scales. All of these mathematical skills are used in working with timelines and time charts.

Similar links are to be found throughout Key Stage 2 where, by Year 5, children are expected in mathematics to interpret readings that lie between unnumbered divisions on a scale, a useful skill in reading historical timelines, which are often numbered in little detail. Quite clearly, the two subjects merge together in this area, and mutually support learning by contributing different dimensions and emphases. While mathematical understanding is essential for working with time and chronology in history, the use of these concepts and skills in history strengthens and deepens children's understanding of mathematics by providing a real-life context for their learning.

Children will also, of course, meet 'old' words used in relation to weights and measures. On the internet, they will encounter material on American websites, they will see films and broadcasts from America and they will read books and stories with references to the terms used in the past in Britain. Sometimes these old terms are still used today, particularly in market places. Children therefore need to be able to distinguish between imperial weights and measures and metric ones, and to recognise some of the more commonly seen terms, such as pounds and ounces, tons, yards and miles, acres, pints and gallons, and so on. These terms are still used interchangeably with metric terms and will continue to appear since the USA still works on imperial measures. To avoid confusion, then, and to be able to work with historical sources, children need to have been introduced to these older terms.

Handling data

As a subject which deals exclusively with very extensive amounts of data, history makes great use of all methods of data handling. In the Early Years children sort objects, such as old toys and new toys, identifying their similarities and differences in both history and mathematics. They learn appropriate vocabulary and also learn to explain why they grouped them in particular ways. Throughout Key Stages 1 and 2, children learn to interpret and create lists, charts, tables and graphs to record their findings. Data handling and organising information in charts and diagrams, specified for Year 2, has many links with the handling of historical data, and the skills learned in mathematics could be transferred for application to an historical topic.

In Years 5 or 6, they might use some census data by converting the numbers of people engaged in different occupations into a bar chart for ease of comparison. Spreadsheets enable them to create charts to illustrate which occupations were most widespread (Noall, 2000). Having used their mathematical skills to handle their data, they might then begin to use their historical skills to interpret the data to decide whether the area where the census was taken was working class or middle class. In Year 5, the language of probability and the skill of constructing line graphs, timetables and calendars have clear links with historical study. Similarly, in Year 6, collecting, processing and interpreting data to solve problems, the language of probability, and using scales have links with history which could enhance learning in both subjects.

REFLECTIVE TASK

REFLECTIVE TASK

Consider one aspect of mathematics from the *Framework for Mathematics*, such as 'Using and applying mathematics', for a chosen age group. Think about how the skills learned in mathematics might be transferred to a history lesson, and what kind of activity in history might make use of them.

Mathematics and the history curriculum: some inescapable connections

Time and measurement of time

Time and chronology in the history curriculum require the ability to use numbers in their thousands and also an understanding of negative numbers. Children learn about time and chronology in many different ways and in many different contexts, gradually making mental links between their experiences to develop their concepts (Historical Association, 2006). Time is an extremely complex phenomenon. It can be considered a physical entity in its own right, dependent on the movement of the planets; it can be considered as a system of measurement; it can be seen as a cultural construct, differing in the way it is recorded and expressed, depending on the part of the world where it is being recorded, for example 'in the melting of a snowflake' for an Eskimo, or 'in the frying of a locust' for an African (Jahoda, 1963). Time can also be a psychological experience, expanding or shrinking depending on the type of activity you are engaged in. For instance, a Year 2 child once told me that 'time seemed longer' when you were in assembly! Nevertheless, the ability to work with chronology and measure time rests on mathematical skills.

The language that surrounds the concepts of time and chronology is rich and varied, and often depends for its accuracy on an understanding of number. Because of this, many children find it difficult to learn how to use temporal vocabulary in an appropriate way. They will make wildly inaccurate statements in their early years, when trying out these new words, such as 'Oh, it was millions and zillions of years ago'. By the ages of eight or nine, however, some of the more able children have developed not only a fairly sophisticated understanding of the concepts, but also of the vocabulary and grasp of number they need to use to describe their understanding.

Problem solving

When using a collection of sources, mathematical skills are sometimes essential in reaching a sensible conclusion. For example, a child may be working on a mystery involving a number of newspaper cuttings which hold the clues to their investigation. To find out the sequence of events that took place and work out why things happened, it would be necessary for the child to be able to place the newspaper cuttings in chronological order, requiring an understanding of numbers and dates.

Similar skills would be needed in looking for reasons for events when using a timeline. The causes of significant events can be illustrated by engaging children in calculations based on information displayed on a class timeline. For example, in looking at a timeline of the Tudor period, a child would need to recognise the significance of the dates of the events that led up to the attempted invasion of England by the Spanish Armada. Understanding the chronology of events would contribute to their understanding of the reasons for England and Spain going to war.

RESEARCH SUMMARY RESEARCH SUMMARY **RESEARCH SUMMARY** RESEARCH SUMMARY

Concern about ensuring that language is taught across the curriculum was clearly stated at the beginning of the twentieth century. As far back as 1921 the Newbolt Report discussed the question of *the relation of English to other studies* (Board of Education, 1921, p1). Since then there have been numerous official documents voicing a similar concern. The Bullock Report (DES, 1975), the National Literacy Project (1997), the Nuffield History Project (Fines and Nichol, 1997), The National Curriculum, (DfEE/QCA, 1999b), and the National Primary Strategy (DfES, 2003b), among many others, have all in differing degrees returned to this issue. *History and the use of language* (School Curriculum and Assessment Authority (SCAA), 1997) gives examples of the links which teachers should be using. It states:

> ... history provides the stimulus of studying people and events in the past on local, national and global scales, as the context for language work. The development of children's historical knowledge, under-standing and skills is closely linked to their ability to use language.

(SCAA, 1997, p1)

The *Framework for Literacy* (DfES, 2006), which is incorporated within the Primary Strategy, maintains this focus and provides greater impetus than was originally to be found in the National Curriculum of 1991. There is an overview of the research into the links between language learning and history in Hoodless (1998a).

Cooper (2007a) provides a useful summary of where links may be found between mathematics and history and Barton (2004) has briefly summarised recent findings in understanding how children learn about time. He explains how children learn to sequence events and to group historical items together within historical periods, eventually learning how to measure time in all its different forms. These changes of opinion about children's abilities have been influenced by recent research which has provided more optimistic findings about children's understandings than were held in the first half of the twentieth century (Hodkinson, 2002). Various experiences and influences affect this learning process, such as using pictures (West, 1981d; Harnett, 1993) and story (Hoodless, 2002).

Despite the positive views coming out of recent academic research, however, Ofsted findings continue to point to a poor standard in the teaching of historical chronology in primary schools (Ofsted, 2007). Children leave their primary schools with little grasp of the sequence of history and many are confused about the broad sweep of events or their causes over time. It is possible that making clearer links with mathematics might impact favourably on teaching and learning in both subjects.

A SUMMARY OF **KEY POINTS**

> There are clear links between the objectives for history and those of the Literacy Framework. These occur both in relation to content, such as the use of stories with historical settings, and in relation to skills, such as the requirement to explore interpretations.

> There are wider links with the National Curriculum for English, through speaking and listening or the use of books.

> There are equally sound links with mathematics, and examples can be given from each strand of the Mathematics Framework to show the potential links with history.

> Time, and all the skills, concepts and language associated with it, is a major link with a study of the past.

> Mathematical skills are needed to solve historical problems, such as those which involve statistics, chronology and reasoning.

MOVING *ON* > > > > > > **MOVING** *ON* > > > > > > **MOVING** *ON*

Standard 127

Carry out an audit of the history curriculum as it is taught in your class or across the school if you are the coordinator for history. Look particularly at the learning objectives that are set and for the use of links with literacy and mathematics. Review the objectives for each topic covered, considering ways in which these links might be extended and strengthened.

FURTHER READING FURTHER READING **FURTHER READING** FURTHER READING

Barkham, J (2002) History book for the literacy hour: a street through time, *Primary History*, 30: 16–17.

Bracey, P (2003) In my view: enjoying a good story, *Primary History*, 34: 6–8.

English Heritage (1998) *A teacher guide to maths and the historic environment.* Northampton: English Heritage.

Miller, C (1998) Pythagoras and number, *Primary History*, 20: 10.

Miller, C (1999) Mathematics from history, *Primary History*, 21: 10.

Miller, C (1999) The magic of maths, *Primary History*, 22: 10.

Nichol, J (2004) Reading a difficult and challenging text using expressive movement and textbreaker: a Nuffield primary history approach integrating history and literacy, *Primary History*, 37: 21–24.

Turner-Bisset, R (2005) Creating stories for teaching primary history, *Primary History*, 41: 8–9.

Walsh, B (2003) Is there a place for the computer in primary history?, *Primary History*, 34: 26–29. This article contains an interesting example of the use of graphs and bar charts in history.

Useful websites

www.standards.dfes.gov.uk/primaryframeworks
   The full *Frameworks* for literacy and mathematics can be downloaded from this site.

www.learningcurve.gov.uk/howto/teacherict.htm
   The Learning Curve website, part of the National Archives, has some statistical resources from the past, useful for linking history and mathematics.

www.history.org.uk/
   Website of the Historical Association.

www.primaryhistory.org/
   The website of the Nuffield Primary History Project.

9
E-learning and ICT in primary history

Chapter objectives

By the end of this chapter you will have:

- **developed your understanding of the requirements for the ICT skills test;**
- **developed your awareness of how to support your teaching and wider professional activities with ICT;**
- **considered ways in which children can develop their ICT skills through history;**
- **considered ways in which children can use ICT to extend their learning in history, such as through e-learning;**
- **developed your awareness of the resources available for both teachers and children;**
- **become aware of the need to safeguard children when they are using ICT.**

Professional Standards for QTS

This chapter will support you as you work towards evidencing attainment against the following Standards:

Q16: To have passed the skills test in ICT.

Q17: Know how to use skills in ICT to support their teaching and wider professional activities.

Q23: Design opportunities for learners to develop their ICT skills.

Q25(a): Use a range of teaching strategies and resources, including e-learning.

The QTS skills tests in ICT

In order to achieve Qualified Teacher Status, it is important to know that you are required to have passed the skills tests, including the test in ICT. This can be done in any of the centres set up in your area for the purpose. In the test, you will have to demonstrate skill in the following:

- word processing;
- using spreadsheets;
- using databases;
- creating presentations;
- using e-mail;
- using browsers.

The Training and Development Agency for Schools (TDA) has a section of its website devoted to providing advice on taking the tests, at www.tda.gov.uk/skillstests which is a useful starting point to achieving this particular Standard. The site is user-friendly and provides information about the content and format of the tests, where to book one at a local centre, information about identity and about the rules governing procedures at the test centre. There are practice materials available on the site so that you can prepare in advance of taking the test.

Access the website and try the benchmark test to see if your ICT skills are 'up to speed'.

Supporting your teaching with ICT

There are several websites which contain background information to support your teaching of history. Information and guidance on current requirements for history and ICT, showing where there are links between the two, are available on the official websites for the National Curriculum (see the list of websites on page 106) and the Becta website, see www.becta. org.uk and www.ictadvice.org.uk.

There are also websites which offer guidance and support with teaching strategies such as presentations. PowerPoint, can be a very effective and motivating presentation tool in the classroom. There is a useful section of the website for Oxfordshire LEA (www.ict.oxon-lea.gov.uk), which gives examples of PowerPoint presentations prepared for teaching purposes, such as an example of a presentation prepared for teaching about the Victorian heroine, Grace Darling.

Sharing information with partner schools is often done via school websites, such as www.coxhoe.durham.sch.uk/Curriculum/Curriculum, which has excellent examples of the work of this primary school. Planning, lesson ideas, resources, local facilities, new creative ideas and assessment can all be shared in this way, hopefully leading to an increasing bank of resources for creative ideas. Another useful site for ideas and examples of planning is www.headlinehistory.co.uk, set up by the Department for Culture, Media and Sport.

A comprehensive list of resources, publishers of books and materials in hard copy and also on-line materials is available at www.CurriculumOnline.gov.uk. This is a particularly useful site, since you can enter the history topic you are working on and be taken straight to relevant materials. There are, of course, websites specific to National Curriculum topics, such as Spartacus (www.spartacus.schoolnet.co.uk), useful for the Victorians and twentieth-century history, and the Romans (www.brims.co.uk/romans/) among many others. The BBC also has web pages specific to each National Curriculum topic.

Carry out some brief research, using the internet, into the life of a person that you think has been significant in recent history, such as Winston Churchill. Prepare a short presentation of five or six slides, using software such as PowerPoint. Ensure that the text would be suitable for a range of reading abilities within a Year 5 or Year 6 class and include images and sound.

Supporting your wider professional activities using ICT

Support for teaching

There are a number of e-resources for teachers looking for subject resources, such as www.homeworkelephant.co.uk/teachers. While the site covers all key stages, you will find material here relevant to primary topics. The site is useful for quickly updating your own subject knowledge before teaching a topic.

Sites which enable chat and forums with other teachers are also developing and include sites such as www.teacherstalk.co.uk. This useful site enables you to write in with your queries as well as to see previous communications. It also offers information about resources and jobs too!

There are websites for the professional associations in each subject and, for history, you need to go to the website of the Historical Association, www.history.org.uk. The primary section of this helpful site provides information about conferences, organising visits, Young Historian awards and on how to join the Association. It also provides additional information and links to articles on teaching history topics from the Association's journals, *Primary History* and *Teaching History*.

PRACTICAL TASK PRACTICAL TASK **PRACTICAL TASK** PRACTICAL TASK **PRACTICAL TASK**

Log on to one of the teachers' chat rooms. Use the site to find solutions to any problems you have encountered.

Resources for teaching

English Heritage (www.english-heritage.org.uk) is a large site with an educational section. Here you will find educational games for children, publications, projects, educational resources and an excellent photograph collection, called Viewfinder. This section of the website provides a broad selection of pictures, historic images, aerial photographs, a photo library, architectural photos and stories. For example, you can search Viewfinder under themes, such as 'seaside', and find images from different periods, showing how a particular resort or seaside town has changed. The 'stories' can be rather dry and factual, but are still an excellent resource for developing creative work on account of their detail and the quality of the images, such as the photograph of London in Figure 21, taken in late Victorian times.

Figure 21. Victorian London (reproduced by permission of English Heritage)

There are, in addition, other organisations which specialise in particular historical themes, such as 'Mexicolore' (www.mexicolore.co.uk). Children can write in to the website with questions, which are answered by a team of specialist consultants. Providers of resources and projects include companies such as Cadbury (www.cadburylearningzone.co.uk/history) and Sainsbury (www.jsainsbury.co.uk/museum.museum.htm) among numerous others.

REFLECTIVE TASK

Select one of the websites listed at the end of this chapter and check out the information it contains. Consider its potential usefulness as a resource for teaching. For example, does it add to your subject knowledge; is it relevant to the National Curriculum history study units?

The whiteboard and other hardware

In addition to software, there are hardware items which can be useful for particular purposes in teaching history. There is much information on the use of the whiteboard on the website of the National Whiteboard Network (www.nwnet.org.uk), part of the National Strategy. A helpful article in the Historical Association journal *Primary History* (Fewster, 2005) outlines ways of getting started with the use of the whiteboard. Additionally, there is equipment which allows children to make decisions collaboratively by voting using 'voting pods', the results of which are shown in graphical form on the whiteboard. These items can add to children's motivation since they can immediately see the results of their actions. Such tools can be useful in situations where children might be asked to make a decision and vote on it to see what the majority think, or when they have been asked to express their opinion on an issue. This technology can also be useful for assessment, in checking whether the class have learned something (for example, you could ask your class to 'vote on which you think is the correct answer, a, b, or c').

Personal Digital Assistants (PDAs), or small hand-held screens which can be used individually by children in conjunction with the whiteboard, can also add to the excitement of a lesson. Children can add data to a map, for example, or to a piece of text, or they might annotate an image while they are sitting in their place, and their work appears on the class whiteboard. These types of activity increase motivation and add to the child's experience of personalised learning, as well as providing additional opportunities for you to assess their understanding and knowledge and for the children to engage in self-assessment.

Digital cameras and video recorders are used increasingly in primary schools to record visits, interviews and special events. When used with the computer for incorporating new material into presentations, they can be a tool for developing considerable creativity and motivation. Podcasts and ways of using them to involve others, such as parents, are discussed by Cooper (2007a).

CLASSROOM STORY

Gemma was introducing the topic of the Second World War to her Year 3 class. She wanted to help the children understand why it is called a world war by enabling them to visualise the huge number of places around the world that were involved. Before the lesson, she downloaded an outline map of the world onto the class whiteboard, and at the beginning of the lesson, she revised the children's knowledge of the different continents to ensure that they had remembered this information from an earlier geography lesson.

Gemma provided information about the involvement of each country, ensuring that the whole range of combatants was included. She gave each child a picture or some simple text about one of the countries involved, ensuring that both Allied and Axis powers were included, along with participants from the British Empire. As the children wrote about their findings and completed drawings, Gemma moved around the class with the PDA. She asked each child to mark with a red dot their country on the PDA. Each red dot appeared on the class whiteboard, showing where on the world map that country was. By the end of the lesson, Gemma was able to draw all this information together on the map and ask the children to form their own conclusions.

Opportunities for children to develop their ICT skills

History is a subject which enables children to develop skills in all aspects of ICT. In writing and editing work, they use word processing. In finding and sorting data they can use databases and spreadsheets, along with using browsers for searching for information on the internet. They can use presentation and multimedia packages for sharing the results of their work with the rest of their class or with a class in another part of the country. There are opportunities for children to make meaningful use of their work, linking modern foreign languages and history through e-mailing, if they contact children in other EU countries, or through making contact with countries such as India or Pakistan where their own families might have originated.

Basic skills, such as becoming familiar with the keyboard, can be developed through history, which makes much use of word processing. The use of icons and the desktop settings are other initial skills which children absorb and put into practice as they work on their history tasks. Collecting and organising data, such as the artefacts found at historic sites, can provide opportunities for children to use spreadsheets. Once the data have been entered they can create different types of bar charts and graphs.

Many children are familiar with searching the internet and using browsers. However, the need to search on more specific topics to find particular information, or to answer specific questions set in class, can help hone their skills. They can begin to use key words in an increasingly sophisticated way to produce more reliable, focused searches, a most useful skill later in their education, and in later life.

Presentations promote the use of ICT, whether it is simply organising and printing information, making posters, or creating PowerPoint presentations. The incorporation of images and text, including the use of digital images, sound and video footage, all develop useful ICT skills.

PRACTICAL TASK PRACTICAL TASK **PRACTICAL TASK** PRACTICAL TASK **PRACTICAL TASK**

Use the information given on the Romans on www.yorkarchaeology.co.uk/. Select data from one database of finds to create a small spreadsheet. Use the facilities of the programme to create a number of different graphs. These graphs could be used to encourage children to consider why more items of particular kinds survived rather than others, and why there were so many of them.

How ICT can support children's learning in history

As Walsh (2003) points out, there needs to be a good reason for using ICT instead of a book or other source. He argues that the purposes of ICT need to be considered carefully in order to justify it as part of a history lesson – it needs to add something to the lesson. Cooper (2007a) discusses these considerations and chapter 6 in her book contains a useful section on ICT, which outlines a range of ideas, sources and useful websites and also gives examples of work carried out in schools and museums.

Chronology

At Key Stage 1, there are simple programmes which allow children to move images around the screen to produce a logical sequence, often in time order. These can provide an impetus to learning because of their colourfulness, interest and sheer speed. The increased level of interest and motivation produced by asking a child to rearrange a sequence of pictures into the correct time order, using the computer instead of paper, is considerable.

At Key Stage 2, there are several good software packages for using and creating timelines, and, again these can give a new, additional dimension to the learning of an important concept because of their motivational power and speed of operation. The BBC have produced an interactive timeline, although this would be useful mainly for very able children in Years 5 and 6 (www.bbc.co.uk/history/interactive/timelines). A very child-friendly interactive timeline programme can be purchased from Soft Teach (www.curriculumon line.gov.uk). This programme provides some sample timelines ready-made, but also permits children to create their own, importing images and inserting text and dates.

Historical enquiry

Every Child Matters (DfES, 2004c) points out that personalised learning is one of the most positive ways forward in ensuring that every child achieves their full potential. The Learning Curve website, part of the National Archives, has some useful ideas and materials for personalised learning in history using ICT (www.learningcurve.gov.uk/howto/teacherict. htm). As one of the largest collections of history resources, the Learning Curve provides resources for National Curriculum topics and contains interactive materials for children. An article by Weights (2000) introduces some of the best websites for classroom use, although, of course, some of these have now been updated.

Claire and Lewis (2004) recommend the pre-selection of websites by the teacher, thus avoiding some of the problems frequently encountered in using the internet, and some schools make use of their own school website or intranet for this purpose. There are many potential difficulties associated with the worldwide web as a source, such as the time sometimes needed to download websites, the terminology used, which can be idiosyncratic and confusing, and often the quality of the material that is obtained. Peat (2003) refers to the difficulties encountered if you were simply to type in 'Tower of London' to find detail about its history. Instead, you might well get a version of the past written by a bus tour company; possibly not the most reliable source of information. Walsh (2003) recommends starting with the websites of the largest and most well-known national institutions, such as the National Archives website (http://learningcurve.gov.uk), the BBC (www.bbc.co.uk/history), the QCA(www.qca.org.uk), the TDA (www.tda.gov.uk), curriculum on-line (curriculumonline.gov.uk) or Becta (www.becta.org.uk). These websites are regularly updated, monitored and controlled for quality and are likely to contain suitable information. Some, such as the BBC, are beginning to include virtual tours – see, for example, www.bbc.co.uk/history/interactive/virtual tours. Cooper (2007a, p112) discusses the use of such sites and also PowerPoint in creating virtual tours.

Artefacts on-line

The British Museum has an outstanding collection of artefacts available on its Compass website (http://www.thebritishmuseum.ac.uk/compass), along with a specific page for children (www.britishmuseum.org/explore/families and children.aspx). The website of the York Archaeological Trust is an excellent site for collections of finds from Roman, Anglo-Saxon, Viking and medieval times in York (www.yorkarchaeology.co.uk/). Peat's article in *Primary History* gives further references to museum websites (Peat, 2003). Historic sites usually have their own websites and are increasingly developing interactive materials. Sites such as Stonehenge (www.stonehenge.co.uk), Sutton Hoo (www.suttonhoo.org/archaeology), Hadrian's Wall (www.hadrians-wall.org) or castles in Wales (www.castlewales.com/) can all easily be explored using the internet.

Texts and databases

The extensive information in the form of texts and numerical statistics that is available for historians often lends itself ideally to database work. In particular, census and similar data are best used on the computer and a useful article on this can be found in *Primary History* (Smart, 1999). Calculations and results can be displayed with such accuracy and speed that learning can be considerably enhanced. For example, a comparison of where servants travelled from in late Victorian times in order to find work, compared with the same information in earlier times, quickly reveals that, after 1860, servants travelled great distances, sometimes from other parts of Europe, which would not have been possible before. Children can then use their knowledge of the period to infer that the reason for this was probably the introduction and large-scale use of the railways, which were convenient and relatively inexpensive.

Census data on a smaller scale could be used by children in Years 2 or 3. For example, they could study the occupations of residents of just one street to produce a simple bar chart to find out about the people who lived in John Street.

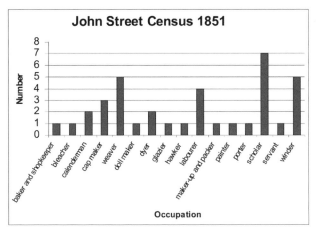

Figure 22. Using census data

Visual sources on-line

In addition to museum websites, the quantity of visual material, including video and film is vast, from BBC and ITV history broadcasts to TV dramas and films, from which appropriate clips can be used. Many books for teachers and resource packs of teaching materials, such as *Ready Resources*, (Hoodless, 2003a) include CD-ROMs with collections of primary sources, such as portraits, sketches, photographs, sound recordings and video clips.

Interactive resources on-line

The use of the computer does not have to be restricted to the search for information. Historical skills, such as inferential ability, can be developed with the thoughtful use of some web-based materials which at first glance do not appear very interactive. For example, the computer is an excellent source of maps and sites which contain geographical information linked to history. The site, http://www.roman-britain.org/maps.htm has a detailed set of maps of Roman Britain, which show the locations of villas, forts, potteries, mines etc., so that a good picture can be built up of Roman settlement patterns. The maps are also an excellent stimulus for encouraging children to make inferences about why there were so many small forts in particular places, such as on the borders and near Hadrian's Wall. Google Earth (http://earth.google.com) is an interesting source for local history work, since you can pinpoint sites of interest to your study.

Games and simulations are also popular ways of linking ICT and history, where historical knowledge, skills and conceptual understanding can be developed in an enjoyable way. For example, there are a number of games and simulations on the website of the Nuffield Primary History project (www.primaryhistory.org/teachingmethods/simulations-and-games,185,AR.html), and on the BBC websites (www.bbc.co.uk/history/forkids/) and (www.bbc.co.uk/historyt/ancient/vikings/launch_gms_viking_quest.shtml).

PRACTICAL TASK PRACTICAL TASK **PRACTICAL TASK** PRACTICAL TASK **PRACTICAL TASK**

Access the maps on the Roman Britain website and explore the features of this part of the site. Consider and plan opportunities for encouraging children to engage in inferential thinking. For example, why did the Romans choose particular places to build their towns and forts? Can the children begin to identify patterns and suggest reasons for these?

Organisation and communication of historical findings

The use of ICT to produce, edit and enhance their work can make a great contribution to children's skill in organising and communicating their work in history. Through the use of text-based web resources such as the Microsoft on-line encyclopedia Encarta (www.encarta.msn.com/), children can summarise and make simple notes, thus avoiding the temptation to simply copy, paste and print, and also extending their skills in literacy. For example, Walsh (2003) describes how, in using the British Museum Compass website (www.thebritishmuseum.ac.uk/compass), children read the notes accompanying each of the artefacts they were studying, and then made their own simple notes for their 'museum display'. Similarly, he explains that children can be encouraged to summarise rather than copy by being asked to produce a list of points under headings such as 'Five Things That Every Person Should Know About Henry VIII' (Walsh, 2003).

Examples of children's own presentations and web pages can be found on the internet at sites such as www.greatrissington.ik.org, www.goldenowlawards.co.uk or www.schools.ik. org. For example, Year 1 children at Great Rissington Primary School placed on their website a photograph of their work on castles as part of their topic on 'homes'. On the website http:// www.coxhoe.durham.sch.uk/Curriculum/Curriculum.htm, there are several excellent examples of work produced for both teaching and learning. Cooper outlines the creation of a website by Year 3 children when visiting an art gallery (www.theherbert.org/learning/).

E-mail is also widely used; many primary schools have links with other countries usually via e-mail, to chat about aspects of their work, especially in relation to modern foreign languages. Clearly, there is great scope for the exchange of understanding about history, both between teachers and children using this kind of technology. Video-conferencing is another potentially exciting medium for exchanging ideas about primary history with schools in other English-speaking countries and with countries in Europe.

Safeguarding children

Ensuring that children are safe when using digital sources is essential. Teachers need to research what is available and then find ways of incorporating these resources into their teaching. There are also issues concerning the use of visual sources and the taking of digital photographs of children. There is much helpful advice available on the internet, some of which can be found at www.becta.org.uk and also at www.bgfl.bridgend.gov.uk. It is always advisable to check on the best procedures and legalities of using e-resources and digital images.

RESEARCH SUMMARY RESEARCH SUMMARY **RESEARCH SUMMARY** RESEARCH SUMMARY

Ofsted reports, particularly *History in the balance* (2007) recommend that the principles of *Every Child Matters* are reflected in the history curriculum in schools, particularly in providing children with the knowledge and skills to understand the world in which they live. Links with other subjects are recommended, particularly with subjects like ICT. There is an emphasis throughout this report on ensuring that the curriculum is revised to meet the needs of modern children and that they acquire the skills they will need in modern society. Publications by Martin, Smart and Yeomans (1997) and Jarvis (2003) explore the background and development of using ICT in teaching history, while Sharp (2002) looks at the use of ICT across the curriculum.

A SUMMARY OF **KEY POINTS**

> It is necessary to have passed the QTS skills tests in ICT to gain Qualified Teacher Status.

> One of the most useful ways of supporting your teaching is to use ICT for information on planning, finding historical information and for communicating with other teachers.

> You can support your wider professional activities through the use of websites with information for teachers on issues such as marking, planning, job hunting. You can also improve your own subject knowledge through the use of good internet websites, such as the website of the Historical Association.

> There are opportunities for children to develop their ICT skills when learning history, in areas such as word processing, the use of databases and spreadsheets, presentation software and the use of internet browsers.

> \> E-learning can support children's learning in history through providing access to a wide range
> of resources and first-hand sources, virtual tours, historic sites and museums.

MOVING *ON* > > > > > > MOVING *ON* > > > > > > MOVING *ON*

Standard 117, Standard 127, Standard 129

Once you have attained the level of expertise in using ICT applications in the six areas required by the QTS skills test, a valuable way forward would be to work on developing your own school's website, particularly the section on history. Look at http://www.coxhoe.durham.sch.uk/Curriculum/Curriculum.htm. Here the history section has a wealth of examples of planning, presentation and different ideas for work across a wide range of ages and different topics in both Key Stages 1 and 2. Use these examples to develop your own school website.

FURTHER READING FURTHER READING **FURTHER READING** FURTHER READING

Cooper, H (2007) *History 3–11: a guide for teachers*. London: Fulton. (Chapter 6 gives a useful overview of some of the key issues and uses of ICT, with additional recommendations for useful websites and software.)

Mills, M (2004) Using the English Heritage Viewfinder website, *Primary History*, 37: 32–36.

Norton, M (1999) Making the most of ICT at Key Stage 2, *Primary History,* 21: 7–9.

Smart, L (1999) ICT – high profile in 1999–2000: but will you use it in your history teaching?, *Primary History*, 22: 6–7.

Useful websites

www.bbc.co.uk/historyt/ancient/vikings/launch_gms_viking_quest.shtml

www.bbc.co.uk/history/forkids/

www.primaryhistory.org/teachingmethods/simulations-and-games,185,AR.html

These sites contain examples of simulations.

www.bbc.co.uk/history/interactive/virtual_tours

This site provides virtual tours of historic sites and buildings, and some reconstructions, all related to the National Curriculum.

www.bbc.co.uk/history/interactive/timelines.

An interactive timeline produced by the BBC. However, this would be useful mainly for very able children in Years 5 and 6.

www.becta.org.uk

www.ictadvice.org.uk

www.bgfl.bridgend.gov.uk

These sites give advice on safeguarding children when using the internet and digital sources.

www.bclm.co.uk

Black Country Living Museum.

www.brims.co.uk/romans/

Contains information on the Romans study unit.

www.thebritishmuseum.ac.uk/compass

The British Museum Compass website is an excellent source of artefacts.

www.cadburylearning zone.co.uk/history
    Website for Cadbury's.

www.castlewales.com/
    Site containing information about the many castles in Wales.

**http://www.coxhoe.durham.sch.uk/Curriculum/Curriculum.htm
www.croft.notts.sch.uk
http://www.nettlesworth.durham.sch.uk/index.html
    Three primary school websites of interest. ** Particularly good.

www.CurriculumOnline.gov.uk
    Becta and Curriculum Online are two websites set up to support the education sector.

http://earth.google.com
    The website for Google Earth.

www.encarta.msn.com/
    The website for Encarta, an on-line encyclopedia.

www.english-heritage.org.uk
    Website for English Heritage.

http://www.eriding.net/history/index.shtml
    Useful for subject resources.

www.headlinehistory.co.uk
    Headline history is commissioned by Culture Online www.cultureonline.gov.uk/ part of the Department for Culture, Media and Sport. A website for children, teachers and parents, it contains examples of hot-seating, worksheets in various topics, lesson plans and links to other useful websites.

www.history.org.uk
    Website of the Historical Association.

http://www.homeworkelephant.co.uk/teachers
    Useful for developing your own background subject knowledge.

www.ict.oxon-lea.gov.uk
    Gives examples of PowerPoint presentations.

www.itnarchive.com
    British Pathé website.

www.learningcurve.gov.uk/howto/teacherict.htm
    The Learning Curve website, part of the National Archives, has some useful ideas for teaching history using ICT.

www.mexicolore.co.uk
    A useful website for the Aztecs study unit.

www.nc.uk.net

www.ncaction.qca.org

These official government websites all provide information and guidance on national requirements.

www.npg.org.uk/live/search

The National Portrait Gallery website has a wide range of portraits that are useful, for example, for
studying the same person at different times in their life.

www.roman-britain.org/maps.htm

www.j-sainsbury.co.uk/museum.museum.htm

Website for Sainsbury's.

www.schoolsliaisonorg.uk

Useful in connection with museum visits.

www.transportarchive.org.uk

The Transport Archive.

www.24hourmuseum.org.uk

News and features from over 3,000 historic sites, museums and galleries.

www.schoolsnet.com

www.standards.dfes.gov.uk

www.teacherstalk.co.uk

www.theteacherscorner.net

Two websites for teacher communication.

www.teachers.tv/ict/whiteboardtips

www.teachingideas.co.uk/history/contents.htm

Useful for ideas and examples of unit and lesson plans.

www.tda.gov.uk/skillstests

The website where you can find information about the Skills Tests.

www.theherbert.org/learning/

An example of a children's website.

http://www.willowbrook.essex.sch.uk/history.htm

Another useful school website, which lists websites for each National Curriculum history unit.

www.yorkarchaeology.co.uk/

The website of the York Archaeological Trust. This website contains pictures of artefacts from
Roman, Anglo-Saxon, Viking and Medieval times found in York.

10
Creative and innovative approaches: history in the Early Years Foundation Stage

Chapter objectives

By the end of this chapter you will have:

- explored ways of developing children's understanding of a sense of time within the context of the Early Years Foundation Stage (DCSF, 2008);
- explored a variety of activities, including the use of artefacts, that support children's understanding of a sense of time.

Professional Standards for QTS

This chapter will support you as you work towards evidencing attainment against the following Standards:

Q8: Have a creative and constructively critical approach towards innovation, being prepared to adapt their practice where benefits and improvements are identified.

Q31: . . .promote learners' self-control and independence.

Introduction

Teaching history as a subject in the early years is often regarded as a challenge for practitioners. History is concerned with times past and as such can be viewed as inappropriate or even irrelevant to young children who are actively discovering the world around them in the here and now (Hoodless, 1996b; Purkis, 1996). However, the study of history requires the ability to investigate, question, explore, discuss and reflect. Good early years practice provides opportunities for young children to do precisely this and so history, far from being dull and irrelevant, becomes a medium through which children have the opportunity to make discoveries about the world around them. Moreover, the social aspect of history enables young children to explore relationships and to develop their understanding of different cultures and beliefs, developing positive dispositions and attitudes.

In the Early Years Foundation Stage (EYFS) history is presented as a sense of time and is one aspect of 'Knowledge and understanding of the world', one of the six areas of learning in the Early Years Foundation Stage. In this chapter we will explore ways of developing children's sense of time within the context and principles of the Early Years Foundation Stage document which is statutory from September 2008 (DCSF, 2008).

In this chapter, a variety of activities will be explored that use children's own experiences as a starting point, such as daily and weekly routines and how these relate to the passing of time. In addition, the use of artefacts will be explored as a way of prompting discussion about the past. An emphasis will be given to the development of the vocabulary of time, and children's ability to use this vocabulary with increasing understanding. We will also explore how practitioners can create an environment that supports children's development of a sense of time.

The Early Years Foundation Stage

The Early Years Foundation Stage (DCSF, 2008) brought together three main documents: *Curriculum Guidance for the Foundation Stage* (DfEE/QCA, 2000), *Birth to Three Matters* (DfES/MMU, 2002) and the *National Standards for Under 8s Daycare and Childminding* (DfES, 2003c) into one coherent and flexible approach to care and learning from birth to five. The EYFS is for every child and its overarching aim is to enable every child to achieve the Government's five outcomes for children.

Four guiding themes underpin the EYFS:

* Unique child – every child is a unique and competent learner from birth.
* Positive relationships – children learn to be strong and independent from the base of a loving and secure relationship with parents and/or key worker.
* Enabling environment – the environment plays a key role in supporting and extending children's development and learning.
* Learning and development – children develop and learn at different rates and in different ways.

In addition the EYFS sets out the six areas of learning and development in the *Curriculum Guidance for the Foundation Stage* document (DfEE/QCA, 2000):

* Personal and social development;
* Communication, language and literacy;
* Problem solving, reasoning and numeracy;
* Knowledge and understanding of the world;
* Physical development;
* Creative development.

Each section is divided into four columns that support practitioners in the ongoing process of assessing, supporting and extending young children's learning and development.

The six areas of learning are interconnected and cannot be delivered in isolation. Moreover, the areas of learning must be presented within the context of planned and purposeful play opportunities that develop from the child's interests, with the emphasis on child-initiated activities.

Practitioners' observations of children enable them to build up an effective picture of the child – a learning journey, reflecting their individual learning styles and needs. In this way practitioners are able to identify where the child is in terms of their learning and development, and what they need to plan and provide for next.

The activities and concepts explored in this chapter will embrace the four themes that underpin the EYFS; identify links to other areas of learning; and identify ways of embedding activities within the learning environment, supporting and extending children's interests.

History in the Early Years Foundation Stage: links to the themes of EYFS

History in the Early Years Foundation Stage – a sense of time – is set within the area of learning 'Knowledge and understanding of the world'. Children find out about the world around them through exploration and discovery, what they see and what they hear. They are supported in developing their understanding by adults who provide opportunities for exploration and enquiry and support and extend their learning through the use of open-ended questions, *getting involved in the thinking process with them* (DfES, 2007, card 4.3).

Parents are the child's first and most enduring educators (DfES, 2007, card 2.2), and all families should be valued and welcomed into the setting. It is important that practitioners recognise children's own unique qualities and provide opportunities for children to talk about their families and their own experiences in an environment that encourages respect for others and challenges cultural, racial, social, and gender stereotypes.

When parents and practitioners work together the results have a positive impact on children's development and learning (DfES, 2007, card 2.2). When the child first enters the setting, practitioners will already have had opportunity to get to know the child and his/her family through home visits and visits to the setting. From this initial knowledge of the child the practitioner will be beginning to build up a picture of the child's unique experiences and how they can be provided for within the setting.

Every child is a competent learner from birth. The practitioner will be aware that some children already have an awareness of a sense of time and the past through their home experiences and extended family, perhaps spending time with grandparents and other family members, and through religious and cultural activities (Thornton and Brunton, 2004). Moreover, through the medium of stories, film and television young children are developing an awareness of time past. Wood (1995) reiterates this point, suggesting that children have a natural awareness of time through such experiences.

REFLECTIVE TASK

Consider the following:

- How do you gather information on a child who is new to your setting?
- How do you involve parents in that process?
- How do you ensure that children have opportunities to talk about their families and experiences?

Make a note of how you would deal with these issues and, if possible, try out some of your ideas in an Early Years setting.

From birth young children actively begin to explore the world around them. Practitioners need to provide a rich and varied environment (DfES, 2007, card 3.3), both indoors and outdoors, which supports children as active learners and allows them to explore, experiment and make connections in their learning. The learning environment should encourage independent learning and should provide opportunities for children to develop their understanding of time, utilising both indoors and outdoors, including the local neighbourhood.

Children also need opportunities to be able to re-enact their experiences through their independent play, both indoors and outdoors. Practitioners must provide a home corner role-play area with resources that reflect the wider community and home experiences of the children in the setting. Outdoors children can have opportunities to make houses with boxes and drapes, and recreate family experiences such as outings and visits making use of wheeled toys, trolleys, prams and makeshift buses and trains constructed from chairs and blocks.

With the development of language, young children begin to question what they observe and experience in order to make sense of the world and their place in it. *When children have opportunities to play with ideas in different situations and with a variety of resources, they discover connections and come to new and better understandings and ways of doing things* (DfES, 2007, card 4.3). Practitioners must provide a learning environment that supports children in making discoveries and provides opportunities for children to talk about, question and reflect upon their experiences.

By providing an environment that supports enquiry and independent play practitioners are able to *observe children to find out about their needs, what they are interested in and what they can do* (DfES, 2007, card 3.1). They then analyse this information in order to provide activities that are meaningful, relevant and exciting, and plan for the next steps in the child's learning.

REFLECTIVE TASK

- Do you provide opportunities in your early years setting for children to talk about and question events in their own lives and those of others?
- Do you provide opportunities for children to explore their experiences through role-play, both indoors and outdoors?
- Do you observe and record children's responses in different situations, for example when engaging in role-play or exploring artefacts, in order to plan the next steps in their learning?

Exploring a sense of time through classroom activities

Chronology – measuring the passing of time

Piaget (1927/1967) suggested that young children could not grasp the concept of time as they were unable to measure time and understand its duration. Anyone who works with young children will know that when children begin to talk about the past – things that happened yesterday or last week – they often become unsure of the terminology that measures time. The examples below illustrate some ways of supporting young children in exploring the passing of time and sequencing events using routines that are familiar to children.

The on-line EYFS materials provide guidance and give examples of ways of developing children's awareness from the earliest stages of learning through to the end of the Foundation Stage (www.standards.dcsf.gov.uk/eyfs/site/resource/pdfs.htm). The following story is based on the 'Knowledge and understanding of the world' (KUOW) area of learning and shows how the guidance can be interpreted in practice in nursery schools and classes.

CLASSROOM STORY
Visual timelines
Links to EYFS – Development Matters – *'Understand some talk about immediate past and future, for example before, later, soon.' 'Anticipate specific time-based events such as mealtimes or home time.'*
(22–36 months – KUOW – Time)

Barbara is a practitioner in a large nursery school. From her experiences in her setting, she often noted how young children have difficulty in understanding the passing of time. She also wanted to help children to settle in to the setting and become familiar with routines. Using the digital camera Barbara supported the children to take photographs of each other involved in the daily routines of the setting – hanging up coats, signing in, snack time, story time and so on. She laminated the cards to create a visual timeline of the routines of the session.

Barbara then used the visual timeline in a variety of activities, both indoors and outdoors, such as during circle times as a pass the parcel game, with children placing the pictures in a bag or box and passing them around to music. When a picture had been selected Barbara encouraged the child to talk about the picture and peg it onto a washing line in chronological order.

Barbara also devised a way of using a skittles game outdoors. She placed the pictures face down with a skittle on top of each one. The children then took turns to knock a skittle down and retrieve a picture. Again the children were encouraged to talk about the picture and peg it onto a washing line in chronological order.

As Barbara encouraged the children to discuss the pictures she introduced vocabulary such as *before, after, later, soon, today, tomorrow, yesterday, morning, afternoon, lunchtime, hometime* and so on. She used some of the pictures to form a display in the entrance hall, encouraging parents and carers to discuss the pictures with the children when they entered the setting. As children discussed the routines of the session with their parents, Barbara was able to note the children's developing understanding and directly involve parents in the observation and assessment process, noting their comments and contributions.

To develop children's language further Barbara involved the children in selecting photographs for their Record of Achievement books. The photographs showed the children involved in the activities in the nursery and through the shared discussion the children were able to further develop the vocabulary of time as they talked about what they were doing and when. Barbara then annotated the photographs with the children's own language, which contributed to the observation and assessment process. Moreover, Barbara was able to involve the children in the observation and assessment process as they reflected on and talked about their learning (DfES, 2007, card 3.1).

Night and day activity
In order to further develop the links between home and the setting Barbara provided a disposable camera for parents to take photographs of the children involved in routines at home, such as mealtimes or bedtime. The camera was sent home along with a pack containing a brief explanation of the activity, some key vocabulary and a format for

parents to record their comments. This allowed working parents, particularly fathers, to be more involved in their children's learning. Barbara then collated the pictures and parental comments into a class book which she shared with the children.

By noting the responses of both children and their parents to this activity and observing children in the role-play area, Barbara identified that the children were interested in night time and darkness. They were interested in the photographs of bedtime, discussing different beds, pyjamas, or toys. In the home corner some children had made a bed using the large blocks and were re-enacting going to bed. Barbara gathered together a variety of objects such as pyjamas, breakfast cereal box, hairbrush, shampoo, book and lunch box. She invited the children to choose an object and talk about when they would use it – in the day time or at night time. She introduced vocabulary such as *day, night, today, tomorrow, yesterday, dark, light.* She then incorporated the objects into the home corner, providing a bed and cot for the children to re-enact their experiences of going to bed and waking up in the morning.

Barbara was then able to extend this interest further by setting up a dark tunnel outdoors using outdoor equipment and large sheets of dark material where children could experiment with torches and luminous materials. In the book area she provided books such as *Can't You Sleep Little Bear* (Waddell, 2005), *Peace at Last* (Murphy, 1995), and non-fiction books on day and night. This prompted more discussion about routines at night and during the day.

To develop this interest and provide further opportunities for children to extend and consolidate their learning, Barbara provided a 'Time' interest box (see Clere, 2005 for more ideas). In the box Barbara put a variety of clocks, including a digital clock and an alarm clock. She also put in a variety of sand timers and kitchen timers, together with some magnifying glasses, some clock mechanisms and some information books about time. The interest box was then used indoors in the investigation area as well as outdoors.

Throughout the activities, both adult and child led, Barbara was able to introduce new vocabulary which supported children's understanding of the passing of time. She was able to provide opportunities for children to practise, consolidate and explore further these concepts, both indoors and outdoors. She was also able to observe children's growing awareness of the passing of time and so plan activities that were meaningful for the children and identify the next steps in their learning and development.

PRACTICAL TASK PRACTICAL TASK **PRACTICAL TASK** PRACTICAL TASK **PRACTICAL TASK**

Using the concept of 'change over time', draw up a simple outline plan for an activity in which you focus closely on developing children's understanding of the concept. Think about how you would provide opportunities for children to explore and consolidate their understanding through practical hands-on experiences, such as through role-play. Plan how you would observe and identify children's responses to the activity and how you would involve parents in the process.

Using artefacts in the Early Years Foundation Stage

Young children learn rapidly about their world from play, which often involves handling artefacts. They can learn about the past by playing with older versions of things that are familiar to them. Domestic items and toys from the past are useful additions to the home corner, along with replicas, like this one, of a teddy from 1902.

Figure 23. A replica Steiff bear

The following classroom story illustrates creative ways of linking personal and family history with the exploration of artefacts through the use of puppets.

CLASSROOM STORY

Investigating the past through exploring artefacts with young children

Links to EYFS *'Find out about past and present events in their own lives, and in those of their families and other people they know.'* (DfES, 2007 Development Matters – Early Learning Goals – KUOW – Time)

Jo, a reception teacher in a primary school, wanted an exciting way to introduce historical artefacts to young children. The children had already explored the language of change over time by bringing in photographs of themselves as babies and discussing how they had changed. The children had also brought in their favourite toy from when they were a baby and their current favourite toy. This experience had produced much discussion about toys and the needs of babies compared to older children.

Building on this experience, Jo wanted to extend the children's knowledge and vocabulary by exploring old toys. She introduced a Granddad puppet (see the Resources section on page 119) called Granddad Bill. Granddad Bill had a special suitcase where he kept his most treasured possessions. The suitcase was very old and worn because Granddad Bill had had it since he was a little boy. The children immediately identified with Granddad Bill and wanted to know what he had brought to show them. Jo had put a wooden moveable toy inside the suitcase and a cloth doll. Granddad Bill showed the toys to the children and explained that they were his favourite toys from when he was a little boy. The children were then able to talk about the differences and similarities between their toys and Granddad's toys. Jo was able to introduce vocabulary such as *old, past*, and *history* and extend the children's

---

discussions with open questions such as 'I wonder what...', and 'What if...?' Jo noted the children's responses to the activity and recorded them as 'learning journeys' (DfES, 2007, card 3.2; CD-ROM resources).

Granddad Bill became a favourite with the children in Jo's class and Jo used the suitcase to introduce other artefacts to the children. The Granddad puppet was used in other areas of the classroom to support children's learning, such as in the book corner and the home corner. Soon Granddad Bill was joined by Grandma Mary and the puppets provided a stimulus for children to talk about their own grandparents and families. Extending the activity further, Jo encouraged parents, grandparents and other family members to bring their childhood toys into the classroom. She was then able to set up an interactive display of old toys and contemporary toys for the children to explore and interact with.

PRACTICAL TASK PRACTICAL TASK **PRACTICAL TASK** PRACTICAL TASK **PRACTICAL TASK**

Links to EYFS – Development Matters – *'Remember and talk about significant personal events in their own experience'*; Effective Practice – *'Talk about and show interest in children's lives and experiences'* (DfES, 2007, – 30–50 months – KUOW –Time)

Several children in an early years setting had recently celebrated a birthday. Through their ongoing observations of children, the practitioners noted that the children were keen to extend this interest in celebrations – in the home corner the children would pretend to blow out the candles on the cake and sing 'Happy Birthday'. At the playdough table the children would make cakes and candles and wrap playdough in paper to make presents.

If you were the practitioner in this setting consider how you would build on and extend this interest, considering both planned activities and enhancements to your continuous provision areas to support children's self-initiated play, for example, in the home corner, model making area, workshop area, or outdoor area.

Using story

All stories are about events and changes which happen over time, in our own lives and in the lives of others, whether recently or long ago in folk memory. Stories are by definition the living past (Cooper, 2007b). Story is a major means of children's learning and understanding about the past from their very earliest days, and the enormous range of stories and picture books available for young children is a testament to this fact. Through story, children become aware of the passing of time within a narrative, the sequence of night and day, the days of the week and, eventually, months and years. These early understandings are the foundation for the development of later, more complex concepts of time, when children begin to understand about change and the reasons for change. Both story-telling and the sharing of story books with young children are vitally important contributors to their emerging sense of the past.

Much has been written about story and story-telling in the early years. For example Lunn and Bishop (2004) write about how story can be used to develop historical skills and concepts in the early years, Turner-Bisset (2005b) and Wilkinson (2006a) give useful advice about creating your own stories about historical characters and events for story-telling sessions, and

Harnett (2005) explores the use of nursery rhymes. The story books listed in the Resources section below are among some of the most popular that are used in the EYFS and should be a useful starting point for your investigation into this important aspect of children's learning. They are grouped according to different topics which will contribute to children's sense of time and change over time.

RESEARCH SUMMARY RESEARCH SUMMARY **RESEARCH SUMMARY** RESEARCH SUMMARY

In this chapter we have explored the skill of the adult in supporting and extending children's learning through the use of open-ended questions. The DfES (2007, card 4.3) makes reference to 'sustained shared thinking', where adult and child work together developing an idea or skill. The *Effective Provision of Pre-school Education* (DfES, 2004a) was a longitudinal study that studied the effectiveness of pre-school practice. One of its main findings concluded that *In the most effective settings practitioners supported and challenged the children's thinking by getting involved in the thinking process with them* (DfES, 2007, card 4.3).

Sylva, Melhuish, Sammons, Siraj-Blatchford and Taggart (2004) have researched the effectiveness of provision and teaching methods and approaches in the early years, and their work is summarised in the publications listed in the 'Further reading' section below.

A SUMMARY OF **KEY POINTS**

Every child is a unique individual. From birth children will be learning from the people and experiences around them, developing their understanding of past and present events in their own and their families' lives.

Early years practitioners are able to support and extend this learning through:

> **well-planned and purposeful activities that take account of children's needs and interests;**

> **a well-resourced learning environment, both indoors and outdoors, that provides opportunities for children to explore, experiment, enquire, rehearse, consolidate and revisit their learning;**

> **encouraging and valuing parents' contribution to their children's learning;**

> **giving children opportunities to talk about their experiences and extending their thinking through the use of effective open-ended questions;**

> **observing and noting children's responses in different situations in order to identify their interests and achievements and plan for the next steps in their learning.**

MOVING *ON* > > > > > > MOVING *ON* > > > > > > MOVING *ON*

Standard I7, Standard I8, Standard I39

As a practitioner, consider how you use language and questioning to support and extend the learning of the children in your setting.

Record yourself whilst interacting with the children and reflect upon your use of questioning and how well you supported children's learning (card 4.3).

Share your reflections with the other adults in your setting and support the development of their use of questioning through staff meetings and peer observations.

Consider the organisation of the learning environment and the balance of adult-led and child-led activities.

Do children have opportunities to follow their interests and are their thinking skills supported effectively by the adults in the setting?

Do children have time to explore their interests and develop ideas?

Do you organise your environment effectively to enable adults to spend time with children, talking about their interests and extending their learning?

FURTHER READING FURTHER READING **FURTHER READING** FURTHER READING

Department for Children, Schools and Families (DCSF) (2007) *Supporting children learning English as an additional language. Guidance for practitioners in the Early Years.* London: DCSF. (www.standards.dcsf.gov.uk)

DCSF (2007) *Confident, capable and creative: supporting boys' achievements.* London: DCSF. (www.standards.dcsf.gov.uk)

Keating, I (2002) *Teaching Foundation Stage (Achieving QTS).* Exeter: Learning Matters.

Primary History (2007) *History in the Foundation Stage and Early Years, 3–8.* London: Historical Association. The whole issue is on early years history.

Siraj-Blatchford, I and Sylva, K (2002) *Researching effective pedagogy in the early years.* London: DfES.

Sylva, K, Melhuish, E, Sammons, P, Siraj-Blatchford, I and Taggart, B (2004) *The effective provision of pre-school education.* London: DfES.

Government response to Paul Roberts Report on 'Nurturing Creativity in Young People' (2006) (links from EYFS CD-ROM).

Resources – Stories

Time

The Very Hungry Caterpillar, Eric Carle

The Sandal, Tony Bradman and Philippe Dupasquier

Dear Daddy, Philippe Dupasquier

The Giving Tree, Shel Silverstein

On the Way Home, Jill Murphy

Owl Babies, Martin Waddell

Can't You Sleep Little Bear?, Martin Waddell

Peace at Last, Jill Murphy

Don't Forget the Bacon, Pat Hutchins

Families

Once There Were Giants, Martin Waddell

Avocado Baby, John Burningham

Grandma's Bill, Martin Waddell

The Trouble with Mum, Babette Cole

When Grandma Came, Jill Paton Walsh and Sophy Williams

Badger's Parting Gifts, Susan Varley

Grandfather and I, Helen Buckley and Jan Omerod

Illustrations which show the past

The Elephant and the Bad Baby, Elfrida Vipont

Peepo, Janet and Allan Ahlberg

The Tiger Who Came to Tea, Judith Kerr

Useful websites

www.standards.dcsf.gov.uk/eyfs/
www.standards.dcsf.gov.uk/eyfs/site/resource/pdfs.htm
   The website for the EYFS. The second of these has the resource cards referred to in the chapter.

www.past-times.com
www.articlesoffaith.co.uk
   Companies which provide artefacts about the past and places of worship.

www.showme.uk/
   UK museums and galleries for children.

www.24hourmuseum.org.uk
   An on-line museum.

www.english-heritage.org.uk
   The website of English Heritage.

www.tlfe.org.uk/clicker/historyks1.htm
   Useful for topics on toys, seaside, Fire of London, homes, Florence Nightingale.

www.puppetsbypost.com
   A source of grandparent puppets.

www.featherstone.uk.com
   Website for the *Little Books* series.

www.everychildmatters.gov.uk
www.surestart.gov.uk/research/keyresearch/eppe
   Useful government sites for information about the EYFS.

11
Creativity and cross-curricular links in Key Stages 1 and 2

Chapter objectives

By the end of this chapter you will have:

- considered the need for creativity and what this term means;
- considered innovative planning in history and opportunities for children in Key Stages 1 and 2 to engage in creative work using historical themes as a stimulus;
- considered the links between history, the arts and other humanities subjects;
- begun to think about the links with wider themes such as citizenship;
- noted opportunities for children to work independently in history.

Professional Standards for QTS

This chapter will support you as you work towards evidencing attainment against the following Standards:

Q8: Have a creative and constructively critical approach towards innovation, being prepared to adapt their practice where benefits and improvements are identified.

Q31: ... promote learners' self-control and independence.

Why teach creatively?

To be effective and meaningful, the school curriculum must be appropriate and relevant to children and the society they live in. A major argument put forward therefore, is that, since society is changing, and since it has changed significantly over recent decades, it is important to ensure that the curriculum adapts and remains appropriate for its age. (See, for example, the QCA *Futures Programme*, 2005.) The curriculum needs to respond to changes and developments in technology and demography, and to take into account modern attitudes, values and beliefs about how children learn, especially in a global society.

One group of major changes, of course, has consisted of those which have affected technology, and the implications of this for primary history. New skills and knowledge are now needed for young people to function effectively in a multidimensional learning environment which changes rapidly and constantly. The second major change is social. With second and third generations of immigrant groups from many parts of the world now growing up in Britain, there is an increasing need for their histories to be reflected in the history curriculum. More recent immigrant groups, such as those from Eastern Europe, bring their own needs and values which, if we are to have an inclusive curriculum, need to be taken into account.

Research into multiple intelligences suggests new approaches for teaching and learning, where visual, auditory and kinaesthetic intelligences are involved in the learning process (Gardner, 1993). Citizenship education, to enable children to understand more fully their rights and responsibilities, has been discussed fully in many works by Hilary Claire. Claire takes a very broad view of the meaning of citizenship education and advocates history as a major linking discipline (Claire, 2004a, 2005). Personalised learning is a major factor in recent initiatives, such as *Every Child Matters* (DfES, 2004c), where an aim is to make use of the perspective, interests and needs of the learners themselves in shaping the curriculum.

Ofsted summarises arguments for creativity in history teaching:

> *The Primary National Strategy proposes a raft of suggestions for schools aimed ultimately at helping children to do better. One of its principle [sic] challenges to schools is to be more creative with the curriculum so as to make it more relevant to their pupils. It is this proposal that is particularly relevant to history . . .*
>
> *In a nutshell, the Strategy, linked to other initiatives, presents a challenge to history teachers and to those considering revisions of the National Curriculum – to be creative with the curriculum so as to meet the needs of all pupils of all abilities. This challenge is timely. The present history National Curriculum reflects the debates and issues of the 1980s, so it is not unreasonable to reconsider the extent to which it needs adjusting by teachers and others to meet the needs of a new generation of pupils. For instance, as suggested earlier, it is not necessary to teach the National Curriculum in discrete periods. Instead, periods can be synthesised around questions that are significant, understandable, and relevant to young people.*

> (Ofsted, 2005, p4–5)

A growing concern about the well-being of children, and the revision of the curriculum to reflect their interests and learning needs, has been reflected in *Excellence and Enjoyment* (DfES, 2003b) and *Every Child Matters* (DfES, 2004c), and will be embedded in the forth-coming review of primary education led by Jim Rose.

What is meant by 'creativity'?

There are numerous definitions of this most complex of ideas. However, one of the most influential for education has been made in a recent publication of the National Advisory Committee on Creative and Cultural Education, *All Our Futures* (NACCCE/DfEE, 1999). *All Our Futures* identifies four key elements within creativity: that it is multidimensional, involving all fields of activity; that it involves 'playing with ideas'; that it involves the imagination and emotions as well as intellectual skills; that it is purposeful, with clear objectives. Hilary Cooper (2007a) makes a strong case for the ways in which history fulfils all of these requirements. She argues that:

- it is multidimensional in the way it involves all aspects of a society and making connections between societies;
- it involves 'playing with ideas'; making possible inferences from sources;
- historical imagination is integral to the process of historical enquiry;
- historical enquiry must be purposeful; sources must be combined to construct and communicate accounts of the past.

> (Cooper, 2007a, p63)

As Turner-Bisset points out, there is a widely held view that creativity relates only to arts subjects (Turner-Bisset, 2005a), a notion which arose because creativity was thought to be a form of divergent thinking. Taking a broader view, she sees creativity as ... *connecting different frames of reference to create humour, discovery or works of art. It is about opening the mind to perceive things in alternative ways*. She believes that creative teaching is about *using those connections to help children learn through a range of representations, teaching approaches and activities, which enable children to be active agents of their own learning*. In history, there is great scope for creative teaching: *All this happens within the structures of history as a discipline: the combination of historical enquiry, interpretation and exercise of the historical imagination to recreate the past while remaining true to the surviving evidence* (Turner-Bisset, 2005a, pvii). In her section on 'An explanation of creativity', she gives a useful overview of books on creativity in the primary curriculum, such as Beetlestone (1998) and Duffy (1998) and a critical evaluation of the QCA website on creativity (www.ncaction.org.uk/creativity/).

Above all, however, creative, innovative practice is best when based on sound, well-tested research or practice, where there is evidence to show its usefulness. Some of the most consistent research and reporting has been carried out by Ofsted, and this work has resulted in the view that there is a need to organise learning around significant questions that are relevant to young people. This is where the innovative practice should emerge, therefore, through creating key questions which, in response to the needs and interests of the children, shape the curriculum.

Innovative methods at Key Stage 1

Creative, innovative practice can involve either creative teaching or creative learning, or a combination of both. One of the main aims of the Key Stage 1 teacher of history is that of bringing it alive and engaging children with the past in a way that is meaningful to them. To this end, the imaginative use of play, technology, story and visual sources are widely employed to answer key questions such as 'What was it like to live at this time in the past?' Teachers are also using well-tried approaches in innovative ways, such as using costume and artefacts in a focused manner in order to involve children's creative imagination, and to engage them in a meaningful way into studying the past. Here both creative teaching and learning are taking place.

PRACTICAL TASK PRACTICAL TASK **PRACTICAL TASK** PRACTICAL TASK **PRACTICAL TASK**

Philip, a Year 1 teacher, managed to acquire from a local drama group a set of costumes related to the Middle Ages and decided to use them as a starting point for work he was about to begin on 'castles'. He had set the question, 'What was it like to live in a castle long ago?'

Consider how you would use resources like these. When you are next in a school or early years setting, collect similar resources and plan some activities which you can test out with children in the Early Years Foundation Stage or Key Stage 1.

Reconstructing the past: an active approach

Much can be done to engage young children's imaginations through recreating the past, both within your own classroom and as part of a visit. For example, a visit to a Victorian school museum will reveal what life was like for children in that age, re-enacting lessons, dressing in Victorian clothes and playing with Victorian toys, as well as offering a unique learning experience (Lawrie, 1998). These unique educational experiences can be found in many excellent museums, and they are explored in issue 35 of *Primary History*, the journal of the Historical Association specifically for primary teachers. A range of different ideas for innovative lessons can be found at www.teachers.tv/.

Innovative methods at Key Stage 2

At Key Stage 2, the primary teacher's aim of bringing the past to life remains important. However, with children's increasing skill in self-directed enquiry, much personalised learning can take place in the development of understanding about the past. Independent research into historical themes is perhaps one of the most rewarding aspects of primary school work. It can, however, be full of pitfalls for the inexperienced trainee or teacher and it is necessary for them to reflect on their own experiences of this kind of learning and the potential difficulties they might encounter when using it as a teaching strategy. There are numerous benefits to be derived from independent work, however, such as increased skill and understanding, a sense of achievement and corresponding confidence and, more importantly perhaps, a growing awareness that learning is a matter of personal commitment. It is necessary though to scaffold work appropriately to ensure that suitable learning takes place, and that language and artistic and creative skills are involved in children's learning outcomes. You can guide their research through devising appropriate questions with them, and using strategies to help them devise their own questions (see Figure 24 below).

Figure 24. What I want to know (Year 5 pupil's work)

CLASSROOM STORY

Amy, a Year 5 teacher, decides to use historical photographs as part of an enquiry into the Second World War. She provides a set of photographs taken at different points in time, particularly focusing on some of the key characters, such as Sir Winston Churchill. The children, who are very computer-literate, are encouraged to find further photographs from the period and to add them to the growing class collection.

Much work takes place in analysing and discussing the pictures, placing them in time and historical context. The historical background to each picture is reviewed and they are placed in chronological sequence, later to be added to the class timeline.

Amy then asks the children to think about the effect of these events on the people involved and to imagine how they felt at the time each photograph was taken. The children devise questions, such as 'What did Winston Churchill feel like at the end of the war?' then add their own 'thought capsules' to the pictures. In Figure 25 the child was using a photograph of Sir Winston Churchill taken at the end of the war.

Churchill - Great not, all this big worry on my mind and I can get on!

Figure 25. What was Churchill thinking? (Year 5 work)

PRACTICAL TASK PRACTICAL TASK **PRACTICAL TASK** PRACTICAL TASK **PRACTICAL TASK**

Make a list of the ways you could use photographs or portraits to promote creative responses from children. These responses could take the form of prose, poetry, art, model making, music or drama.

Classroom-based activities can also involve active learning, such as the classroom 'dig' described by Harriet Martin (1996) or the use of fascinating primary sources, such as the 'lists' discussed by Ian Mason (1999). Very often, there is an historic place or character in the locality, which children might 'discover' on a visit to local archives. The real excitement generated by finding out and communicating something new and original is probably one of the most creative experiences possible for a child. For a very informative short article on how to use local archives, see Halewood (2000). The use of drama, interviews, re-enactments and information technology are all part of well-tried approaches. However, these can become innovative if both the teacher's and children's enthusiasms are shared and good questions are devised that meet the children's needs. Teachers TV includes examples of innovative lessons at Key Stage 2, such as that described by Falck (2006).

Cross-curricular links with the humanities

Most young children learn in a holistic way, and so cross-curricular work is a sound, creative means of addressing their needs. For example, geography was a necessary part of a study of Ancient Egypt where the children used the subject as part of their work of locating on maps significant historic sites along the Nile (see Figure 26).

Figure 26. Map of Ancient Egypt (Year 3 work)

Religious Education is an essential part of studying many history units at Key Stage 2, such as Ancient Egyptian, Greek, Roman, Anglo-Saxon or Tudor societies. Religion impacted significantly on daily life for most people in the past and influenced events that took place. The different religious and cultural groups that make up many British urban populations also provide a rich resource for study as part of a local history theme.

Wider cross-curricular links

There are links with science in both methodology and content. For example, the enquiry methods used in both subjects are very similar, involving the use of evidence to formulate hypotheses and conclusions. History might be linked with science when, for example, following an experiment, similar experiments carried out in the past could be explored within a history lesson, looking at how scientific knowledge and understanding has its roots in history. Many important scientific developments are necessarily part of the history curriculum, such as developments in understanding about health and medicine, the universe and space travel. These are themes which will excite and appeal to young children, particularly many boys, and will enable them to see the true value of history.

There are many excellent science museums which could be used in a history topic. These include the Science Museum in South Kensington in London, the Manchester Museum of Science and Industry, and many others. Anthony Richards of the Science Museum in London has produced an informative article on how history teaching can benefit from the use of the vast resources available in these museums (Richards, 2003). Other scientific sites, such as Jodrell Bank, also have great links with history and offer excellent opportunities for combining these subjects in creative new ways. For example, investigations could be based on questions like, 'How did we begin to find out about our universe?'

There are equally important links with the other curriculum subjects, known as the foundation subjects.

Art

When used in display work, presentations for another class, parents or the school, art is a powerful creative medium through which children can express their understanding of their learning in history. Art features in the creation of project books and posters, in pottery and other sculptures, all of which can be used imaginatively to contribute to children's rich experience of history.

Figure 27. Life in Ancient Egypt (Year 3)

Be an Archaeologist

Pots found from ancient Greece show everyday life and story of gods. This pot shows a chariot race.

Figure 28. Pottery from Ancient Greece (Year 6)

Design and technology

Figure 29. Model houses (Year 2 work)

Children's creative skills and imagination can be combined when history topics involve the making of models and working items from the past, such as an Ancient Egyptian shaduf, or a water wheel. The children who made the model houses shown in Figure 29, based on a topic on local history, thoroughly enjoyed the activity and developed their skills effectively, enhancing their achievement in both curriculum areas.

Drama

A widely used dramatic technique in teaching history is role-play, which involves taking on the character of another person and acting as they might have done. As a form of play it comes naturally to young children, who will often spontaneously act out their learning in the playground. Obviously, some knowledge of the period and the person involved is needed if it is to be part of work leading up to some drama. Once they are aware of the historical context, children can then assume different roles to work out how they think people in the past might have been affected by events, or how they might have behaved in certain situations. Conflicts can be used as situations for role-play and the children asked to decide how best to deal with problems. Simulations and games can be found on the internet (see the list of useful websites on page 132). These interactive games create a situation where the child acts in the role of a participant in an historic situation. For example, in some Viking simulations, the child makes decisions to do with invasion and settlement, which are played out on the computer game. The child can then see the results and effects of the decisions made.

'Hot-seating' is a form of role-play where one person takes on a role for a specific purpose. For example, the teacher themselves might take the 'hot seat', wear an item of clothing to indicate when they are in role, and then speak as if they were, for example, Henry VIII. This activity provides also an opportunity for children to find out more about a specific topic, and offers teachers a creative and interesting way of imparting knowledge.

'Freeze-frames' are still scenes, where the children create a pose, which they hold for a short time. These are useful for exploring specific events or key moments in the past. Children can mime, through their poses and expressions, the feelings of the characters involved in an event, exploring these ideas and emotions themselves and ultimately, understanding the situation more deeply.

'Conscience alley' is dramatic technique where thoughts are voiced openly. In a decision-making situation, children form two rows and a central character walks down between them. As this takes place, the children whisper or speak their thoughts, trying to exert their influence. The process of thinking through dilemmas and voicing their thoughts helps children to relate with issues that frequently arise in history. (See issue 48 of *Primary History*, Historical Association, 2008.)

REFLECTIVE TASK

Read some of the articles on drama recommended in *Primary History*. Consider how you might use some of these dramatic techniques to enliven your history lessons and motivate your class.

Music

Children's dramatic reconstructions often make use of music and dance, which are often the most distinctive features of past ages. Either as an accompaniment, or as a piece created by the children themselves, music is a valuable part of a child's response to an historical theme. Music can be used to accompany story-telling and poetry and dances from the past, which can be performed as part of a wider expression of children's learning, perhaps as part of a Tudor day, or a class assembly.

While performance is of supreme importance in music, for the purposes of the history curriculum, what is of value is the use of music, songs and dance as first-hand sources of evidence (Turner-Bisset, 2005a). Musical artefacts can tell the child historian much about a past civilisation, for example. A replica flute or pipe from Aztec times, when investigated, can reveal the musical abilities of the people, the similarities and differences between Aztec and modern Western music, and also the Aztecs' craftsmanship and love of imagery. The lives of composers throw further light onto the characteristic features of the age.

The texts of songs contain a wealth of historical information. The songs from working life or about Irish immigration can provide real insight into aspects of Victorian life, for example. The hardships of labourers, mineworkers and railway builders are outlined in specific detail in these verses, and with a little research into their meanings, much can be understood from thinking about them. Ballads, folk songs and love songs tell a story in their own way, again providing a rich source of historical information.

Simply listening to musical pieces characteristic of different periods in the past can contribute to children's awareness of the context of that time, the kinds of instruments that were played and the musical forms used. For example, Tudor music or the distinctive sound of medieval music can be evocative of those times in the past. Music in all its forms appeals to children whose learning style is predisposed towards the enactive and emotional.

Physical education

Games from the past can become a practical element within history lessons. For example, we know from artefacts that have been found that the Vikings played certain games. These include playing with a football, among many others. Dances, both from folk traditions and courtly dances, are another exciting way of involving children physically and mentally in re-enacting the past. *To understand fully a past society or culture, one needs to know something of that culture's music, song and dance* (Turner-Bisset, 2005a, p123). Dance in its many forms can also be experienced by watching extracts from broadcasts and film, set within its historical context.

Modern foreign languages

When studying a modern foreign language, a knowledge of the history and culture of that country and its society contributes to children's learning. A European theme, on a topic such as France, for example, provides opportunities to look at some of the major events in French history, especially where they connect with British history (sadly, most of these are wars!) and also to introduce the relevant vocabulary and phrases in French. An excellent 'topic week' I once observed focused on the theme of France, looking mostly at modern culture, and made use of virtually the whole curriculum through looking at maps and café culture, which involved food, menus and money and dress. Dramatic scenes referred to episodes in the history of France.

Modern British local history could also incorporate modern foreign languages in the form of modern Asian languages, such as Urdu, Gujerati and Hindi. Many urban conurbations include substantial populations of Asian descent, and even when descendants are second and third generation, people still know and use their families' 'mother tongue'. This would be a valuable way of encouraging an inclusive approach to teaching history in school.

Citizenship

The year 2000 saw a renewed emphasis on this aspect of children's education. A clear statement was included in Curriculum 2000: *The school curriculum should pass on enduring values, develop pupils' integrity and autonomy and help them to be responsible and caring citizens capable of contributing to the development of a just society* (DfEE/QCA, 1999b). Citizenship should help children in: developing confidence and responsibility and making the most of their abilities; preparing to play an active role as citizens; developing a healthy, safer lifestyle; developing good relationships and respecting the differences between people.

Since 2000, a great deal of work has been carried out in this area, with teachers looking for the opportunities that work in other subjects offers for exploring citizenship. It also features in the Professional Standards for teachers; teachers must model good citizenship and those going into the profession need to consider the implications of this.

The role of history in citizenship education

History is a study of human behaviour in the past and naturally incorporates issues of citizenship. Past problems, conflicts and solutions provide a context for present-day notions of citizenship. The rights and responsibilities of citizens are key issues in citizenship education. History provides us with examples of societies where there has traditionally been a lack of human rights, but also provides the story of how human rights have been slowly won.

There are varied opportunities to incorporate citizenship within a history theme. Cooper (2000, 2007a) gives examples of how local history work can provide opportunities for developing practical links with the citizenship curriculum. An interesting view of citizenship is discussed by Brown and Harrison (1998), who have researched the experiences of children in different times and places in relation to their rights as citizens. Claire (2005) provides a detailed and comprehensive overview of the concepts and skills of citizenship. She also looks at how history can support citizenship education through the content of themes and topics, and finally at ways of teaching about issues such as equality.

CLASSROOM STORY

Julie was working on a topic about the 1960s with Year 5. She had begun to work with the class on the notion of equality, and what this meant in the past compared with the present day. As she looked further into the subject of equality, she realised that past and present notions of this idea are very different. Julie decided to begin to discuss equality as we understand it today, so that the children might be clear about the focus of the work.

At the beginning of a lesson on the ship, the *Empire Windrush*, Julie asked the children if anyone could explain what we mean by equality. The children explained that it means all people are equal. Julie explained that in a democratic system, everyone is entitled to equal rights under the law.

She told the class that they were to imagine they were all immigrants from Jamaica, arriving on the *Empire Windrush*. The children read extracts about how the excited new arrivals had dreamed of a new life in the 'mother country'. Julie then gave them extracts from newspapers at the time, which raised all sorts of concerns about the arrival of immigrants from the Caribbean. She followed this activity with showing the class, using the whiteboard, some of the signs the immigrants saw when they tried to find accommodation in London and other large towns around the country; signs such as 'No Blacks', or 'No Blacks, Irish or dogs'.

Many children expressed dismay at what they read. Some murmured quietly that they had sometimes heard these things said in private. There then followed a lively discussion about how ideas of equality have changed in Britain since the 1960s, with Julie adding information about changes to the law, such as the Race Relations Act, preventing such discrimination taking place.

Assessing creativity

Creative work in history takes many forms. These include: creating a research topic and devising questions; writing a personal interpretation of why and how things happened; creating a personal response in the form of a diagram, picture, model, song, display or presentation. Methods of assessing creative achievement include the methods used in all good assessment strategies. However, for making qualitative judgements it is often most useful to talk to the child to see how well they can explain their work. Self-assessment can be a useful tool, in that it can encourage children to recognise their own strengths and talents.

The assessment of children's work in history all requires qualitative judgement, since it is the process skills and concepts they have used, as well as the end result, that is being assessed. For example, the thinking involved in setting up and organising their work can be revealed through a simple 'mind map' where the child identifies what they want to find out:

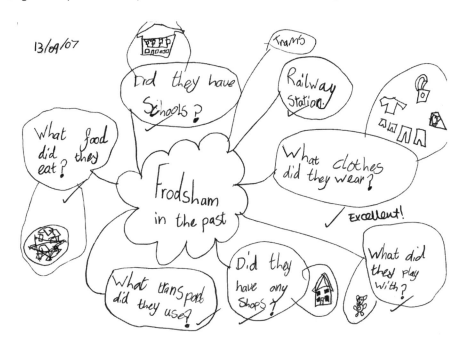

Figure 30. Mind map (Year 2 work)

RESEARCH SUMMARY RESEARCH SUMMARY **RESEARCH SUMMARY** RESEARCH SUMMARY

Research into multiple intelligences, such as that of Gardner (1993, 2006) has influenced views about the need for introducing more creativity into the classroom. The NACCCE Report (1999) provided a sound analysis of creative practice for teachers of history to use as a set of principles. Cooper (2007a) has shown how these can be applied to the history curriculum, while Turner-Bisset (2005a) developed this concept of creative teaching in history in detail. Earlier work by historians which began to consider issues surrounding creativity and cross-curricular approaches includes Husbands (1996), Blyth and Hughes (1997), Hoodless (1998a), and Bage (2000). The QCA website ncaction, the QCA *Futures Programme* (QCA, 2005) and Teachers TV, among many others, also explore ways of making cross-curricular links and introducing innovative methods.

A SUMMARY OF KEY POINTS

> A clear rationale is needed for introducing new creative approaches. Innovative methods need to be based on research and effective classroom practice.

> Creativity is multidimensional and involves 'playing with ideas', imagination and enquiry.

> Innovative methods in history at Key Stages 1 and 2 involve imaginative use of play, technology, story and visual sources. Historical reconstructions and individual research feature more prominently at Key Stage 2.

> Cross-curricular links can be made between history and the core subjects, and the other foundation subjects.

> Cross-curricular themes, such as thinking skills and citizenship, can be delivered through history.

MOVING *ON* > > > > > > MOVING *ON* > > > > > > MOVING *ON*

Standard 18

You may have been using a good unit plan effectively in the past, and yet have now been asked by your history coordinator to ensure that you are incorporating innovative and creative methods. Devise an action plan, which will help you to critically evaluate your planning and teaching of this unit in the past, identifying aspects that have been less effective or less engaging for the children. Plan one or two new approaches or strategies which will enable each child to shape their work in an individual way.

FURTHER READING FURTHER READING FURTHER READING FURTHER READING

Claire, H (2004) History and citizenship, in Claire, H (ed), *Teaching citizenship in primary schools.* Exeter: Learning Matters.

Dean, J (2007) Teaching styles and pupil learning: the Nuffield Primary History Project's creative, interactive pedagogy – the pupils' voice. *Primary History*, 47: 14–15.

Hughes, R (2005) The Foundation Stage, Key Stage 1, citizenship in the early years, in *Leading Primary History.* London: Historical Association.

Primary History, issue 48 (2008) London: Historical Association.
This issue is devoted to the use of drama in history.

Primary History, issue 35 (2003) London: Historical Association.
This whole issue is devoted to the use of museums as an educational resource.

Useful websites

www.bbc.co.uk/history/interactive/games/
   A good starting point for games and simulations.

www.ncaction.org.uk/creativity/

www.ofsted.gov.uk/publications/annualreport0405/
   Contains the subject report for history in primary schools.

www.teachers.tv/
   A user-friendly site with useful ideas for innovative lessons.

12
Equality, inclusion and diversity as part of the history curriculum

Chapter objectives

By the end of this chapter you will have:

- considered ways of overcoming potential barriers to learning;
- considered the diverse needs of children within classrooms today, from those of children with differing abilities and learning styles, to those of children from different social, ethnic and religious backgrounds;
- begun to understand the range of different learning styles;
- looked at the use of varied teaching strategies to meet the needs of children with SEN;
- considered the use of histories from other parts of the world and other communities as a means of enriching the curriculum.

Professional Standards for QTS

This chapter will support you as you work towards evidencing attainment against the following Standards:

Q18: Understand how children and young people develop and that the progress and well-being of learners are affected by a range of developmental, social, religious, ethnic, cultural and linguistic influences.

Q19: Know how to make effective personalised provision for those they teach, including those for whom English is an additional language or who have special educational needs or disabilities, and how to take practical account of diversity and promote equality and inclusion in their teaching.

Q20: Know and understand the roles of colleagues with specific responsibilities, including those with responsibility for learners with special educational needs and disabilities and other individual learning needs.

Overcoming barriers to learning

There are many ways of working which will help you overcome the barriers to learning experienced by children with special educational needs (SEN), such as:

- creating stimulating and informative learning environments;
- ensuring children are motivated and concentrating;
- providing equality of opportunity through teaching approaches;
- using appropriate assessment approaches;
- setting targets for learning which build on children's knowledge and interests, but which are attainable and yet challenging. Effective target-setting should help children to develop their self-esteem and confidence in their own abilities.

It is important to make provision where necessary to support individuals or groups to enable them to participate effectively in the curriculum and assessment in both classroom and fieldwork activities. The support of additional adults as discussed in Chapter 7 will be vital in this aspect of your work. It is essential to take account of the type and extent of the difficulty experienced by the child with SEN and greater, more varied differentiation of tasks and materials will be necessary. Where children need access to specialist equipment or adapted activities you will need to make use of their statements of special educational needs and work closely with other supporting adults or agencies. It is also helpful to assist children in managing their behaviour and emotions so that they can take part in learning history effectively and safely.

Children with different learning styles

It is important to differentiate your teaching for all children, either individually or working in groups, but it is especially important for children with special educational needs. Effective learning and behaviour both rely on work being set at an appropriate level for children to be challenged, yet also have a sense of achievement.

The *visual*, *auditory* and *kinaesthetic* methods (VAK) frequently used for teaching children with these different learning styles are mentioned in Chapter 5. Some children learn holistically; in other words they learn by first looking at the whole 'picture' and then analysing it. Yet others learn systematically, or sequentially. History is an excellent subject for meeting all these different learning needs since the range of sources and methods commonly used in the study of history includes all of them. However, it is helpful to understand the styles of learning within a class or group that you are teaching and to ensure that you differentiate accordingly. It is also helpful to use the whole range of teaching strategies so as to address all the learning needs and preferred styles of learning within a group.

Children with special educational needs

It is important when thinking about special educational needs (SEN), to realise that this term covers a very wide range of learners, from the most able to the least able. SEN can include an enormous variety of different kinds of need, some of which are listed below:

- the gifted and able child;
- children with specific learning difficulties (SLD);
- children with hearing or visual difficulties;
- children with moderate learning difficulties (MLD);
- children with physical or medical difficulties;
- children with emotional and behavioural difficulties (EBD)

Children with SEN are equally entitled to study the whole curriculum, and tasks will need to be very carefully differentiated for them. However, history, with its wide range of sources and strategies, provides scope for meeting their needs.

Children with specific and moderate learning difficulties

Children of normal intellect in mainstream classes sometimes have difficulties in specific areas:

- poor drawing and writing skills;
- language difficulties – either in understanding verbal instructions or in expressing themselves clearly;
- emotional immaturity.

Children with specific learning difficulties may develop behavioural problems such as anxiety, withdrawal or aggressive behaviour, particularly if their needs are not addressed. Children with moderate learning difficulties are common in most primary classrooms, and often include children with a reading age below that of their peers. Thinking about the reading levels of history textbooks and resource sheets and adapting these to an appropriate level will help the weaker reader.

History can be accessed by children with these learning difficulties in a number of ways. For example, a child with poor writing skills can be given scaffolded tasks, with considerable support for their writing. The teacher might provide 'sentence starters' for the child to complete, or cloze activities where the required words can be chosen from a list. Children with poor drawing skills can be taught using the 'apprenticeship' approach, where the teacher may work alongside the child to produce a drawing, demonstrating techniques at the same time. A child with low self-esteem, who is emotionally insecure, or who is reluctant to read, can be included in historical work, by the greater use of visual sources, the provision of more opportunities for speaking and listening in pairs or groups, and by more verbal support and discussion with the teacher. Many different approaches other than those involving reading and writing can be used to enable a child to achieve conceptual understanding in history.

Children with severe physical or medical difficulties

These children are likely to be taught in a separate, specially designed unit or school. They may include children with moderate or severe autism, children with ADHD, or children with Downs' syndrome. However, if they are being taught within a mainstream class, they are likely to be supported by a full-time classroom assistant with special training in managing their needs. The support staff will need effective liaison with the class teacher to ensure learning in history is achieved by these children, as discussed more fully in Chapter 7. Good practice in history teaching also applies to children with SEN, who, like others, need stimulating, challenging, interactive methods to promote their interest and learning across the humanities.

Children with dyslexia

Dyslexia can affect children's reading, spelling, handwriting and their ability to read and interpret charts and diagrams and can affect progress in history in particular, where there is often a heavy emphasis upon the use of written sources and sometimes tables or charts. The teacher, therefore, needs to be aware of potential difficulties in this area, being constantly alert to the fact that a child with dyslexia may not have been identified. Children with dyslexia need support in reading and structured tasks. A variety of tasks need to be planned, which do not exclusively rely on skill in reading, writing or using data. It is important to be clear on the purpose of the children's activities. If writing is not the main focus of demonstrating understanding, then other methods could be used to achieve the same outcome, such as using a camcorder, oral presentation, word-processing, or cut and paste exercise. Various methods of assessment such as talking, artwork, presentations, drama and display may enable the child with these difficulties to fully demonstrate their abilities in history.

Children with hearing difficulties

Children with hearing difficulties, or using hearing aids, will need to work hard at their listening skills. Listening is a vital skill which requires paying attention and attaching meaning to what has been heard. History lessons might make use of sound recordings and videos, stories, oral accounts, interviews, drama, role-play, and children talking about their research. In these lessons, it is helpful to use quiet corners for listening and small group work and to use visual cues at the same time. Children with poor hearing should sit near to the teacher and away from sources of noise. Remember to direct your speech to children with these difficulties, making sure that they can see you, since they may partially rely on lip-reading. Speaking slowly and clearly can be helpful, as well as quickly confirming that the child has understood any instructions or guidance that has been given verbally. The use of additional visual material to accompany spoken communication will also be helpful.

Children with visual impairment

Visual impairment can have serious consequences for children's learning in history if not fully taken into account. As a normal part of planned activities, history includes visits out of school, and the use of a considerable amount of visual material. Clearly, the implications of these activities for children with visual impairment will need to be carefully thought through, with additional verbal explanation provided as much as possible. The classroom story below provides an example.

CLASSROOM STORY

Jill, the history coordinator for her school, was taking history lessons with a mixed ability Year 5 class which included Millie, a child with sight impairment. She was naturally apprehensive as to how to adapt her teaching style and resources to enable Millie to fully participate in her history lessons.

Jill took advice from the Senco, and ensured that her lessons became more orally focused. When work was written on the board, she read aloud the information. Showing a broadcast about the Victorians, she made sure the sound was accessible to all. Regularly during the video, pauses were made, and volunteer children recapped what had happened so far. When working on follow-up activities, Jill allowed time to work individually with Millie to ensure she had fully grasped the task and had appropriate resources to use.

Jill also took into account the following strategies:

- always make sure Millie is at the front of the class for any demonstrations, video films;
- all written tasks and reading needs to be in large print, font 16 point or above;
- allow more time for reading instructions;
- direct questions clearly to Millie by using her name;
- check whether black and white or colour helps her better to distinguish features in pictures, charts or maps.

Where children may have difficulty in discriminating between colours the teacher needs to make use of black and white illustrations and avoid colour coding within tasks. When coloured pencils and paints need to be used, have labels on them to aid the child.

Those 'left behind'

There are some children in most classes who seem simply to be 'behind' their peer group. These children may lack motivation due to poor self-esteem and regularly underachieve, yet they might appear to be as intelligent as others in their class. The reasons for their difficulties are many and varied: the child might have had a prolonged period of absence; their parents might not send them to school regularly; they might have suffered from emotional or behavioural difficulties when younger and thus failed to learn at that stage; they might have started their schooling already 'behind' their peers through lack of stimulation at home. In some extreme cases, there might be a child with sight or hearing impairment, for example, which has not been detected earlier, or which has suddenly developed.

These children will need to work at an earlier stage in the history curriculum. This will not, of course, apply to the study units being taught, but to the level of expectation you have in each of the statements of attainment. By starting at an appropriate point for the level of development of the child, it might be possible, through the use of various resources and additional support, to enable them to move ahead more quickly, and also to build up their self-esteem.

Teaching the gifted and able child in history

The Every Child Matters agenda DfES (2004c) has implications for the education of gifted and talented children, in that they are entitled to a challenging and demanding curriculum that meets their needs. The government has set up Gifted and Talented (G&T) partnerships in local authorities and a national academy for the Young, Gifted and Talented (YGT). However, as Jon Nichol points out, the crucial factor in all of this is what happens in schools and classrooms, since this is where the needs of the G&T will be met (Nichol, 2007). Gifted and talented children tend to learn quickly, have a very retentive memory, have a wide general knowledge and enjoy problem solving. They often have a strong imagination and show strong feelings and opinions. They set themselves high standards and are perfectionists, and generally possess keen powers of observation and reasoning, seeing relationships and generalisations.

Teachers need to create opportunities to interest, motivate and challenge the very able children in order to provide equality of opportunity for all. Having within the classroom a selection of resources from the next year group or key stage is a good idea, to help extend individual children's research skills. You can also draw on material from higher levels of study, making use of higher statements of attainment from the history attainment target. Another approach is to extend the breadth and depth of study, with an expectation that the gifted and talented child will research further, working independently and looking beyond the content covered by the rest of the class.

Children from disadvantaged backgrounds

Children may come from families or have parents who have themselves underachieved or failed to achieve for one reason or another while at school. These are not always necessarily children from poor urban backgrounds living on 'problem' estates. There is also much rural poverty, with households which are not highly literate. While children from middle-class homes usually receive most parental support, some children lack support due to pressure of work on their parents. Similarly, while many single-parent families are highly successful, other single parents struggle to provide the quality time needed for each child at home.

It is important to take account of these factors when talking and questioning children and making assumptions about their out-of-school learning and activities, and giving homework. It may be helpful to see the parents and discuss the work you are sending home, or to send regular information home to the parents or carers, but above all to ensure that the work can be managed by the child working independently. Many children from poorer homes have no computer or internet link, and this can disadvantage them if homework requires ICT. Others come from homes where their parents or carers cannot read or are not proficient enough to be able to give adequate support for demanding tasks.

PRACTICAL TASK PRACTICAL TASK **PRACTICAL TASK** PRACTICAL TASK **PRACTICAL TASK**

Pam had set her class the task of enlisting the help of their parents or other carers at home in a library visit. Her aim was for each child to visit the library and to familiarise themselves with how materials are laid out and how to find information they need. She had set them a small enquiry based on their current history topic on Roman Britain. Each child had selected an item of interest, such as Roman roads, villas or forts, and their task was to return to school the following week with some information found in the library.

To her dismay, Pam received a visit from one child's parents soon after setting this task. They came into school at the end of the day and explained that they had always worked on a farm. They had grown up in farming families and had never actually visited a library themselves. They admitted that they would have personal difficulties of all kinds in helping their child carry out this task.

Imagine you are in Pam's shoes. Consider what you would say to these parents. Plan the advice or support you could give to them in order to avoid embarrassment and failure on the part of the child to complete the set task.

Issues of class

Children from poorer social class backgrounds will almost certainly be acutely aware of any disadvantages they suffer compared with their middle-class peers, and you will need to employ positive strategies to ensure these children feel fully included and respected. History offers a wide range of opportunities to achieve this aim. For example, a study of societies in the past where there was little concern about equality among social groups could give rise to discussion about the issue. Stories, biographies and autobiographies by people from working-class backgrounds are an important item to include where relevant, in order to value their contribution to history.

Foreign holidays may not be part of some children's prior knowledge, and so this needs to be taken into account when making assumptions about their experience when questioning children about the modern equivalents of Ancient Egypt or Ancient Greece. Access to the internet and books needs to be available in school time, as many families do not have these. The cost of school trips may be an issue, and alternative plans may need to be considered if fieldwork is a regular feature of the school's work in history.

Issues of gender

There is a need to ensure the schemes of work do not exclude the interests of groups of children, either boys or girls. Despite a considerable move towards greater equality, the fact is that certain topics *do* interest girls more while others appeal to boys. It is important, therefore, to be aware that topics which may have appealed to you as a girl or boy may not motivate all the children in your class. Topics about the Second World War, for example, will inspire Key Stage 2 boys to research all the finer details about aircraft or guns, while dress and changing fashions may well appeal to many of the girls. Resources also need to be selected and balanced and avoid stereotypes. For example, books and visual sources need to be selected to ensure a gender balance, with males and females undertaking the whole range of roles and activities.

The role of women in history is usually secondary to that of men and often invisible. It is helpful therefore to include women among your choice of significant people, key characters in history units and the resources selected to teach these topics. There are some interesting instances in history of women disguising themselves as men, simply to be able to follow their interests, such as English novelist Mary Ann Evans, who had to write under the pen name of George Eliot. Another interesting impersonator, who had a career as a female pirate, is discussed in an article by Kirkland and Wykes (2003). We also need to invite contributions from women who are active in the local community, as well as find examples of those who have made a contribution to national and international history. Some ways of doing this might include:

- finding visual resources which contain images of women in history;
- asking local women community leaders to talk about their roles;
- identifying women in history or contemporary society who play a leading role within their tradition, such as women ministers in Christianity or women rabbis in Judaism.

Children from minority ethnic and cultural backgrounds

History can contribute to the elimination of racism, sexism and other forms of discrimination by promoting an understanding of how these prejudices arose through examples from past societies, and how they may have been overcome. For example, a study of Rosa Parks would be an interesting choice of a significant person from the past (Claire, 2006). Local history study and the study of world history units can contribute to this learning by enhancing children's understanding of the global community.

The different cultures often found in the modern classroom are a rich resource to be used in history. You will need to ensure the schemes of work do not exclude particular groups of children (see for example, Lewis and Coxall, 2001). Valuing our multicultural heritage can start with place names and children's names, which can give us an insight into the multicultural links of our community. The language of our local area links in with the local place names. In the names of streets and buildings there is evidence of Roman, Viking and Anglo-Saxon names as well as recent heroes, such as Nelson Mandela.

Children with English as an additional language

The impact on children of learning English as an additional language (EAL) is an important aspect of work in history, especially in inner-city, multicultural schools, where there is a school population which is constantly changing. The refugee who has recently arrived, for example from Pakistan or Poland, will be considerably affected by moving to a very different culture and language. Class and EAL support teachers need to plan collaboratively in order to agree their specific roles in providing targeted support in history lessons. There are groups and organisations which provide support in the form of materials for children and teachers facing these difficulties, and some suggested websites can be found below.

In terms of assessment, a child with EAL may have a good grasp of a subject but not be able to communicate this knowledge. Assessment tasks need to be practical, visual and as accessible as possible, and in marking work, you need to be aware that you are not assessing skill in language use, but in the child's understanding of history.

Children on the move: children from traveller backgrounds

Schools on the fringes of towns and in rural areas may include the children of traveller families (Bowen, 2001). While they are similar to child refugees or asylum seekers in the sense that they do not have a settled home life, each of these children has different needs but also in terms of their different experience great potential for enriching work on local, personal or family history.

Promoting equality

History offers a wide range of opportunities to address issues of equality. One of the principal aims of history teaching is to encourage children to reflect on their own values and experiences and to develop empathy towards others. Empathy involves the ability to understand the perspectives of others and to be able to see things from their point of view, even if you do not share it. Good history teaching provides children with opportunities to share their individual perspectives and learn from the perspectives of others. Claire has researched and written extensively about these aspects of personal, moral and social education (Claire, 1996, 2001, 2005).

REFLECTIVE TASK
REFLECTIVE TASK

Look through the outline history study units. Identify units or parts of units which might be suitable contexts for introducing notions of equality to your class and consider how you might use these opportunities.

An inclusive classroom

Inclusive practice involves treating each individual with respect, including them equally in whatever is taking place, and responding appropriately to their different needs. It requires a detailed knowledge of the abilities, interests and backgrounds of each child, best achieved by building up a profile for each one. This profile might include the results of tests and assessments, day-to-day records of development and improvement, for example in their use of historical enquiry skills, notes which you have made while observing the child at work and at play, and marked examples of the child's work. Individual Education Plans would be included in the building up of these child profiles. Personal and family histories, of course, provide excellent material for building up this detailed knowledge and understanding of individuals which can in turn influence respect for all within your classroom.

An inclusive curriculum

The National Curriculum for history appears quite limited, mostly to white, British history. It would certainly be easy to teach the curriculum with this kind of focus. However, there are limitless ways of ensuring that the curriculum for history is culturally rich and varied. Resources can be selected to represent many different cultures. For example, there are story books which could be used in teaching history in the early years or at Key Stage 1, which draw on the lives of single-parent families, working-class children, families from different parts of the world, and families from different religious and cultural backgrounds. Examples of significant people could be drawn from cultures across the world, both black and white, such as Mary Seacole's career as a nurse during the Crimean War (see Seacole, 1857/1999).

At Key Stage 2, the multicultural nature of British history is very evident. For example, the Romans brought to Britain a different culture, as did the Saxons, Vikings, Danes and Norman French. In later periods, notably the Victorian, there was considerable emigration and also immigration, which included Jewish populations and Asian populations, with many from India and China. In twentieth-century Britain, the Second World War is an excellent example of how multicultural history is; people from Asia, Africa, Australia and the Caribbean all volunteered to join the British forces, many returning to live in Britain during the 1960s.

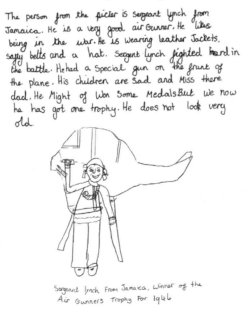

The person from the picter is Sergeant Lynch from Jamaica. He is a very good air Gunner. He likes being in the war. He is wearing leather Jackets, safty belts and a hat. Sergent Lynch fighted hard in the battle. He had a Special gun on the frunt of the plane. His children are sad and Miss there dad. He Might of Won Some Medals But we now he has got one trophy. He does not look very old.

Sergeant lynch From Jamaica, winner of the Air Gunners Trophy For 1946

Figure 31. Drawing of Sergeant Lynch (Year 4 work)

Figure 32. Photograph of Sergeant Lynch

The individual piece of writing shown in Figure 31 summarises the thoughts and conversation of a Year 4 child when studying the photograph in Figure 32.

In learning about the war, of course, it is important to maintain a balance by also looking at the effort and hardships of those in Germany, Italy and Japan.

Many history units allow for a culturally inclusive approach. For example, present-day local studies in urban centres have a naturally inclusive focus, where immigrants, refugees and asylum seekers all play their part in forming local communities. There are often local community organisations which provide information and resources for teaching. At a national level, the lives of significant people might include those of Mother Teresa or Martin Luther King.

Figure 33. Olaudah Equiano

The world history units are a good opportunity to study the past of another society and to begin to understand the reasons for how they evolved. The history of the Indus Valley civilisation is one of increasing interest in areas where there is a growing Asian population, and the history of Benin might provide a way into some study of the slave trade and its eventual abolition. While the work of William Wilberforce is fundamental, children could be introduced to the work of Olaudah Equiano, who grew up in Benin, was taken as a slave, won his freedom, and then joined Wilberforce in London to assist in his abolitionist work. Equiano has produced a fascinating autobiography, in which he describes his early memories of an idyllic existence in Benin (Equiano, 1789/1995). Ways of including the slave trade in your curriculum are described in an interesting article about the slave trade in Bristol by Dresser (2002).

Written and visual sources and displays should include people from different cultures and races, and from diverse social backgrounds. This indicates the fact that they are treated equally and need to be studied equally. An important point to note here, however, is that sometimes resources are difficult to find or may give a distorted picture. Major charities produce materials to attract attention and raise funds. These naturally tend to emphasise the desperate plight of children, often in Asia and Africa, giving a negative impression of what life is like. While such resources may fill a need, it is also worthwhile trying to ensure that an equal number of images appear which give a positive view. For resources on this aspect of the curriculum, see www.nationalarchives.gov.uk/pathways/blackhistory/.

RESEARCH SUMMARY RESEARCH SUMMARY **RESEARCH SUMMARY** RESEARCH SUMMARY

Hilary Cooper indicates in her article on learning and assessment how gifted and able children might further their historical thinking through work on sources (Cooper, 2007c). Issue 47 of the journal *Primary History*, which is devoted to history for the gifted and talented, contains much useful information, ideas for practice and interesting case studies from the classroom (Historical Association, 2007). Freeman (2002) stresses that meeting the needs of the most able has a positive effect on all children. Gilespie's work on special needs in history can be found on the History Initial Teacher Training (HITT) website (www.historyitt.org.uk/).

Hilary Claire (1996, 2001, 2004a) has written extensively on issues of equality, inclusion and diversity. She sees these issues as of central importance in the education of the young child. Her research into issues such as equality and inclusion in history shows how the curriculum need not marginalise women, minority groups or those with disabilities. She suggests further reading and a wide range of resources to assist you in planning for an inclusive curriculum.

A SUMMARY OF **KEY POINTS**

> It is important to consider barriers to learning for children with SEN and find ways of overcoming these.

> You will need to differentiate work to suit different learning styles.

> There are many types of special need. It is important to find out about the needs of children with different types of special educational need and consider strategies for meeting these needs.

> You can devise positive strategies in history to ensure the inclusion of children from disadvantaged backgrounds.

> It is important to ensure equality of opportunity for boys and girls through equal access to the curriculum and to resources.

> Issues of gender, class and race are important considerations when developing an inclusive classroom and curriculum.

> You will need to do some research into English as an Additional Language (EAL) if you are not familiar with the subject.

> Multicultural classrooms provide a rich resource for teaching and learning.

MOVING *ON* > > > **> > >** MOVING *ON* > > > **> > >** MOVING *ON*

Standard 118, Standard 119, Standard 120, Standard 121

Carry out an audit of your history curriculum and identify the opportunities to make it more culturally inclusive. Locate resources and plan activities which will broaden the history curriculum in your classroom. If you coordinate history across the school, carry out this activity for the whole school curriculum.

FURTHER READING FURTHER READING **FURTHER READING** FURTHER READING

George, D (1999) *Gifted education: identification and provision.* London: Fulton.

Gravelle, M (1996) *Supporting bilingual children in schools.* Stoke-on-Trent: Trentham Books.

Rutter, J (2000) *Refugee children in the classroom: a handbook for teachers.* Stoke-on-Trent: Trentham.

Useful websites

www.bbcactive.com/schoolshop

The website of BBC Active, containing information about recent resources on black history.

www.historyitt.org.uk/

Website of the History in Initial Teacher Education Project.

www.nagty.ac.uk/

Website of the National Academy for Gifted and Talented Youth.

www.nationalarchives.gov.uk/pathways/blackhistory/

This site has resources for black and multicultural history.

www.qca.org.uk/qca_12071.aspx

This web page gives details of a bibliography produced by the QCA on teaching about multi-ethnic histories suitable for Key Stage 2.

www.standards.dfes.gov.uk/primary/publications/inclusion/newarrivals/
www.schoolsweb.gov.uk/locate/pupilsupport/eal/
www.literacytrust.org.uk/Database/EALindex
www.literacytrust.org.uk/Database/EALres.html
www.teachers.tv/video/

These websites provide information on methods and resources for supporting children learning EAL.

www.schoolhistory.co.uk/forum/

This website is for teachers to share tips and advice on teaching history to children with SEN.

13
Contexts for out-of-school learning in history

Chapter objectives

By the end of this chapter you will have:

- considered a broad view of what constitutes out-of-school learning, to include school visits and incidental learning at home and homework;
- been introduced to a rationale for out-of-school learning;
- considered the organisation of out-of-school learning, including safety, risk assessment and liaising with other professionals;
- considered the wide range of contexts and opportunities for out-of-school learning;
- thought about catering for children with SEN and EAL on field trips and visits;
- been introduced to the idea of extended schools;
- thought about planning homework based on history;
- considered the variety of incidental experiences from which children learn about history.

Professional Standards for QTS

This chapter will support you as you work towards evidencing attainment against the following Standards:

Q30: ... identify opportunities for learners to learn in out-of-school contexts.

Q24: Plan homework or other out-of-class work to sustain learners' progress and to extend and consolidate their learning.

What does out-of-school learning include?

Infants and young children are active learners from birth, rapidly absorbing information from their surroundings. Out-of-school learning therefore builds on this prior learning and also helps them relate their school work to real-life experience. Planned activities include day trips, residential visits and homework. Outside learning experiences involve contexts ranging from the school playground to distant localities. The school grounds offer a wealth of opportunities; buildings can be studied for types of materials and design elements that help us to place the building in its historical context. Follow-up work can incorporate earlier photographs, prints, maps and plans to extend the study out into the locality. Beyond the school, children can learn about houses, shops, work places, parks, and historic buildings. Taking children out of the classroom helps to develop a range of skills, such as close observation, making inferences and decision making as well as skills in engaging in group work. The increased sensory experiences available to them help all kinds of learners, including those with special needs or English as an additional language, to remember and learn from the out-of-school context. Children learn from television, film and drama, literature, art, music and visits to museums and places of historical interest as well as when participating in organised activities.

Why plan out-of-school experiences?

Learning outside the classroom is part of the National Curriculum:

> *Pupils should be taught how to find out about the past from a range of sources of information . . . historic buildings and visits to museums, galleries and sites . . .*
>
> (DfEE/QCA, 1999a, p104/105)

The Professional Standards also require teachers to engage children in this kind of learning. History benefits greatly from the use of fieldwork as a teaching strategy. It provides a wide range of learning contexts, such as historic sites, stately homes, castles, museums, industrial sites and local town or village centres. Children learn with enjoyment from their experiences out in the environment, and the resources it offers are often very rich. The management of school outings is critically important however. Parental permission must first be obtained in writing, both to inform the parents and to meet insurance requirements. The safety of the children is paramount. Adequate support from other adults is important to ensure a low child to teacher ratio; higher quality learning takes place in small group activities with adult support. Clarity in your aims and objectives for the visit will ensure a more enjoyable experience, while risk assessment and pre-visits by the teacher are key aspects of planning and preparation. You can plan activities to help children question and understand their surroundings further and in a more structured way.

A major decision in planning history fieldwork is how much direction you wish to give in relation to the amount of freedom of choice allowed for the children. For example, many museums and galleries produce packs of worksheets, such as the 'I spy' variety, where children find different display items and perhaps answer a few questions or complete a few cloze procedure sentences. As teacher, you will need to decide whether this is the most productive way of using the children's time while they are on their visit.

You may, instead, wish to plan a route around the site yourself, stopping and discussing points of interest with the children. This provides opportunities to ask and answer questions and for children to choose their own objects of interest. It also opens up endless possibilities for variety in the method chosen for recording these observations: digital cameras; sketches, drawings or paintings; rubbings or prints; notes; or audio recordings. Very young children, or children who do not have good writing skills, might be supported by an adult helper who could make notes or write sentences and descriptive passages for them by scribing what they want to say. Helpers could assist with photography, sketching or taking rubbings of interesting features. (It is important to note that for activities such as making rubbings, such as brass rubbings in a church, permission may be required.) Alternatively, you may decide to guide the children around the site to introduce and explain it to them, and allow them to select a section which they find interesting.

Organising an historical field trip in the locality

The well-organised history coordinator will have included in the subject handbook the necessary arrangements for planning a trip. However, it is worth bearing in mind the following points when planning a local study:

- be clear about your objectives for the trip;
- make a visit to the site yourself in advance;
- draw up a risk assessment (there may be one available in your school);
- write a letter to parents and make sure that there is time for replies to be returned;
- plan activities for the children;
- design resources and prepare any necessary materials;
- prepare the additional adults with guidance, a pre-visit or information about the route;
- prepare the children by making practical arrangements for their clothing and their behaviour while out of school. Provide them with resources, such as maps to look at or clip boards.

CLASSROOM STORY

Catherine had planned a visit to a reconstruction of a Roman fort with her Year 4 class. The fort was situated at Murton Park, just outside York. The day was spent in role, with the children being new recruits to the fort. Activities involved finding out about life in the fort, drill training, working in the stores and learning about the daily routine of a Roman soldier. The new recruits were also addressed by the centurion during the day. While on the visit, Catherine discovered that Murton Park also provides Viking days and Second World War experiences.

Figure 34. Roman site visit (Year 4)

Risk assessment

Safety is the most important aspect of any planning involving a visit outside school. Field trips and site visits can be hazardous, since the management of children is different once they are out of the classroom and different issues arise. The number and type of hazards rises once children are out of the classroom. The major risk on school outings is traffic, especially on a local study outing to a town or city centre. Other risks can include slippery or uneven pathways, walking near waterways, obstacles such as roadworks or footpath repairs, and danger of falling from heights or tripping. Castles and archaeological sites in particular can pose serious dangers to young children. There are sometimes great heights, with little protection from falling; narrow, winding stairs in towers; the danger of falling into deep water in wells or moats; jagged stonework; and uneven walking areas.

Many of these risks can be minimised by ensuring that children wear suitable clothing, such as trainers or shoes with a good grip, long-sleeved waterproof clothes and warm clothing when necessary; by ensuring that children listen carefully to instructions about crossing roads; and by planning what is said to children before they leave their coach, and the method of lining up. Risk assessment, therefore is of vital importance on history field trips, along with careful planning and the support of additional adults.

First-aid equipment is needed, along with clear outline plans and instructions for other adults accompanying the class. For children in the early years, one adult to two or three children would be advisable, while for children in Key Stages 1 and 2, an adult for each small group of four or six children is best. It is always a good idea for accompanying adults to wear bright clothing, since this helps children to locate you, and for traffic to see you in advance. Clear written guidance for helpers is very important, and if possible a meeting with them before-hand to ensure they are all clear about their role and responsibilities. A pre-visit to the site is always advisable, since it is a requirement that you draw up a risk assessment. You will need to be aware of any special needs or requirements of individuals and make sure that these will be suitably catered for during the outing.

Advice on risk assessment and planning trips can be obtained from your local education authority, teaching unions and the Department for Children, Schools and Families (DSCF) (www.dfes.gov.uk/childrenandfamilies).

Liaising with other professionals

Once you have arrived, there are often others available to provide support. However, it is necessary to confirm this in advance. Museums will have an education officer with knowledge of the collections your class is visiting. These professionals can greatly enhance children's learning while at a museum with their extensive specialist knowledge and also with their enthusiasm for the subject. They will have the skills to introduce children to a wide range of resources, such as artefacts, to motivate the children and provide a good learning experience for you too. At historical sites there is often a field officer or ranger with specialist knowledge of the site.

Risk Assessment Sheet

School: ....

Class: ....

Teacher: ....

Other adults: ....

....

....

....

....

1) HAZARDS	
2) PERSONS AT RISK	
3) RISK CONTROL METHODS	
4) ACTION TO BE TAKEN BY	
5) FURTHER ACTION REQUIRED	
6) CLOTHING, EQUIPMENT, MEDICATION OR OTHER SPECIAL REQUIREMENTS FOR CHILDREN WITH SEN OR EAL	

NAME AND TITLE OF ASSESSOR	SIGNATURE	DATE
SIGNATURE OF HEAD TEACHER		DATE

Figure 35. Risk assessment sheet

REFLECTIVE TASK
REFLECTIVE TASK

Look at the sample risk assessment sheet on page 149 and consider whether you feel it is sufficiently detailed to cover all possible eventualities. Make amendments as you think appropriate.

PRACTICAL TASK PRACTICAL TASK PRACTICAL TASK PRACTICAL TASK PRACTICAL TASK

Walk from your school for 15 minutes. On your return journey make a note of possible risks. For each risk plan how you would minimise the risk. Use the risk sheet above to record your findings and action.

Out-of-school contexts for history

Out-of-school contexts for teaching and learning in history include historic buildings, such as castles, palaces, churches, cathedrals, stately homes, and the homes and workplaces of ordinary people in the past. There are also museums, galleries, archaelogical sites, libraries and archive collections, such as local record offices. In addition, there is an increasing number of 'reconstructions'. These are places which have either been restored or converted into a place where life in the past can be experienced. They include places such as the Black Country Living Museum (www.bclm.co.uk/) or the Back-to-Backs (www.birminghamheritage.org.uk/back2back.htm), a reconstructed nineteenth-century street in Birmingham. There are several very useful guides to aspects of local history, such as the 'teacher's guides' produced by English Heritage (Alderton, 1995; Copeland, 1994; Corbishley and Watson, 1997; Durbin, 1993; Purkis, 1993a, 1995).

Further examples of the kinds of work that can be undertaken in history can be found in *Teaching humanities in primary schools* (Hoodless, 2003b), where chapter 10 includes examples of out-of-school activities. Catling (2006), Halewood (2000), Hasted (2007), Knights (2005), Lomas (2002), Starkey (2002), Whitworth (2006), Valerio (2005) and Vass (2005a) have all written informative short articles on different aspects of work on local history.

CLASSROOM STORY

A Year 3 class was engaged in a local history study unit investigating how their cathedral had changed over time, with a focus on chronology. A fieldwork activity was planned in the cathedral, where the children were to study different areas inside the building, selected in advance by their teacher. She had decided to plan the children's activities very precisely, to ensure that they were well occupied and well behaved in such an important location, and to create a usable timeline from the children's work. Before the visit, permission had been arranged through the Dean. Children were carefully briefed about the visit, including instructions on safety and appropriate behaviour in the cathedral. In the previous lesson, the children's fieldwork tasks were discussed including:

- recording written information about the things they would see in the cathedral;
- noting when each part of the cathedral was built and how far particular features date back.

Several parents and two classroom assistants had agreed to help with the visit. This allowed children to be divided into small groups of six, each with their own adult helper. A short briefing sheet was prepared for adult helpers, who met in advance of the visit to confirm the arrangements. For the visit the children were equipped with notebooks and a simple task sheet, where they were asked to 'spy' particular features and write a few words about them. They then chose their favourite item to draw at the end of the sheet. The pictures would then be cut out to make a large timeline of the cathedral as follow-up work in school.

At the cathedral, the children enthusiastically looked around before being taken by their group helper to their own section for more detailed study. Here they made both written and visual records. The children worked surprisingly independently, since the cathedral was a very supportive environment with plenty of information available, a very calming atmosphere conducive to study, and plenty of places for them to sit and work either independently, or in groups. The teacher was pleasantly surprised at how this atmosphere promoted the children's self-discipline and enthusiasm in their work.

PRACTICAL TASK PRACTICAL TASK **PRACTICAL TASK** PRACTICAL TASK **PRACTICAL TASK**

Visit a place of interest in your own locality, such as a church or cathedral. Study the features of the building and its interior, including special exhibits, furnishings, pictures and windows. Consider the organisation of your time in the building and what you would make your priorities for study. Plan the visit, keeping activities interesting and well focused.

Catering for children with SEN and EAL on field trips and visits

The particular needs of children with SEN must be addressed during visits, in order to overcome barriers to learning. Teachers will take account of a disability, or children's progress in learning English as an additional language by making provision where necessary to enable them to participate effectively. Children with visual or multisensory impairment or mobility difficulties will need support from teachers and other adults to help them observe and gain understanding about historical features and the environment. Description of places and features of interest, along with the use of appropriate hearing equipment or other technological support, will be important in these outside learning environments. Making use of expert support will also be invaluable.

Extended schools

According to the National Foundation for Educational Research (NFER):

> *Out of school learning (OSL) refers to any school-linked activity that takes place outside normal school hours – that is, outside school time reserved for compulsory curricular education. As such, OSL activities can take place before school starts in the morning, during lunch breaks, after school, at weekends or in the school holidays. A central feature of OSL is that participation is voluntary.*
>
> (www.nfer.ac.uk/research-areas/out-of-school-learning/)

Features of this type of out-of-school learning which might contribute to children's learning in history could include:

- homework and homework clubs;
- study clubs – extending curriculum;
- particular interests – such as archaeology;
- family learning – parents and other family members learning with their children;
- residential activities – study weeks or weekends.

An extended school is a key means of delivering the Every Child Matters agenda (DfES, 2004c). An extended school works with the local authority and other schools to provide access to a varied range of activities including study support, sport and music clubs and childcare in primary schools. There is evidence that extended services can help to improve children's attainment, self-confidence, motivation and attendance and a school's success in this area is now included in Ofsted reports. Evaluations of extended schools in Britain in recent years have shown that these services can have positive effects on children and families, effects that can also benefit schools and improve children's attainment. Ofsted has found that these extended services have enhanced self-confidence, raised children's attainment and improved attitudes towards learning (Ofsted, 2006). Extended schools services can help remove barriers to learning and give support to children with problems outside their academic work. The Government has provided additional funding for schools to support personalised learning both during and after the normal school day, with the aim of providing support especially for children from disadvantaged areas.

In history, extended schools provide opportunities to learn beyond the classroom in many ways, such as the potential to organise short visits after school to sites of interest in the local area or to investigate historical features around the school and its grounds. The focus on developing core skills and study skills for children from disadvantaged backgrounds will help children raise their attainment and motivation in subjects such as history, where study skills are fundamental.

Residential activities

There are large numbers of residential centres across the UK which include opportunities for work in history. Alongside new and exciting learning activities, the experience of a residential trip has personal and social value. Children can learn to be independent in a safe environment, thus building their self-esteem. They can also learn to interact with their peers and with adults on a more personal level, acquiring important social skills along the way. A search on the internet will quickly enable you to find your nearest centre. Alternatively, a visit to your local library, local teachers' centre, or local authority website will produce useful information about educational residential centres; see, for example, www.devon.gov.uk/devondiscovery.htm. Activity and action centres are also widely available, with experienced organisation and leadership provided by charity organisations such as www.actioncentres.co.uk.

Archaeology

There are many clubs and organisations across the country for children with an interest in archaeology. There is a national Young Archaeologist's Club (www.britarch.ac.uk) which has many local branches. These clubs are for children and young people up to the age of 18 and they run many exciting visits and residential 'digs'. These holidays allow children to meet people with similar interests, as well as providing great new learning experiences. Nicky Milsted (2006) provides an informative description of what archaeology really is, namely, *the use of physical evidence of human activity to try to understand the past, and to understand human culture.* There are also ideas and activities for the classroom, and information about the Young Archaeologist of the Year Award. The journal *Primary History* also has frequent articles and information about archaeology and the Young Archaeologist's Club (YAC).

Planning homework

While most schools regularly set homework for literacy and numeracy, it can also be beneficial for children's learning and their attitude towards learning to set them homework tasks in history. The quality of learning that can take place at home, as well as the personalised learning that is facilitated, can enhance children's progress, in terms of wider understanding, linking learning to real-life contexts, and improved motivation to learn using the knowledge and support of adults at home.

Some children may not have access to the same resources as others, or may not have a suitable place to work. Therefore it is sometimes useful to give tasks which may be simpler to achieve, with support in the form of pre-prepared outlines for the children to complete. Other children may be fortunate in having good support at home, and more open-ended enquiry tasks might be more effective here. Sensitivity and care is needed in the setting of homework tasks, to ensure that they can be effectively completed and to avoid frustration and failure.

Developing work started in a lesson

Overall medium-term planning and lesson plans should include reference to homework. This needs to be carefully structured and sequenced in the same way as the lessons themselves to ensure continuity of learning and progression in understanding and the development of skills. Sending work home can take many forms. One teacher decided that she could develop her children's understanding of time and chronology by asking them to complete their work at home (see the Classroom Story below).

CLASSROOM STORY

Janice was working with her Year 2 class who were creating personal timelines. She wanted the children to extend their understanding of chronology beyond the notion of time passing over a day or week to that of their whole lifetime. She had drawn up a simple structure for the timeline, based on the idea of a folding booklet. She used a shared writing lesson to create the first page, about the birth of the child. She gave the children their birthdates from her class register and they composed a sentence together.

She then sent the timelines home for completion. She included a note to the parents and carers of the children explaining that they would need to sit with their child and talk about the things that had happened to them when they were younger, selecting one key event for each year. They were encouraged to use family photos to help complete the visual images on the timeline.

Janice gave the class a week before they needed to bring back their timelines. The children were full of enthusiasm, having spent time talking at home about their lives. The timelines themselves were a source of enjoyment for the rest of that half term.

Incidental learning out of school

Most children learn about history in an incidental way as well as through structured teaching in school.

TV, broadcasts, costume drama, films

Films, dramas and television broadcasts often have an historical theme or context. Even if the content is fictitious the background, period and costume are usually from the past and many children and trainees refer to such experience as a factor in what they know about the past. These visual stimuli help children and young people build up their own picture and concept of different times in the past. These are very often stereotypical, but they do help begin the process of developing historical awareness in the minds of the young. Many, however, are very accurately researched, such as the BBC 'costume dramas', and children can absorb accurate notions of what it was like in the past.

Reading story books and fiction

Story books and fiction frequently use a historical context. They are also an excellent medium for the development of children's chronological understanding. Many picture books and fictional stories use time and chronology in different ways, a technique which can be used to teach in greater depth and detail about this very complex concept. For example, flashbacks, ellipses (condensing time), parallel time, omissions of periods of time producing 'jumps' in time, and flash forwards are used to allow authors to 'play with time'. These devices are commonly used in time travel stories, and if they are discussed thoughtfully with the child reader, a deep understanding of the nature of time in narrative can be achieved (Hoodless, 2002).

Family learning: visits to sites with families

Any visit to a museum or place of interest, particularly at weekends, shows how popular this is with people of all ages, but particularly with parents who are keen to develop their children's learning. This, and all other kinds of incidental learning within the family, are sources of knowledge and information which can be used effectively in the classroom, both through sharing of experiences with the class, or through the encouragement of individual work, in the form of project books or computer-based resources.

RESEARCH SUMMARY RESEARCH SUMMARY **RESEARCH SUMMARY** RESEARCH SUMMARY

Out-of-school learning has always been a major part of the National Curriculum for history. The NFER has carried out research into issues surrounding this type of learning, identifying a number of barriers to its inclusion in school curricula, such as time and cost considerations; fears about children being injured and schools/teachers facing legal action; bureaucracy; low awareness of the benefits and the opportunities available; and a lack of confidence and training for teachers (www.nfer.ac.uk/research). Despite these concerns, the local area and environment are a major source for historical enquiry. Purkis (1993b) has written extensively on the subject, arguing that answering questions and examining buildings in the local area, such as looking at the materials they are made from, the building styles and so on, will encourage children to look more closely, to be more aware of their surroundings and learn from them. As she points out, they are an endless and incredibly useful source for studying the past.

English Heritage is one of the leading organisations which manages historic sites. It has an extensive education service and aims to *help teachers and those involved in education at all levels to use the historic environment as a resource, right across the curriculum* (www.english-heritage.org.uk/). It has begun to work on an exciting new range of 'discovery visits' (Whitworth, 2006). It is also a major partner in the new government initiative aimed at encouraging further use of the environment as a learning resource:

> *The Learning Outside the Classroom Manifesto partnership was launched by the Secretary of State for Education and Skills on 28th November 2006... Its aim is to ensure that all young people have a variety of high quality learning experiences outside the classroom environment.*
>
> (www.english-heritage.org.uk/)

National Trust out-of-classroom learning is gaining momentum and is benefiting from an increasingly higher profile. The National Trust recently commissioned its own research in this area (www.national trust.org.uk/).

Research in the United States has found that structured programmes for out-of-school learning have bene-fited children from poorer backgrounds more than those from more affluent families (www.standards.dfes.gov.uk/research/). These disadvantaged children have responded well in terms of attendance, motivation and enthusiasm, while those from better-off families had sufficient activities based at home that they did not need the programmes to the same extent.

A SUMMARY OF **KEY POINTS**

> Out-of-school learning takes place either as part of the planned curriculum for history, as part of independently organised activities or as part of family or personal individual interest.

> Safety is a crucially important consideration in OSL. The help of additional adults needs to be enlisted and risk assessment must be undertaken prior to any planned out of school learning.

> Professionals on site with specialist knowledge and skills should be consulted prior to a visit.

> Preparation and planning need to be detailed for all out-of-school learning. This needs to include a pre-visit. Survey any locality where you are teaching for places of interest and potential educational value.

> Contexts for OSL in history are many and varied and include residential visits and special interests such as archaeology.

> Special provision must be made for children with SEN or EAL on a planned out-of-school activity.

> Homework and incidental learning with family or friends can contribute to children's learning about the past.

MOVING *ON* > > > > > > MOVING *ON* > > > > > > MOVING *ON*

Standard I28, Standard I37(c)

If you are a teacher in your induction year, you might find it useful to talk to other teachers and your history coordinator about how they incorporate personalised learning into their planning. Make notes and consider how you might make use of some of their strategies in your own teaching.

If you are the history coordinator for your school it might be helpful to make out-of-school learning and personalised learning the topic for one of your staff meetings. Since this is now one of the factors in determining teachers' progress within the profession, discussion and sharing of ideas on these subjects would be beneficial for the whole staff.

FURTHER READING FURTHER READING **FURTHER READING** FURTHER READING

Andrews, K (2001) *Extra learning: out of school learning and study support in practice.* London: Routledge Falmer.

Malkin, A (2000) Homework – the way forward. *Primary Practice*, 25: 8–14.

Sharp, C, Keys, W and Benefield, P (2001) *Homework: a review of recent research.* Slough: NFER.

Primary History (2003) *Learning through museums and galleries.* Issue 35. London: Historical Association.

Useful websites

www.birminghamheritage.org.uk/back2back.htm

> Website for the 'Back-to-backs' in Birmingham, a courtyard of back-to-back houses, now owned by the National Trust.

www.bclm.co.uk/

> Website of the Black Country Living Museum.

www.devon.gov.uk/devondiscovery.htm

www.actioncentres.co.uk

> Examples of websites about residential visits.

www.dfes.gov.uk/childrenandfamilies

> Website of the Department for Schools, Children and Families.

www.everychildmatters.gov.uk/

> The website for *Every Child Matters*.

www.english-heritage.org.uk/server/show/nav.1571

> Website for English Heritage's education pages. English Heritage provide free publications, which includes resources and information sheets for teachers. Many of their other publications for teachers are excellent and some are listed in the references section below. There is a section on learning outside the classroom on their education website.

www.nationaltrust.org.uk

www.ntseducation.org.uk/pupils

> The National Trust provides resources for education.

www.nfer.ac.uk/

> Website of the National Foundation for Educational Research (NFER).

www.nfer.ac.uk/research-areas/out-of-school-learning/

> NFER pages on out-of-school learning.

www.standards.dfes.gov.uk/research/

> Useful website for an overview of government research.

www.teachernet.gov.uk/wholeschool/extendedschools/

> This website gives further information on extended schools.

www.britarch.ac.uk

> Website of the Council for British Archaeology.

References

Alderton, D (1995) *A teacher's guide to using industrial sites.* English Heritage.

Alexander R, Rose, AJ and Woodhead, C (1992) *Curriculum organisation and classroom practice in primary schools. A discussion paper.* (The three wise men report) London: DES.

Ashby, R, Lee, PJ and Dickinson, AK (2002) 'Progression in children's ideas about history', in Hughes, M (ed) *Progression in learning* (BERA Dialogue), Clevedon: Bristol PA, and Adelaide: Multilingual Matters.

Bage, G (1999) *Narrative matters: teaching and learning history through story.* London: Falmer.

Bage, G (2000) *Thinking history.* London: Routledge-Falmer.

Barton, KC and Levstik, LS (1996) "Back when God was around and everything": Children's understanding of historical time, *American Educational Research Journal*, 33 (22): 419–454.

Barton, KC (2004) Helping students make sense of historical time. *Primary History*, 37: 13–14.

Barton, K, McCully, A and Marks, M (2004) Reflecting on elementary children's understanding of history and social studies, *Journal of Teacher Education*, 55 (1): 70–90.

Beetlestone, F (1998) *Creative children, imaginative teaching.* Buckingham: Open University Press.

Blyth, J and Hughes, P (1997) *Using written sources in primary history.* London: Hodder & Stoughton.

Blyth, J (1998) Life in Tudor times; the use of written sources. Chapter 9 in Hoodless, P (ed) (1998) *History and English in the primary school.* London: Routledge.

Blyth, WAL et al. (1976) *Curriculum planning in history, geography and social sciences.* Bristol: Schools Council Publications.

Blyth, WAL (1990) *Making the grade for primary humanities.* Milton Keynes, Open University Press.

Board of Education (1921) *The Teaching of English in England* (The Newbolt Report). London: HMSO.

Bowen, P (2001) English canal-boat children and the education issue 1900–1940: towards a concept of traveller education? *History of Education,* 30 (4), 359–378.

Brown, M and Harrison, D (1998) Children's voices from different times and places, in Holden, C and Clough, N (eds), *Children as citizens. Education for participation.* London and Philadelphia: Kingsley.

Bruner, JS (1974) *Beyond the information given: studies in the psychology of knowing.* London: Allen and Unwin.

Bruner, JS (1977) *The process of education* (new edition). Harvard: Harvard University Press.

Bruner, JS (1990) *Making sense: the child's construction of the world.* London and New York: Routledge.

Catling, S (2006) Geography and history: exploring the local connection, *Primary History*, 42: 14–16.

Claire, H (1996) *Reclaiming our pasts: equality and diversity in the primary the history curriculum.* Stoke: Trentham Books.

Claire, H (2001) *Not aliens: primary school shildren and citizenship/PHSE curriculum.* Stoke: Trentham Books.

Claire, H (2004a) *Teaching citizenship in primary schools*. Exeter: Learning Matters.

Claire, H (2004b) Oral history: a powerful tool or a double edged sword? *Primary History*, 38: 20–23.

Claire, H (2005) Learning and teaching about citizenship through history in the primary years, in *Leading primary history*. London: Historical Association.

Claire, H (2006) How should we remember Rosa Parks? *Primary History,* 43: 18–20.

Claire, H and Lewis, B (2004) Using the web constructively and imaginatively to learn about Britain since the 30s, *Primary History*, 36: 16–18.

Clere, L (2005) *The little book of bags, boxes and trays.* Lutterworth: Featherstone Education.

Coltham, JB and Fines, J (1971) *Educational objectives for the study of history: a suggested framework*. London: Historical Association.

Cooper, H (1991) Young children's thinking in history. Unpub PhD thesis. University of London.

Cooper, H (2000) *The teaching of history in primary schools. Implementing the revised National Curriculum* (3rd edn). London: Fulton.

Cooper, H (2007a) *History 3–11: a guide for teachers*. London: Fulton.

Cooper, H (2007b) Thinking through history: story and developing children's minds. *Primary History*, 45: 26–29.

Cooper, H (2007c) Thinking through history: assessment and learning for the gifted young historian. *Primary History*, 47: 36–38.

Copeland, T (1994) *A teacher's guide to using castles*. English Heritage.

Corbishley, M and Watson, I (1997) *Using Roman sites: a teacher's guide*. English Heritage.

DCSF (2008) *The Early Years Foundation Stage*. London: DCSF.

Deary, T (1994) *The rotten Romans* (horrible Histories series). London: Scholastic. (Some books in this series are now available from the BBC as audiobooks.)

Department for Children, Schools and Families (DCSF) (2007) *The children's plan: building brighter futures*. London: DCSF.

Department of Education and Science (DES) (1975) *A language for life* (The Bullock Report). London: HMSO.

DES (1991) *History in the National Curriculum (England)*. London: HMSO.

DfEE/QCA (1998) *A scheme of work for Key Stages 1 and 2: History*. London: QCA.

DfEE/QCA (1999a) *History: the National Curriculum for England*. London. HMSO.

DfEE/QCA (1999b) *The National Curriculum: handbook for primary teachers in England: Key Stages 1 and 2* (including the National Curriculum attainment targets). London. DfEE.

DfEE/QCA (2000) *Curriculum guidance for the Foundation Stage*. London: QCA.

DfES (2003a) *Every child matters*. London: DfES.

DfES (2003b) *Excellence and enjoyment: a strategy for primary schools*. London: DfES.

DfES (2003c) *National Standards for under 8s daycare and childminding*. London: DfES.

DfES (2004a) *Effective provision of pre-school education: Final report*. London: DfES.

DfES (2004b) *Every child matters: the next steps*. London: DfES.

DfES (2004c) *Every child matters: change for children*. London: DfES.

DfES (2006) *Primary framework for literacy and mathematics*. London: DfES.

DfES (2007) *Early Years Foundation Stage materials: booklets, poster and cards*. London: DfES.

DfES/MMU (2002) *Birth to three matters: a framework to support children in their earliest years*. London: DfES.

Donaldson, M (1978) *Children's minds*. London: Fontana.

Dresser, M (2002) Bristol and the slave trade: a virtual slavery trail for school children and their teachers. *Primary History*, 32: 32–36.

Duffy, B (1998) *Supporting creativity and imagination in the early years*. Buckingham: Open University Press.

Durbin, G (1993) *A teacher's guide to using historic houses*. English Heritage.

Durbin G, Morris S and Wilkinson S (1990) *A teacher's guide to learning from objects*. London: English Heritage.

English Heritage (1998) *Story telling at historic sites*. Northampton: English Heritage.

Equiano, O (1789/1995) *The interesting narrative and other writings*. New York: Penguin. (The autobiography of Olaudah Equiano, a slave from Benin, who earned his freedom.)

Falck, I (2006) ''Wolfgang's story'': an innovative Year 6 history lesson, coming soon on the small screen via Teachers TV, *Primary History*, 43: 21–22.

Fewster, S (2005) Using a whiteboard, *Primary History*, 39: 8–20.

Fines, J and Nichol, J (1997) *The Nuffield history project: teaching primary history*. London:

Heinemann.

Fisher, M (2005) *Britain's best museums and galleries: from the greatest collections to the smallest curiosities*. London: Penguin.

Fox, A and Gardiner, M (1997) The arts and raising achievement. Paper presented to Arts in the Curriculum Conference. London.

Freeman, J (2002) The education of the most able pupils: A creative future, *Education Review,* 15: 2.

Fuerstein, R et al (1980) *Instrumental enrichment: an intervention program for cognitive modifiability*. Baltimore. Md: University Park Press.

Galton, M (1998) *Inside the primary classroom: twenty years on*. London: Routledge Falmer.

Galton, M, Simon, B and Croll, P (1980) *Inside the primary classroom.* London: Routledge.

Galton, M and Williamson, J (1992) *Group work in education*. London: Routledge.

Gardner, H (1993) *Frames of mind: the theory of multiple intelligences.* London: Fontana Press.

Gardner, H (2006) *Multiple intelligences: new horizons in theory and practice.* New York: Basic Books.

Halewood, J (2000) A treasure trove of local history – how to use your local record office. *Primary History*, 24: 10–11.

Harnett, P (1993) Identifying progression in children's understanding: the use of visual materials to assess primary school children's learning in history, *Cambridge Journal of Education,* 23, 2: 137–154.

Harnett, P (1998) Children working with pictures. Chapter 5 in Hoodless, P (ed.), *History and English in the primary school.* London: Routledge.

Harnett, P (2005) Polly put the kettle on: using nursery rhyme to develop children's knowledge and understanding of the past, *Primary History,* 41: 34–35.

Hasted, N (2007) Case study 5: local history – a pupil-led study with 9–10-year-olds. *Primary History,* 47: 32–34.

Hibbert, C (2000) *Queen Victoria in her letters and journals.* Stroud: Sutton.

Historical Association (2005) The power of a good story: history and literacy, *Primary* History, 41.

Historical Association (2006) Time and time again, *Primary History*, 43.

Historical Association (2007) Thinking through history: opportunity for equality, *Primary History*, 47.

Historical Association (2008) History, drama and the classroom, *Primary History*, 48.

Hodkinson, A (1995) Historical time and the National Curriculum, *Teaching History*, 79: 18–20.

Hodkinson, A (2001) Enhancing temporal cognition in the primary school, *Primary History*, 28: 11–14.

Hodkinson, A (2002) A coordinator answers: the development of chronological understanding in primary history, *Primary History,* 31: 8–9.

Hoodless, P (1988) Primary school children's use of language in problem-solving. M.Ed dissertation, University of Liverpool.

Hoodless, P (1994a) Language use and problem solving in primary history, *Teaching History*, 76: 19–22.

Hoodless, P (1994b) A Victorian case study: simulating aspects of Victorian life in the classroom, *Primary History*, 7: 14–16.

Hoodless, P (1996a) *Time and timelines in the primary school*. London: Historical Association, Teaching of History Series, TH 69.

Hoodless, P (1996b) Children talking about the past, in Hall, N and Martello, J (eds) *Listening to children think*. London: Hodder and Stoughton.

Hoodless, P (ed.) (1998a) *History and English in the primary school: exploiting the links.* London. Routledge.

Hoodless, P (1998b) Children's awareness of time in story and historical fiction, in Hoodless, P (ed) *History and English in the primary school.* London: Routledge.

Hoodless, P (2001) *Teaching with text.* Leamington Spa: Scholastic.

Hoodless, P (2002) An investigation into primary school children's developing awareness of time and chronology in story and historical fiction, *Journal of Curriculum Studies*, 34: 2, 173–200.

Hoodless, P (2003a) *Ready resources, Key Stage One and Key Stage Two. Books 1–8*. Leamington Spa: Scholastic.

Hoodless, P (ed.) (2003b) *Teaching humanities in primary schools*. Exeter: Learning Matters.

Hoodless, P (2006) Materiality and ideology in children's perceptions of past historical writing. *The Curriculum Journal,* 17(4): 335–350.

Husbands, C (1996) *What is history teaching? Language, ideas and meaning in learning about the past.* Buckingham: Open University Press.

Inhelder, J and Piaget, B (1958) *The growth of logical thinking from childhood to adolescence*. London: Routledge and Kegan Paul.

Jahoda, G (1963) Children's concepts of time and history, *Educational Review*, 15: 87–104.

Jarvis, M (2003) *Using ICT in primary humanities teaching*. Exeter: Learning Matters.

Jarvis, P and Parker, S (eds) (2005) *Human learning: an holistic approach.* London: Routledge.

Jenkins, K (1995) *On 'What is history?'* London and New York: Routledge.

Jenkins, K (2003) *Rethinking history*. (2nd edn) London and New York: Routledge.

Johnson, P (1998) *A book of one's own*. London: Hodder Arnold H&S.

Kirkland, S and Wykes, M (2003) Grace O'Malley, alias Granuaile, pirate and politician, c. 1530–1603, *Primary History,* 34: 34–35.

Knights, R (2005) Developing a local history project based on a local industry, *Primary History,* 39: 32–33.

Kyriacou, C (1998) *Essential teaching skills.* Cheltenham: Nelson Thornes.

Lawrie, J (1998) Sevington school – a unique history resource, *Primary History*, 19: 19.

Lee, PJ (1992) "A lot of guesswork goes on": children's understanding of historical accounts. *Teaching History*, 29–36.

Levstik, LS and Pappas, C (1987) Exploring the development of historical understanding. *Journal of Research and Development in Education*, 21: 1–15.

Lewis, L and Coxall, H (2001) Ways of making Key Stage 2 history culturally inclusive, *Primary History*, 29: 11–13.

Lomas, T (2002) How do we ensure really good local history in primary schools?, *Primary History,* 30: 4–6.

Lomas, T, Burke, C, Cordingly, D and McKenzie, K (1996) *Planning primary history*. London: Murray.

Lunn, P and Bishop, A (2004) Teaching history through the use of story: working with early years practitioners, *Primary History*, 37: 30–31.

Martin, A, Smart, L and Yeomans, D (1997) *Information technology and the teaching of history*. London: Routledge.

Martin, H (1996) An active approach to ancient history: the Greeks, *Primary History*, 14: 15–17.

Marwick, A (2001) *The new nature of history: knowledge, evidence, language.* London: Palgrave.

Mason, I (1999) Learning through lists: the example of Richard Aldworth, *Primary History*, 21: 22–24.

McNaughton, AH (1966) Piaget's theory and primary school social studies, *Educational Review*, 19 (1): 24–32.

Miller, C (1998) Pythagoras and number, *Primary History*, 20: 10.

Miller, C (1999a) Mathematics from history, *Primary History*, 21: 10.

Miller, C (1999b) The magic of maths, *Primary History*, 22: 10.

Milsted, N (2006) Young archaeologist of the year award: don't just dig things up! Values and virtues of archaeology, *Primary History,* 43: 23–24.

Murphy, J (1995) *Peace at last.* London: Macmillan Children's Books.

NACCCE/DfEE (1999) *All our futures: creativity, culture and education*. NACCCE Report. London: DfEE.

The National Literacy Project (NLP) (1997) *The National Literacy Project: framework for teaching.* National Literacy and Numeracy Project: Crown Copyright.

Nichol, J (2000) Literacy, text genres and history: reading and learning from difficult and challenging texts. *Primary History*, 24: 13–18.

Nichol, J (2004) Assessing children: profiling progression. *Primary History*, 36: 18–22.

Nichol, J (2005) Reading into writing: history, imagination and creativity – a Nuffield primary history project approach. *Primary History*, 41: 28–32.

Nichol, J (2007) Thinking through history: opportunity for equality. *Primary History,* 47: 4.

Nichol, J and Dean, J (1977) *History 7–11: developing primary teaching skills.* London: Routledge.

Noall, R (2000) How can the use of spreadsheets enhance children's learning in history? A case study, *Primary History*, 26: 16–17.

Ofsted (2002) *Primary subject reports 2000/01: History*. London: Ofsted.

Ofsted (2005) *The annual report of Her Majesty's Chief Inspector of Schools 2004/05: History in primary schools.* London: Ofsted.

Ofsted (2006) *Extended services in schools and children's centres.* London: Ofsted.

Ofsted (2007) *History in the balance. History in English schools 2003–2007.* London: Ofsted.

Peat, J (2003) A quick guide to museums and galleries on the internet, *Primary History,* 35: 8–10.

Peters, RS (1967) *Ethics and education.* Atlanta: Scott Foresman.

Piaget, J (1926) *The language and thought of the child* (3rd edn 1959). London: Routledge.

Piaget, J (1927, trans. 1967 by A J Pomerans) *The child's conception of time.* London: Routledge and Kegan Paul.

Piaget, J (1928) *Judgement and reasoning in the child.* London: Kegan Paul.

Plowden, B (1967) *Children and their primary schools.* (The Plowden Report) London: HMSO.

Purkis, S (1993a) *A teacher's guide to using school buildings.* London: English Heritage.

Purkis, S (1993b) Outside interests, *Junior Education,* May, 18–21.

Purkis, S (1995) *A teacher's guide to using memorials.* London: English Heritage.

Purkis, S (1996) History in the Early Years, in Whitebread, D (ed), *Teaching and learning in the Early Years*. London: Routledge.

QCA (1998) *Maintaining breadth and balance at Key Stages 1 and 2*. London: QCA.

QCA (2005) *The futures programme: meeting the challenge.* London: QCA.

Richards, A (2003) Identity crisis: History through science, strange bedfellows or obvious partners?, *Primary History*, 35: 11–12.

Royston Pike, E (1966) *Human documents of the industrial revolution in Britain*. London: Allen and Unwin.

School Curriculum and Assessment Authority (SCAA) (1997) *History and the use of language.* London: SCAA Publications.

Seacole, M (1857/1999) *The wonderful adventures of Mrs Seacole in many lands.* London: The X Press. (The autobiography of Mary Seacole, a nurse from Jamaica.)

Selley, NJ (1999) *The art of constructivist teaching in the primary school: a guide for students and teachers.* London: Fulton.

Sharp, J (2002) *Primary ICT: knowledge, understanding and practice.* Exeter: Learning Matters.

Smart, L (1999) Any place for a database in the teaching and learning of history at KS1, *Primary History*, 23: 8–10.

Starkey, D (2002) Exploring the history on your doorstep with 4Learning. *Primary History,* 32: 11–13.

Steffe, P and Gale, J (eds) (1995) *Constructivism in education.* Hillsdale, Hove: Erlbaum.

Taba, H et al (1971) *A teacher's handbook to elementary social studies: an inductive approach.* Philippines: Addison-Wesley.

Thornton, L and Brunton, P (2004) *The little book of time and place.* Lutterworth: Featherstone Education.

Turner-Bisset, R (2005a) *Creative teaching: history in the primary classroom.* London: Fulton.

Turner-Bisset, R (2005b) Creating stories for teaching primary history. *Primary History*, 41: 8–9.

Valerio, E (2005) Scheme of work for a local history of Southall. *Primary History*, 39: 22–25.

Vass, P (2005a) Piecing together the puzzle: some thoughts on historical sites, *Primary History,* 39: 34–36.

Vass, P (2005b) Stories about people: narrative, imagined biography and citizenship in the Key Stage 2 curriculum, *Primary History*, 41: 13–16.

Vygotsky, LS (1962) *Thought and language.* New York: MIT Press.

Waddell, M (2005) *Can't you sleep, little bear?* London: Walker Books.

Walsh, B (2003) Is there a place for the computer in primary history?, *Primary History*, 34; 26–29.

Weights, R (2000) Know your dot/coms: historical websites, *Primary History,* 26: 14–15.

West, J (1981a) Children's awareness of the past (unpublished PhD thesis, Keele University).

West, J (1981b) Time charts. *Education, 3–13*, 10: 48–51.

West, J (1981c) *History 7–13.* Kingswinford: Dulston Press.

West, J (1981d) Authenticity and time in historical narrative pictures, *Teaching History*, 29: 8–10.

Whitworth, K (2006) "Discovery visits": What's new at English Heritage for schools?, *Primary History,* 43: 14–16.

Wilkinson, A (2006a) Putting the story back into history, *Primary History,* 43: 26–27.

Wilkinson, A (2006b) Teaching sensitive issues in history, 3–19, *Primary History*, 44: 25.

Wood, E (1995) History, in Anning, A (ed), *A National Curriculum for the Early Years.* Milton Keynes: Open University Press.

Wray, D and Medwell, J (1998) *Teaching English in primary schools: a handbook of teaching strategies and key ideas in literacy*. London: Letts Educational.

adult support on school outings 146, 147, 148
*All our Futures: Creativity, Culture and
    Education* 28, 30
archaeology 152–3
architecture 75–6, 92
art 75–6, 126
artefacts 5, 41–2, 52–3, 73–4
    cross-curricular links 128, 129
    EYFS 114–16
    on-line 103
assessment 58–9, 59–61, 66–8, 85
    contribution of teaching assistants 77
    evaluation of teaching 68–9
    feedback 63–4
    self-assessment 64–6
    strategies 61–3, 100, 113, 130–31
    tasks 38, 51, 61, 140
Attainment Target for History 59, 60, 61, 66

Bage, Grant 8, 61
balance 142
barriers to learning 133–4, 151
Barton, K.C. 95
behaviour 134, 135
behaviourist theory 42
bias 54, 84
Blyth, Joan 86–7
Blyth, W.A.L. 20, 30
books 5, 71–3, 86–7, 88, 154
    see also written sources
breadth of study 17–19
British history in KS2 18
broadcasts 27, 75, 104
Bruner, J.S. 6, 7, 44, 55, 82
built environment 54, 91, 92

calculation 92
carers 78–9, 113
caretakers 78
cause and effect 14–15
celebration of learning 49, 79
change and continuity 2, 14–15, 17, 40–41
Chata Project 61
child-centred learning 46–7
Children Act (2004) 1, 19
Children's Plan 19
chronology 7, 13–14, 40–41, 95, 154
    skills 14, 43, 93, 94
    see also timelines
citizenship 86, 120–21, 129–30
Claire, Hilary 120–21, 143
classroom organisation 48, 55–6
cleaners 78
Climbié, Victoria 19
cognitive development 5, 6, 55
cognitive theory 42
communication of historical findings 17, 52,
    104–5
    see also language
comparison of texts 84
computers *see* ICT; internet resources
concepts 7, 12–13

assessment 60
    progression in understanding 40–41
    research into 20
conceptual development 2
conscience alley 128
constructivist theory 6
'content' versus 'process' approach 12
context
    classroom 48–9
    schemes of work 24
Cooper, Hilary 121, 143
creativity 8, 20, 28, 30
    in teaching 120–25
    writing 75
critical evaluation of information 3
cross-curricular work 3, 19, 29, 30, 47–8, 125–9
    Innovating with history 25–6
    planning 36
    teaching strategies 47–8
    see also literacy

dance 128, 129
data
    handling 93–4, 101, 103
    local and national 68
databases 103
decentring 5
design and technology 127
differentiation for ability 50–51, 134
digital cameras 100
disadvantaged backgrounds 137–8, 152, 155
discrimination 130, 139
discussion and questioning 62–3, 85
displays and illustrations 48–9, 126, 143
diversity 109, 111, 120
    in the curriculum 29, 129, 139, 141–3
Donaldson, M. 20
drama 86, 127–8
dyslexia 135–6

e-mail 105
Early Years Foundation Stage (EYFS) 38, 109–
    110, 111–12
    artefacts 114–16
    chronology 84, 112–14
    concepts 40
    mathematics 89, 93
    NC areas of content 17, 110
    story 116–17
Education Act (2002) 19
Education Reform Act (1988) 11
emotional difficulties 49
empathy 3, 140
English as an Additional Language (EAL) 29,
    78, 140, 151
English Heritage 50, 99, 154–5
enquiry skills 43, 126
    internet use 102–3
    questioning 50, 52, 85, 124
equality 71, 130, 138–43
Equiano, Olaudah 142–3
European history 18, 129

evaluation
    lessons 38
    teaching 68–9
evaluation sheets 64–5
Every Child Matters: Change for Children 1, 7–
    8, 19–20, 137
    extended schools 151–2
    personalised learning 29, 102
evidence *see* interpretation; sources
*Excellence and Enjoyment - A Strategy for
    Primary Schools* 1, 8, 19, 28–9, 30
extended schools 151–2

family learning 154
feedback 63–4, 68
fiction 86, 154
fieldwork 145–8, 150–51
film 75, 86, 154
Fines, John 85
formative assessment (assessment for learning)
    59, 62–3, 67–8, 85
Foundation Stage *see* Early Years Foundation
    Stage (EYFS)
Framework for Literacy and Mathematics 30,
    54, 83–4, 93
freeze-frames 128

Galton, M. 51, 55
games and simulations 104, 127
Gardner, H. 51
gender 139
general teaching requirements 20
geography 125
    see also maps
gifted and able children 137, 143
group work 43, 48, 51, 56

hazards *see* health and safety
health and safety 20
    borrowed artefacts 73
    internet 105
    school outings 146, 148, 149
hearing difficulties 136
Historical Association 99
historical sites 55, 86, 146–7, 148, 150
history
    nature of 3–5
    school 2–3
holistic learning 8, 20, 30, 125, 134
homework 153
hot-seating 86, 127
human rights 129–30

ICT 20, 49, 101, 102–5
    hardware 100
    historical findings 104–5
    QTS skills tests 97–8
    see also internet resources
identity 2
improving own learning performance 43–4
inclusion 20, 29, 120, 140–43
    language 129
    resources 71
    social class 138
    see also diversity

independent work 47, 50, 123–4, 138
    EYFS 111–12
indexes 71
Individual Education Plans (IEPs) 141
individual work 51–2
information books 5, 71–3, 86–7
information processing 43, 50
Innovating with history 25–6
innovative practice 120–25
interactive resources 104, 127
internet resources 5, 27, 35, 73
    National Curriculum in Action website 27,
        40
    pupils' use of 101, 102–5
    support for teachers 98–100
interpretation 3, 4, 15–16, 76
    guidance 23
    language of reasoning 84

key skills 13, 43–4
    see also skills
Key Stage 1
    assessment 61, 62
    breadth of study 17–18
    concepts 40–41
    innovative methods 122–3
    mathematics 89, 93
    QCA schemes of work 24–5
    subject knowledge 38, 40
Key Stage 2
    breadth of study 18–19
    concepts 41
    innovative methods 123–5
    mathematics 89–90, 92, 93
    QCA schemes of work 24–5
    self-assessment 64–6
    subject knowledge 40
knowledge, skills and understanding 12–17, 18,
    23
    assessment 60–61
    planning 35, 38
knowledge and understanding of the world
    (EYFS) 109, 111, 113–14
KWL grid 64, 66

language 3, 7, 94
    across the curriculum 20, 82–3, 84, 85, 95
    EYFS 112, 113
    foreign 129
    names 139
league tables 68
learning 7–8, 42
    celebration of 49, 79
    holistic 8, 20, 30, 125, 134
    informal 6–7, 154
learning difficulties *see* special educational
    needs (SEN)
learning environment 48–9
    EYFS 111–12
    outside the classroom 145–6
learning mentors 78
learning objectives *see* learning outcomes
learning outcomes 82–3
    assessment 63, 64
    planning 34, 35, 38, 44

learning styles 6, 29, 50–51, 134
level descriptions 61
listening 86, 136
literacy 3, 7, 30, 75, 82–8
    pictures 54
literacy hour 83
literature 75, 86, 154
local archives 125
local history 18, 129, 130, 142, 150–51
    mathematics 90–91, 92
long-term planning 33–4

maps 92, 104
marking 63, 64, 140
mathematics 30, 89–95
measurement 93, 94
Media Museum, Bradford 75
medium term planning 34–5, 36–7, 153
Miller, Colin 90, 92
mind maps 131
minority ethnic and cultural backgrounds *see*
    diversity
modelling tasks 49–50
modern foreign languages 129
monitoring 58, 59, 68
moral and ethical questions 4–5
multiple intelligences 120, 131
museums 55, 74, 86, 126, 150
    liaison with professionals 148
music 26, 75, 128

National Curriculum in Action website 27, 40
National Curriculum (NC) 11, 52, 98, 121, 129
    Attainment Target for History 59, 60, 61, 66
    guidance 23
    inclusion 141–3
    out of school learning 146, 154
    Programmes of Study 12–19
National Foundation for Education Research 79
National Teacher Research Panel 79
Nichol, J. 61
non-fiction *see* information books
number 89–92
nursery nurses 78

observation 62, 113
Ofsted
    evaluation of teaching 68
    innovative practice 121, 122
    reports and recommendations 27–8, 68–9,
        105
oral history 54, 75, 85–6
organisation of learning 17, 104–5
organisational/methodological concepts 13, 20
out of school learning 145–6
    contexts for history 150–51
    extended schools 151–2
    homework 153
    incidental learning 6–7, 154
    planning for 146–8, 151–3, 154
    residential activities 152

paired work 43, 51
parents 5, 7, 137–8
    EYFS 111, 113–14

permission for outings 146, 147
    reporting to 59, 66, 67
    support by 73, 78–9
past tense 84
Personal Digital Assistants (PDAs) 100
personal targets 59, 63, 64, 133
personalised learning 29, 47, 52, 121, 123
    ICT 100, 102
    out of school 152, 153
perspective and bias 54, 84
photographs 75, 105, 113–14, 124
physical education 129
Piaget, Jean 5, 44
planning 26
    for assessment 68
    homework 153
    long term 33–4
    medium term 34–5, 36–7
    out of school learning 146–8
    for progression 38, 40–43
    short term 35, 38, 39
    subject coordinators 76–7
play 52
play workers 78
plenaries 66
Plowden Report 55
poetry 87
portraits 4, 53, 75
PowerPoint presentations 98
pre-school learning 7
presentations 98, 101, 105, 126
problem solving 43, 44, 94–5
Professional Standards for Teachers 1–2, 129,
    146
profiles 141
Programmes of Study *see* National Curriculum
    (NC)
progression 33, 38, 40–43, 82–3
published materials *see* fiction; information
    books
Purkis, S. 154
puzzles 90
Pythagoras 89

QCA schemes of work 24–5, 35
    Innovating with history 25–6
QTS skills tests, ICT 97–8
questioning 50, 52, 85, 124
    assessment 62–3, 66

reading 72, 86–7, 154
reasoning 3, 30, 43, 84
reconstructions of the past 55, 86, 122–3, 150
recording and reporting 66–7
religious education 125
reporting to parents 59, 66, 67
research and investigation 50–52
residential activities 152
resources 5, 139
    inclusive 141, 143
    learning environment 49
    local archives 125
    out of school learning 145, 146, 150
    people 76–9
    see also internet resources; sources

risk assessment 146, 148, 149
role-play 127
Rose, Jim 121

school history 2–3
school websites 98, 102
schools broadcasts 27, 75, 104
Schools Council Projects, 'Place, time and
    society' 20, 30
science 126
self-assessment 52, 59, 64–6, 100, 130
Selley, N.J. 6
sensitive issues 4–5, 55
sensory curriculum 52–3, 145
sequencing 84
severe physical or medical difficulties 135
shape and space 92
sharing effective practice 79
short-term planning 35, 38, 39
skills 3, 5, 13, 41–4, 53
    assessment 60
    change and causation 15
    chronology 14, 43, 93, 94
    historical interpretation 15
    learnt out of school 145
    literacy 84–5
    number 90–91
    organisation and communication 17
    planning for progression 41–3
    research into 20
    source analysis 16
    transferable 30
    see also enquiry skills
slave trade 142–3
social class 138
social and emotional development 5
songs 128
sources 4, 5, 15, 16, 56
    primary 52–3, 54, 72, 73–6, 128
    secondary 52, 54, 71–3
    skills in use of 41–2
special educational needs (SEN) 49, 52, 133–8
    formative assessment 59, 62–3
    school outings 151
special needs coordinators (SENCO) 77
specific and moderate learning difficulties 134–
    5
spiral curriculum 44
spreadsheets 101
statements of special educational need 134
statistics 92
Steffe, P. and Gale, J. 6
stories 5, 8, 85–6, 154
    EYFS 116–17
subject coordinators 33, 76–7, 146
subject knowledge
    pupils 38, 40
    teachers 18–19, 38, 44
subject-led work 47–8
substantive concepts 13, 20
summative assessment 59, 61
support staff 78, 134, 135, 140
    school outings 146, 147, 148

Taba, H. 12–13, 20, 44
talk *see* discussion and questioning
targets 59, 63, 64, 133
teacher-designed enquiry 50–51
teacher-led lessons 46–7
Teachernet 27, 79
teachers
    exposition 49–50
    subject knowledge 18–19, 38
Teachers' TV 27
teaching assistants (TA) 77
teaching strategies 6
    research and investigation 50–52
    teacher exposition 49–50
    teaching and learning approaches 46–9
    using sources 52–5, 56
team working 79
thematic learning 8, 20
thinking skills 42–3
time concept 2, 7, 13–14, 40–41, 95
    in fiction 154
    in mathematics 93, 94
    see also Early Years Foundation Stage
    (EYFS)
timelines 40–41, 74
    EYFS 40, 113
    internet/software resources 102
    mathematics 90, 91, 92, 95
topic work *see* thematic learning
Training and Development Agency for Schools
    (TDA) 97
transferable skills 30
traveller backgrounds 140
truth 4
Turner-Bisset, R. 121–2
TV broadcasts 27, 75, 86, 104, 154

VAK (visual, auditory, kinaesthetic) learning
    styles 51, 52, 134
video recorders 100
video-conferencing 105
visitors 85–6
visual impairment 136–7
visual sources 5, 53–4, 74–5, 104, 143
    see also photographs
vocabulary 2, 3, 13, 88
    EYFS 113, 114, 115
    links with mathematics 93, 94
voting pods 100

Walsh, B. 102
whiteboards 100
whole class work 51
women in history 139
word-processing 101
working with others *see* group work; paired
    work
world history 18, 142
writing 75, 84, 87
written sources 54, 75, 86–7, 143

Young Archaeologists Club 152–3